Criminology Explains Human Trafficking

CRIMINOLOGY EXPLAINS

Robert A. Brooks and Jeffrey W. Cohen, Editors

This pedagogically oriented series is designed to provide a concise, targeted overview of criminology theories as applied to specific criminal justice–related subjects. The goal is to bring to life for students the relationships among theory, research, and policy.

Criminology Explains Human Trafficking

Sarah Hupp Williamson

UNIVERSITY OF CALIFORNIA PRESS

University of California Press
Oakland, California

Library of Congress Cataloging-in-Publication Data

Names: Hupp Williamson, Sarah, 1991- author.
Title: Criminology explains human trafficking / Sarah Hupp Williamson.
Description: Oakland, California : University of California Press, [2024] |
    Includes bibliographical references and index.
Identifiers: LCCN 2023048022 (print) | LCCN 2023048023 (ebook) |
    ISBN 9780520392397 (cloth) | ISBN 9780520392410 (paperback) |
    ISBN 9780520392427 (ebook)
Subjects: LCSH: Human trafficking. | Criminology.
Classification: LCC HQ281 .H893 2024 (print) | LCC HQ281 (ebook) |
    DDC 364.15/51—dc23/eng/20231101
LC record available at https://lccn.loc.gov/2023048022
LC ebook record available at https://lccn.loc.gov/2023048023

33 32 31 30 29 28 27 26 25 24
10 9 8 7 6 5 4 3 2 1

Thank you to Thomas for your love and support throughout all my writing.

CONTENTS

FIGURES

Introduction

Academic interest in human trafficking grew dramatically in the years following two major pieces of legislation. In the United States, the Trafficking Victims Protection Act of 2000 defined and criminalized human trafficking at the federal level. That same year, the United Nations also passed a convention that defined the crime of human trafficking under international law. In the decade prior to 2000, the annual number of academic publications on human trafficking wavered between two hundred and three hundred. As figure 1 shows, the number of new publications on the topic of human trafficking in the two decades following 2000 grew to over sixteen thousand.

More detailed analyses of the human trafficking literature have found similar increases. One literature synthesis found 218 research-based journal articles published between 1975 and 2007, with 91 percent of those being published between 2000 and 2007 (Gożdziak and Bump 2008). Another study of 1,231 articles published between 2000 and 2014 found a steady and substantial increase over time. These articles spanned a wide variety of disciplines, though the top five over time included law, international relations/human rights, criminology, medicine/health, and social science (Russell 2018). New scholarly journals have also been introduced specifically on the topic of human trafficking, including *Anti-Trafficking Review* in 2011 and the *Journal of Human Trafficking* in 2015.

Beyond increasing in volume, scholarly research on human trafficking has expanded its focus over time, though stark differences can still be seen. As figure 2 shows, the number of new publications appearing in Google Scholar differs dramatically by whether the focus is sex trafficking or labor trafficking.

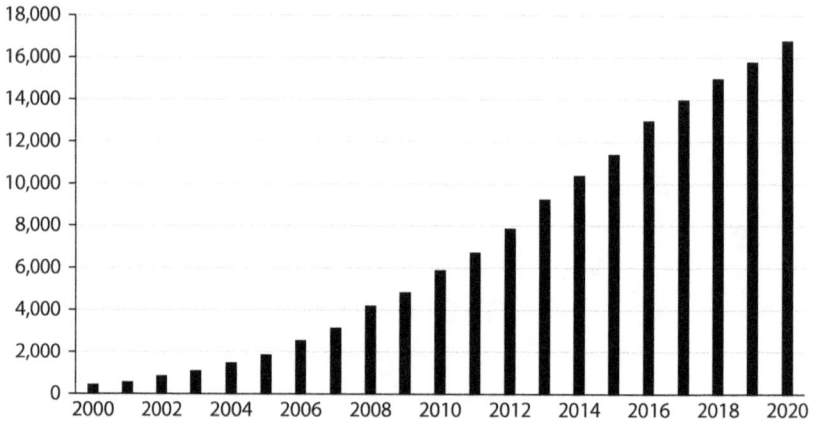

FIGURE 1. Number of new publications, by year, generated by Google Scholar using the search term *human trafficking*, 2000–2020.

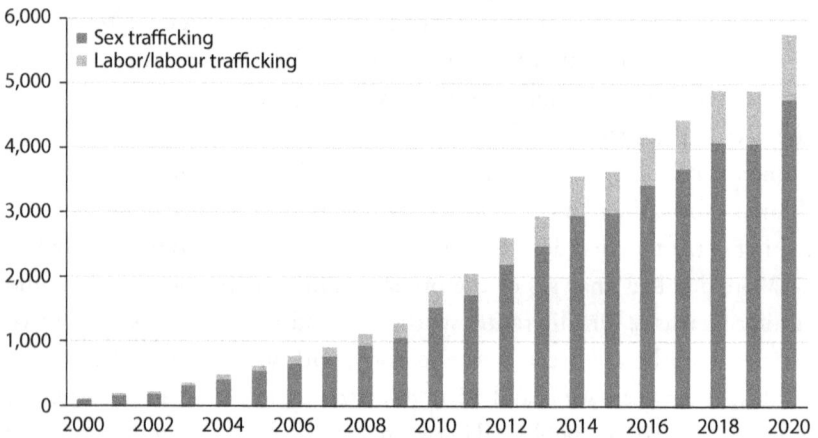

FIGURE 2. Number of new publications, by year, generated by Google Scholar using the search terms *sex trafficking* and *labor/labour trafficking*, 2000–2020.

Most of the growth has been in the area of sex trafficking, though research on labor trafficking has increased within the past decade.

This trend is again reflected in others' findings of the state of the literature (Goździak and Bump 2008; Goździak and Graveline 2015), with one review finding that 70 percent of labor trafficking articles were published in the years after 2009 (Russell 2018). Articles in the discipline of criminology were no different, with one study finding that among 159 criminology articles published on human trafficking between 2000 and 2014, 53 percent focused on sex trafficking, 43 percent on human trafficking in general, 3 percent on labor trafficking, and 1 percent on organ trafficking (Russell 2018).

The human trafficking literature has importantly centered on documenting trafficking routes; estimating the scope of the problem; classifying countries as source, transit, or destination; and understanding legal and policy responses to human trafficking. Research on victim experiences and needs has grown, as has research around awareness, training, and education (Russell 2018). The extent of a criminological and criminal justice focus is seen in the high number of articles that emphasize issues with trafficking laws, legal reform, new policy development, and evaluation of current policies (Russell 2018).

THEORY AND HUMAN TRAFFICKING

A major issue within the human trafficking literature that has been identified by scholars is the lack of a comprehensive theoretical framework. Theorizing on human trafficking remains underdeveloped and fragmented across disciplines (Goździak 2015; Kakar 2017; Limoncelli 2009a). A study of over one thousand scholarly articles found that less than 5 percent of the total sample was based on a theory (Russell 2018). No specific theories have been developed to explain human trafficking. Instead, among trafficking research that has made use of theory, it has applied a variety of existing theories (Kakar 2017).

This fragmentation has led to different disciplines applying their own theories and frameworks that emphasize different concerns. This includes theories such as anthropological theory, political theory, feminist theory, anomie/strain theory, theories of corporate responsibility, economic theories, and life course theory (Franchino-Olsen 2021a; Russell 2018). Limoncelli (2009a, 72) notes of these different approaches, "Criminologists see trafficking as an issue of crime and law enforcement, migration scholars see it as a corrupted form of labor migration, human rights scholars see it as a violation of individual rights, and feminists tend to see it as a gender issue." The development and integration of theory into the study of human trafficking is important to the advancement of the field. Theory is necessary to fully understand and grapple with the wide array of complex factors that go into a crime like human trafficking, explaining both the causes and persistence of trafficking. Criminological theories in particular have been noted for their ability to address the motives of traffickers, victim vulnerabilities, and other patterns within this crime type (Russell 2018).

The purpose of this volume, as part of the larger *Criminology Explains* series, is to provide the reader with a book that is both comprehensive and accessible in regard to the intersections between theory, research, and policy. The topic of human trafficking is used to allow the reader to apply theory to explore issues such as sex versus labor trafficking, victims versus offenders, migration and globalization, domestic and international law and policy, and the wide array of anti-trafficking efforts. Through this book readers will gain an understanding of theory as it applies to the field of human trafficking, including how various levels of analysis from the local to the global are often linked. As human trafficking is a topic that is often cross-disciplinary in nature, literature outside of criminology has been incorporated when it reflects the principles or concepts of criminological theory.

Following the format of other books in the series, this book may be read alone or in conjunction with the corresponding chapters of a criminology textbook. Chapter 1 offers an overview of human trafficking, describing the nature and extent of the issue, measurement issues and challenges, and how the topic of human trafficking has been socially constructed. Chapter 2 applies deterrence theory, rational choice theory, routine activities theory, and victimization theories to human trafficking. This includes exploration of issues such as various policy models of prostitution and sex trafficking, the risks and rewards of trafficking, situational crime prevention, and the intersection between intimate partner violence and human trafficking. Chapter 3 considers psychological theories, examining the question of whether traffickers are psychopaths, the grooming and trauma of trafficking victims, and the victim-offender overlap that often occurs among survivors. Chapter 4 discusses social structure theories, including social disorganization theory and spatial patterns of trafficking, the application of various anomie and strain theories to different types of trafficking, and the use of subcultural theories in explaining the role of organized crime and gang involvement in trafficking. Chapter 5 looks at social process theories, including the role of family and peers in control and learning theories and how labeling theory can be used to understand moral panics of trafficking. Chapter 6 explores various

critical perspectives. This includes cultural criminology and media representations of trafficking, conflict theories and questions of justice, feminist and
queer perspectives to understand both victims and offenders, and critical race
theory as it applies to intersectional inequality and carceral responses to
human trafficking. Finally, chapter 7 addresses various integrationist perspectives, including life-course and development theory, and finally, social-
ecological theory. Each chapter also contains a policy box that showcases how
theory can be linked to real cases or policies on human trafficking, as well as
resources and discussion questions for further thought.

ONE

Defining, Researching, and Responding to Human Trafficking

DEFINING HUMAN TRAFFICKING

What do you think of when you hear the words *human trafficking*? What images come to mind? What does a victim of human trafficking look like and what do they experience? In reality, human trafficking is a complex and multifaceted phenomenon, though there are several myths that persist about it. One prominent myth is that human trafficking only occurs for sexual exploitation (Stickle, Hickman, and White 2020). While sex trafficking does occur, human trafficking actually takes many forms. Definitions of human trafficking have come to include not only sexual exploitation, but also practices around labor exploitation, organ trafficking, forced marriage, child soldiers, and debt bondage. Women and children have often been the focus of anti-trafficking efforts, but the reality is that trafficking affects persons of all races, ages, genders, sexualities, and nationalities (Stickle, Hickman, and White 2020).

Human trafficking also does not have to involve travel across state or national borders, or movement of any kind (Kakar 2017). In fact, someone may be trafficked in their own hometown. While international trafficking has been placed high on the agenda of governments around the world, internal or domestic trafficking may be a greater problem for most countries (Aronowitz 2009). Human trafficking is often thought of as a crime occurring in seedy, underground places, but it frequently occurs in legal industries (Kakar 2017). While things like brothels and red-light districts may come to mind when thinking about the issue, human trafficking happens in work such as agriculture, restaurants, and domestic work. Finally, unlike frequent media depictions, human trafficking does not have to involve physical force or bondage (Stickle, Hickman, and White 2020). There are many ways in which traffickers may exert control over victims, and physical violence is just one. Other common tactics of control include psychological abuse, threats, and fraud or deception (CTDC 2021). To better understand where some of these stereotypes may have emerged from, as well as current definitions of human trafficking, one can look at how the issue of human trafficking has been approached and defined throughout history.

Early Laws on Human Trafficking

The historical roots of human trafficking can be linked to slavery, meaning it is not a new social condition (Farrell and Fahy 2009). However, human trafficking as a distinct social issue can be traced back to the late nineteenth century. At this time in Europe and North America, societal shifts and the growth of industry and urban living had caused an increase in migration, and with that, worries about the movement of White women (Outshoorn 2015). Concern about human trafficking revolved largely around trafficking women for the purposes of prostitution and became an avenue for groups demanding the abolition of brothels and prostitution. This all culminated in the 1904 international treaty titled the International Agreement for the Suppression of the White Slave Trade (Boris and Berg 2014; Outshoorn 2015). The 1904 treaty addressed only the recruitment of women for prostitution in another country through fraudulent or abusive means (Doezema 2002). The treaty focused not on providing protection for women as victims, but on creating systems to investigate and, ultimately, repatriate foreign women who were suspected of prostitution (Lammasniemi 2020).

In the United States, the White-Slave Traffic Act, also known as the Mann Act, was passed in 1910. The Mann Act was passed at a time when the prostitution debate and the White-slave trade were high-profile issues in the country. It was in response to the fear of "White slavery" specifically that Congress passed this act. The Mann Act prohibited unmarried women from crossing state lines for immoral purposes and its primary stated intent was to address prostitution, immorality, and human trafficking, particularly where trafficking was for the purposes of prostitution. In practice, however, the law's broad and ambiguous language about "immorality" resulted in it being used to criminalize even consensual sexual behavior between adults (Kakar 2017; Lutnick 2016). One study of 87 percent of the cases prosecuted under the Mann Act between 1927 and 1933 showed that 46 percent of the cases involved women who identified as prostitutes and were arrested for aiding in the transportation of another woman across state lines for the purpose of prostitution, 23 percent involved women traveling across state lines with their boyfriend when one or both of them was married to someone else, 16 percent of the cases involved women whose sporadic engagement in prostitution was to finance their travels, and 15 percent involved women who were working as prostitutes (Beckman 1983). The misplaced fears over White slavery that led to the passage of the Mann Act also led to the law being used to target and harass Black men traveling with White women (Chacón 2006). It is not surprising that concerns about sex trafficking linked to mobility spiked during this time, which saw increases in internal and international migration, expansion of the use of railroads and automobiles, and the introduction of new communication technologies (Saunders and Soderlund 2003). Overall, these cases show how early anti-trafficking laws were, in practice, not about women and girls being abducted and forced into the sex trade, but about the values and morals surrounding prostitution and women's increased freedom of movement.

Other international agreements under the predecessor to the United Nations, the League of Nations, dealt with similar concern about the movement of women. This included the Suppression of the Traffic in Women and Children (1921) and the Suppression of the Traffic in Women of Full Age (1933). The 1933 convention condemned all recruitment for prostitution or immoral purposes in another country. This abolitionist stance was repeated in 1949 when the United Nations passed the Convention for the Suppression of the Traffic in Persons and of the Exploitation of the Prostitution of Others. This convention called on countries to put an end to both trafficking and prostitution more generally, with a requirement that countries criminalize prostitution under national law (Lammasniemi 2020). However, it was this abolitionist approach that led to many countries not signing on to it (Doezema 2002; Outshoorn 2005).

Ultimately, there were many similarities among these early anti-trafficking efforts. The concerns that led to their passing were often rooted in racism and sexism, focusing on the prostitution of White women regardless of consent (Boris and Berg 2014; Outshoorn 2005, 2015). These early laws also did not formally define the term trafficking, focusing instead on the recruitment or coerced movement of women abroad for the purposes of prostitution. However, with no pressure on nations to implement the protocols of the convention, the issue of human trafficking declined in political and public spheres (Outshoorn 2005).

A resurgence in awareness of the issue of human trafficking began in the late 1980s to mid-1990s when media and women's rights organizations began to draw attention to human trafficking (Farrell and Fahy 2009; Hua 2011). With this, the identity of the victims had changed. While sex trafficking was still the focus of such organizations, victims were now stereotyped as non-White women from relatively poorer countries (Gallagher 2010). The 2000 Trafficking Victims Protection Act (TVPA) was the first piece of federal legislation in the United States dealing with human trafficking. In the same year that human trafficking was made a federal crime in the United States, it was defined for the first time in international law with the passage of the United Nations Protocol to Prevent, Suppress and Punish Trafficking in Persons, Especially Women and Children (also known as the Palermo Protocol) in 2000.

The definition of human trafficking in both laws imposed no gender restriction or border crossing requirement. They focused more on the progression of the act from beginning to end, and divided the definition of trafficking into three elements. Human trafficking is defined as having an act, a means, and a purpose. The act includes every stage of the trafficking process. It includes things like recruiting individuals through deception or fraud, the process of transporting or transferring individuals, or harboring and receiving trafficked individuals. This extends the law to those involved in moving a person into a situation of exploitation as well as maintaining them in that exploitation. This means that "it is not just the recruiter, broker, or transporter who can be identified as a trafficker, but also the individual or entity involved in initiating or sustaining the exploitation" (Gallagher 2010, 47). This differs from early acts and treaties that focused on the initial recruitment. The means include a range of behaviors that work to carry out the acts, such as violence, threats, and deceit. Force, fraud, and coercion are central concepts to the means of trafficking, and it is often required to prove one under law for a trafficking charge. The one exception for this in the United States is that establishing force, fraud, or coercion is not required in cases involving the sex trafficking of minors (Gallagher 2010). Finally, there is a purpose, or the end goal of the acts and the means. Purpose includes various forms of exploitation that can be sexual, such as forced prostitution, but also nonsexual, such as labor exploitation or organ trafficking.

When all of these three elements are together, you have human trafficking. We can see these elements in both the US federal law and the UN international law. Under the US TVPA, the term "severe forms of trafficking in persons" is defined as

(A) sex trafficking in which a commercial sex act is induced by force, fraud, or coercion, or in which the person induced to perform such act has not attained eighteen years of age; or

(B) the recruitment, harboring, transportation, provision, or obtaining of a person for labor or services, through the use of force, fraud, or coercion for the purpose of subjection to involuntary servitude, peonage, debt bondage, or slavery.

The UN Palermo Protocol defines "trafficking in persons" as

> the recruitment, transportation, transfer, harbouring or receipt of persons, by means of the threat or use of force or other forms of coercion, of abduction, of fraud, of deception, of the abuse of power or of a position of vulnerability or of the giving or receiving of payments or benefits to achieve the consent of a person having control over another person, for the purpose of exploitation. Exploitation shall include, at a minimum, the exploitation of the prostitution of others or other forms of sexual exploitation, forced labour or services, slavery or practices similar to slavery, servitude or the removal of organs (UN 2000a, 319).

Both follow the act, purpose, means model in their definitions. However, one distinct difference between the two is that the US law separates out sex trafficking from other forms of labor exploitation. The UN law emphasizes the element of coercion rather than the type of work a victim is trafficked into or exploited in (Chacón 2006). Under the US law, trafficking into commercial sex is symbolically privileged over other forms of trafficking (Peters 2013). Such a moral division has the outcome of minimizing and marginalizing the experiences and harms that labor trafficking victims experience (Barnhart 2009). This separation has also had significant and real impacts on the way that criminal justice officials and service providers conceptualize what trafficking is and who trafficking victims are. This includes negative impacts on victim identification and protection, as will be discussed later in this chapter. A well-studied outcome of this separation under the law is how human trafficking is often reduced to sex trafficking, with training and resources prioritizing it as such, and labor trafficking treated only as an afterthought (Peters 2013). Further, this distinction between sex and labor trafficking under the law is also not always clear cut in practice, as many victims of labor exploitation also experience sexual abuse as a form of coercion and control, and exhibit similar forms of psychological trauma (Barnhart 2009; Peters 2013).

Human Trafficking versus Related Concepts

With human trafficking now defined by law, it is possible to understand how it is distinct from related concepts. Human trafficking as a crime is often conflated with related, but separate, issues. Frequently these include sex work, and prostitution especially, migrant smuggling, and slavery. Here, the differences between each and human trafficking are briefly outlined.

Given human trafficking's historical roots with moral concerns over the prostitution of women and sex trafficking, it is not surprising that this conflation continues today (Cockbain and Bowers 2019). Stereotypes about human trafficking are replayed in media, with victims portrayed as innocent females lured into a life of sexual exploitation (Doezema 2010). In regard to prostitution, it is the means—the force, fraud, and coercion—that separate human trafficking from criminalized sex work. Some sex workers may enter the industry willingly but become victims of trafficking later. While poverty, homelessness, and other precarious life circumstances may influence individuals' decisions to enter sex work, most individuals in the sex trade do not fit the statutory definition of human trafficking (SWAN and GHJP 2020).

Modern human trafficking stereotypes also focus on the international aspects of the issue, leading to a confusion between migrants who are trafficked and migrants who are smuggled. The UN Protocol Against the Smuggling of Migrants by Land, Sea, and Air defines smuggling as "the procurement, in order to obtain, directly or indirectly, a financial or other material benefit, of the illegal entry of a person into a State Party of which the person is not a national or a permanent resident." While human trafficking refers to a crime that is committed against another person, when we speak of smuggling, we are talking about a crime against a nation's laws regarding entry. Thus, one immediate difference between the two is that smuggling must involve the crossing of international borders, while trafficking does not (Aronowitz 2009).

Another difference is that human trafficking involves force, fraud, or coercion to carry out the crime—the victim does not participate willingly (Gallagher 2010). With smuggling, the individual is generally a willing participant who is consenting to the movement. Once they are in the country, smuggled individuals are free to leave their smuggler, change jobs, and so forth (Stickle, Hickman, and White 2020). While smuggling and trafficking are defined as separate crimes, in reality, they are often interrelated (Aronowitz 2009; Scarpa 2020; Skilbrei and Tveit 2008). Deception and fraud may be used by smugglers to recruit individuals, blurring the lines of consent, and what may have begun as voluntary migration may turn into a situation of exploitation that the individual is no longer able to leave. Consider this story of a trafficking victim from the 2015 Trafficking in Persons Report:

> Over a period of several years, five Ukrainian brothers fraudulently promised 70 Ukrainians well-paying janitorial jobs at retail stores in the United States. They further lured the workers with promises to pay for their room and board and all their travel expenses. Once the workers arrived in the United States, however, the traffickers exacted reimbursement for $10,000–$50,000 in travel debts, making them work 10 to 12 hours per day, seven days a week to repay the debt, almost never providing compensation. The brothers abused the workers physically, psychologically, and sexually, and threatened to hurt the workers' families if they disobeyed. The brothers brought many of the workers into the United States illegally through Mexico. Over time, several new recruits were detained at the border and other victims bravely came forward, exposing the trafficking ring. Four of the brothers were convicted on charges of human trafficking; one remains a fugitive and is thought to be in Ukraine (U.S. Department of State 2015).

Are you able to separate the crimes of smuggling, labor trafficking, and sexual exploitation clearly? With this case as an example, it becomes easier to conceptualize human trafficking as a continuum, "with the use of force and coercion at one end and voluntary movement for economic opportunities at the other end" (Derks, Henke, and Vanna 2006, 32). It is in this middle ground that many migrants' experiences of exploitation may be placed.

Human trafficking has also been equated with "modern-day" slavery since the reemergence of the anti-trafficking movement in the 1990s. Despite this push to frame trafficking as slavery, legal advocates have pointed out that, with the exception of only the most extreme cases, human trafficking does not meet the legal threshold for slavery under international law (Chuang 2014). As Weitzer (2015a, 227) states of the conflation between the two terms, "Some analysts use the term *slavery-like conditions* to describe circumstances that are less comprehensive or onerous than outright slavery. These conditions include confiscation of legal documents, tight restrictions on one's freedom, poor working conditions, low pay, and debt that accelerates rather than diminishes over time. In this category, the worker does not suffer absolute slavery in terms of ownership, routine physical violence, total control, confinement, or dehumanization, but is subject instead to milder forms of control." The UN 1927 Slavery Convention defines slavery as "the status or condition of a person over whom any or all of the powers attaching to the right of ownership are exercised." Slavery can be distinguished from human trafficking with respect to six elements: ownership, profits, availability, relationship, responsibility, and discrimination (Kakar 2017). Under slavery, there was legal and documented ownership over the person that does not exist under the criminalized nature of human trafficking. Profits under human trafficking are much higher than under slavery—with human trafficking there is no responsibility over the maintenance of the person as they are seen as disposable due to a surplus of availability. Under slavery the control dynamics tended to be long term and more permanent, based in a discriminatory system that targeted racial minorities. Under human trafficking the control dynamics are by comparison short-lived, and all races and ethnicities are vulnerable. In this way, we can see that while human trafficking certainly bears some resemblances to slavery, it is important definitionally to recognize their differences as well.

CAUSES OF HUMAN TRAFFICKING

Research on the causes of human trafficking comes from a variety of disciplines, including criminology, sociology, social work, political science, and economics. Yet the findings across these disciplines are consistent in what they have found to be recurring causes of human trafficking. There are several root factors that are connected to vulnerability to human trafficking, including globalization, economic inequality, gender inequality, racial/ethnic discrimination, conflict, and corruption. These causes will be explored in-depth in each of the following chapters, illuminating how various criminological theories allow us to understand these causes. Briefly, however, some of the major causes of trafficking are reviewed here.

Globalization

Globalization can be defined as a set of processes that hinder or facilitate the international flow of individuals, items, and information (Ritzer 2010). The structural and cultural changes associated with globalization have exacerbated inequalities while also creating a demand for unmet labor needs, which drives migration (Lee 2011). Structurally, the industries of local economies have been transformed under globalization as migration and trading across borders increases. There is a demand for cheap, low-skilled labor in industries like domestic work, agriculture, construction, and manufacturing—the same sectors that are also likely to experience trafficking (Aronowitz 2017).

Unequal economic development from globalization has also created a wide gap of global inequalities between countries, and even within countries there is a widening gap between poor and rich communities (Chuang 2006a; Zhang 2007). Further, global capitalism has meant that rules and policies largely stemming from nations in Western Europe and North America as well as international financial institutions have greatly influenced the global flow of goods, services, and capital (Centeno and Cohen 2010). This exacerbates an inequality gap between countries that then creates a growing population of individuals who use migration as a means to attain economic gain (Chuang 2006a; Surtees 2008). Through globalization it is important to consider the ways in which migration is linked with vulnerability to human trafficking, including demand for labor and increased hopes or aspirations for a better future (Chuang 2006a; Shelley 2010). When human trafficking is placed within the larger global migratory movement, it becomes possible to understand how the pull of unmet labor demands across borders combined with restrictive immigration policies leads individuals to seek out alternative routes, placing them at risk of trafficking victimization (Chuang 2006a; Lee 2011; Shelley 2010).

In addition to structural changes, globalization and urbanization have led to massive cultural changes as the spread of global media and the internet allows for communities to receive an influx of messages that promise better chances and opportunities elsewhere (Aronowitz 2017; Chuang 2006a). Growing structural inequalities combine with these cultural aspirations to foster an environment that encourages decisions to migrate (Cameron and Newman 2008; Chuang 2006a; Mishra 2015). Individuals become vulnerable to trafficking through false promises of job and educational opportunities. In this way, globalization creates a structural environment that limits the opportunities of some and a cultural environment that contributes to fostering hopes and expectations. Together these may inform individuals' willingness to migrate, increasing their trafficking victimization risk (Cameron and Newman 2008; Chuang 2006a).

Economic Inequality

Globalization has worsened economic inequalities and further marginalized vulnerable populations (Farr 2004; Kara 2010b; Limoncelli 2009a; Shelley

2010; Stone 2005; Truong 2003). One way this has occurred is through economic restructuring that removes important government social safety nets
(Corrin 2005; Hupp Williamson 2017; Kligman and Limoncelli 2005;
Surtees 2008). Institutions like the International Monetary Fund (IMF)
and World Bank have been instrumental in guiding economic policy in developing countries. The outcomes of such policies, however, have often had the
adverse effect of worsening economic inequalities (Hupp Williamson 2022).

Economic deprivation and insecurity can exacerbate vulnerability and
make migration for work or other economic opportunities appear as a viable
option (Chuang 2006a; Surtees 2008). Risky migration decisions linked to
trafficking victimization go hand-in-hand with economic-based disparities
such as poverty and blocked job or educational opportunities (Bales 2004;
Cameron and Newman 2008; Farr 2004; Jac-Kucharski 2012; Mishra 2015;
Outshoorn 2015; Truong 2003; Zhang 2007). Traffickers can ultimately
exploit these vulnerable populations by deceiving individuals with promises
of jobs or education (Cameron and Newman 2008; Hughes 2000). Conditions
of poverty not only drive trafficking flows from poor to wealthier countries,
but also from rural to urban areas within countries (Aronowitz 2017).

Gender Inequality

Gender-based inequality, including discrimination and violence, is also an
important cause of human trafficking (Chuang 2006a; Corrin 2005; Farr
2004; Kara 2010b; Lee 2011; Limoncelli 2009a). Research shows that a lack
of economic and social rights and opportunities—including property rights,
educational access, and political participation—are important factors in the
trafficking of women and girls (Shelley 2010). Gender-based inequalities are
also connected to the "feminization of poverty," where women and children
are disproportionately impoverished in a population (Chuang 2006a; Corrin
2005; Hughes 2000; Hupp Williamson 2017; Lee 2011).

Under such circumstances, the concept of "feminization of survival" is
used to refer to family and community reliance on women to migrate for economic sustenance (Sassen 2002). Also referred to as "survival migration," it is
the need for work that combines with the contradictory demand for workers
and tightening migration restrictions in destination countries that leave these
migrants at risk of trafficking victimization. For women, these circumstances
are only magnified by gender-based employment discrimination that pushes
them to informal economic sectors, which lack legal migration routes (Chuang

2006a). Both the feminization of poverty and the feminization of survival demonstrate that globalization is gendered, often leading to the "feminization of irregular migration" (Lee 2011). In short, poverty and discrimination are often compounded for women, leading them to seek ways to migrate for more prosperous opportunities (Outshoorn 2015). Such migration leaves women vulnerable to trafficking not only during their movement, but also once they have reached their destination.

Racial and Ethnic Inequality

Racial- and ethnic-based discrimination, stereotypes, and cultural oppression can also contribute to an individual's vulnerability to human trafficking. Such discrimination can block equal access to income, education, housing, and legal protections, leading to marginalization (Bryant-Davis and Tummala-Narra 2017). For example, in Latin America, Indigenous populations are at greater risk for labor trafficking (Cameron and Newman 2008), while ethnic minorities in Thailand and Moldova experience high rates of sex trafficking (Shelley 2010).

Racism also intersects with, and intensifies, class- and gender-based inequalities, making it important to look at issues of poverty, gender, and race together. Too often, women of color face marginalized access to education and employment. This vulnerability is capitalized on by the sex industry, as sexist stereotypes based on race and ethnicity create a demand for women from nations in the Global South and the East (Bryant-Davis and Tummala-Narra 2017; Chong 2014; Kempadoo 2001; Limoncelli 2009b). Women of color may be forced or coerced into sexual labor, contributing to their overrepresentation "at the bottom, most dangerous levels" (Limoncelli 2009b, 266). Ultimately, much of the research on racialized victimization in human trafficking notes that it is a compounding of vulnerabilities through discrimination and marginalization in multiple areas that places them at a high risk of trafficking (Butler 2015b; Chong 2014; Chuang 2006a; Corrin 2005; Kara 2010b; Limoncelli 2009a; Todres 2009).

Conflict

Human trafficking has been documented as the direct or indirect result of armed conflict in countries such as Afghanistan, Libya, the Philippines, and Somalia (Kangaspunta et al. 2018). More specifically, conflict in the form of

civil conflict, war, violent militarization, and social unrest has been impli-
cated in creating human trafficking flows (Bales 2004; Cameron and
Newman 2008; Lee 2011; Mishra 2015; Shelley 2010). Such conflicts create
social disorganization and weaken social institutions, leading to deterioration in the rule of law, community and family, and social and economic protections (Kangaspunta et al. 2018).

Along with militarization and displacement, these conditions are associated
with an increase in both the supply and demand of human trafficking
(Limoncelli 2009a). That is to say, these conditions often act to drive individuals
to seek migration out of the area, placing them at risk of victimization by trafficking. As conflicts erode economic and social institutions, displaced individuals and refugees are populations vulnerable to trafficking through migration and
exploitation (Akee et al. 2010). Further, studies show that measures of conflict
and a high presence of displaced persons and refugees in a country are predictive
of that country's likelihood of experiencing human trafficking, meaning the
link between conflict and trafficking cannot be ignored (Akee et al. 2010).

Corruption

Corruption is not so much a cause of human trafficking as it is a facilitator.
Corruption acts to enable and exacerbate human trafficking. A country's
level of corruption has been shown to play a role in allowing the offenders of
trafficking to continue their crimes, which can erode perceptions of the
legitimacy of law enforcement and the law among victims, ultimately undermining anti-trafficking policy and law enforcement within a country (Farr
2004; Jac-Kucharski 2012; Malarek 2011; Surtees 2008). Globalization has
created favorable contexts for crime by facilitating corruption, including
organized crime groups' involvement in transnational crimes such as trafficking (Lee 2011; Shelley 2010). The action or inaction of law enforcement and
public officials through corruption allows the traffickers to continue to
exploit individuals (Malarek 2011). Consider the role corruption played in
the story of M, a female minor trafficked from Moldova to the Balkans:

> First, actual blank passports had been allegedly corruptly obtained by her
> traffickers from a neighbouring Balkan country and used to transfer her into
> the location where she was sexually exploited. Second, even though the pass-
> ports were filled out incorrectly and obviously improper, with the wrong
> official stamps and other glaring mistakes, and even though M. did not speak

any of the local languages of where she was exploited, she was passed through several border crossings without question, allegedly through corrupt facilitation. Third, the brothel where M. was exploited was across the street from the local police station. No action to investigate was taken; some police officers were allegedly obtaining sexual services from M. and other victims of trafficking (UNODC 2011, 11).

In addition to corruption being influential in traffickers' ability to evade prosecution for their crimes, the legal framework often works in their favor as well. Studies have shown that levels of compliance with anti-trafficking laws vary by country and are impacted by factors such as corruption and the rights of women (Avdeyeva 2012; Cho, Dreher, and Neumayer 2014). Research also shows that countries may be selective in their enforcement, focusing on aspects that reflect economic interests, such as border control, rather than the protection of human rights or prosecution of offenders (Cho and Vadlamannati 2012; Hacker 2015).

RESEARCHING HUMAN TRAFFICKING

Researching human trafficking is often a difficult task, and gathering data on the issue presents several obstacles. First, and perhaps most influential, is the fact that the nature of the crime of human trafficking means that it generally goes undetected and undocumented (Kakar 2017; Laczko and Gramegna 2003). Human trafficking victims are a hidden population, a group whose size and boundaries are unknown and whose membership often falls into stigmatized or illegal categories, such as being undocumented or a sex worker (DoCarmo 2020; Tyldum and Brunovskis 2005). In regard to research, gaining access to trafficked individuals is extremely difficult. Victims are a vulnerable population, and service providers, attorneys, and law enforcement may resist their participating in research to protect them from the possibility of further exploitation or adverse impacts from recounting their experiences (Goździak 2015). These issues are only further exacerbated when working with minor victims of trafficking (Rothman et al. 2018).

Overall, there is also a lack of systematic and comparable data on the issue (Kakar 2017). Popular writing on human trafficking tends to remain anecdotal, simple, and sensationalistic (Weitzer 2014). Reports from government agencies and nongovernmental organizations often fail to detail the sources of the numbers they report and cannot be verified (Goodey 2008; Weitzer 2014; Zhang 2009). Among academic studies, the literature that originally developed largely focused on generating estimates, describing cross-national routes of trafficking, and reviewing legal responses (Goździak 2015). Though a growing body of research has taken a more applied perspective (see, for example, the public health approach discussed in chapter 7), studies have still been criticized for sampling issues, poorly designed survey questions, limited scope, empirically unsupported claims, and a skewed focus toward sex trafficking (Cockbain, Bowers, and Dimitrova 2018; Tyldum 2010; Zhang 2009).

One issue contributing to the lack of comparable data is that within the United States, and at the regional and international levels, there is no single agency that acts as a focal point for the collection of statistics on human trafficking (Bales, Murphy, and Silverman 2020; Laczko and Gramegna 2003). Instead, different organizations collect information and research on trafficking, each through the lens and interests that are the focus of that organization and its mandate. For example, the International Organization for Migration (IOM) is likely to focus on issues related to restrictive migration policies, labor demands, and the potential for exploitation, while the United Nations Office of Drugs and Crime (UNODC) may focus on tracing international trafficking routes and the country patterns of international trafficking.

Among what data is available, definitional issues lead to problems of data validity and make comparisons difficult. Existing data is often program specific, meaning that the data is based on the various definitions of human trafficking used by each individual agency and organization (Bales, Murphy, and Silverman 2020; Laczko and Gramegna 2003). When there is a lack of uniformity among the various definitions of human trafficking used by governments, organizations, and researchers, estimates on the nature and extent of human trafficking will vary (Kakar 2017). The issue of human trafficking covers a wide range of processes, actions, and outcomes. Organizations may differ in the data they collect due to this, focusing on different stages such as recruitment, transportation, or control in the final destination. Further, individuals may appear in data from multiple organizations, leading to accuracy problems in estimates (Laczko and Gramegna 2003).

In addition to variations in definitions across organizations, definitions also vary across countries. In many countries' data collection, it is still common to commingle data on trafficking, smuggling, irregular migration, and sex workers (Doezema 2010; Weitzer 2014). Some countries include transportation of a woman across a border for the purpose of prostitution in their definitions of trafficking, regardless of the consent of the woman. In other cases, migrants working in the sex trade may be subsumed under the trafficking definition regardless of their consent and conditions of labor (Chapkis 2003; Doezema 2010; Petrunov 2014). Other countries may not even recognize labor trafficking in their legal codes (Savona and Stefanizzi 2007).

Conflation of human trafficking with other issues, such as smuggling, prostitution, and even slavery, creates issues with data. As discussed previously, human trafficking is often discussed as slavery. However, when there is slippage between these two distinct phenomena, data changes. For example, the US government recently began equating human trafficking with slavery in its reports, with the terms trafficking and slavery being used interchangeably in the State Department's 2012 and 2013 annual reports. This change resulted in a large spike in the number of estimated victims (Weitzer 2015a). Such conflation can lead to dramatic increases in estimates of human trafficking that are not accurate reflections of the potential population.

Countries may also be resistant to cooperating with and coordinating data collection efforts at a cross-national level. Trafficking data may be regarded as classified or privacy laws may prohibit sharing what is often personal information (Laczko and Gramegna 2003). Nations may also be unwilling to share data that they feel will reflect negatively on their government or be used against them in the form of sanctions (Feingold 2011). The sharing of data between source and destination countries can be very beneficial but often occurs only when necessary, or not at all due to concerns about authorities and agencies in the source country being involved in trafficking themselves (Laczko and Gramegna 2003).

Data on the number of persons being trafficked are often only estimates and are generally regarded as unreliable (U.S. GAO 2006; Gożdziak 2015). National estimates of human trafficking are often extrapolated from the number of criminal cases, which represent only a small portion of identified cases. These estimates are often repeated without verification and may even be misinterpreted as actual and known numbers of human trafficking victims (Fedina 2015; Zhang 2009).

The Global Slavery Index (GSI) perhaps best represents these methodological issues. Started in 2013 by an NGO, the GSI ranks 167 countries on their prevalence of slavery. The index demonstrates definitional issues before even getting to the estimates, as they define slavery to include human trafficking, forced labor, and slavery practices (Weitzer 2014). To create its estimates, the GSI draws on a variety of sources, ranging from news media, NGO reports, surveys, and official government agencies, each of which may work from different definitions and viewpoints, leading to noncomparable data. For the 139 countries without this data, the GSI assigns an estimate based on the estimate from a country deemed comparable and relevant (Gallagher 2017; Weitzer 2014). Such a system ultimately means that the estimates presented by the GSI are inaccurate representations of human trafficking in a country.

DATA ON HUMAN TRAFFICKING TODAY

So where does our knowledge about human trafficking come from and what does human trafficking look like based on this data? There are a variety of data sources that human trafficking researchers may make use of for both quantitative and qualitative studies. Quantitative studies tend to focus on estimates, frequencies, trends, and opinions of human trafficking (Russell 2018). Official government statistics are one data source that quantitative researchers may make use of. In the United States, the FBI established the Human Trafficking (UCR-HT) data collection as part of its Uniform Crime Reporting (UCR) Program in 2013. State and local law enforcement agencies that participate in this collection provide counts of offenses, case clearances, and arrests for human trafficking for the purpose of commercial sex acts or involuntary servitude. The 2019 report shows a total of 1,883 incidents of human trafficking were reported that year, with 85 percent reported in the category of commercial sex acts.

As with other crimes, there are several drawbacks to the use of official statistics. Data from official sources, such as criminal justice agencies, are likely to be undercounts of the true number of human trafficking cases. This is in large part due to law enforcement deficiencies in identifying and reporting cases of human trafficking (Farrell and Reichert 2017). Because of this, the number of victims recorded by law enforcement may be a better indicator of the effectiveness and functionality of law enforcement in a country, rather than a good estimate of the number of human trafficking victims (Tyldum and Brunovskis 2005). Often, however, official reports may be one of the few sources of data on identified victims available in a particular country.

Globally, organizations like the United Nations and Interpol can act as sources that bring together statistics from a variety of cross-national sources. The UNODC SHERLOC Database hosts a database of legislation on human trafficking in countries around the world, as well as a case law database. This data can be used to not only study differences and similarities in the laws in various nations, but also to examine details on victims and perpetrators, verdicts, and other information from prosecuted cases of trafficking across the world. For example, cases from the 2020 UNODC Global Report on Trafficking in Persons tell us that the majority of persons investigated or arrested, prosecuted, and/or convicted of trafficking in persons are male, comprising over 60 percent of the total. Thirty-six percent of those prosecuted for trafficking were female and were more likely to be involved in the recruitment phase.

The UNODC has produced seven of these global reports on human trafficking since 2009, with the aim to provide an overview of patterns, flows, and current issues of human trafficking around the world. Data for the 2020 report is drawn from information on the detected victims and convicted traffickers across 148 countries. Globally, victims are typically trafficked within geographically close areas, with most detected victims being citizens of the countries where they are detected. Data shows that domestic trafficking is a growing issue compared to the often-focused issue of cross-national trafficking. Sixty-five percent of trafficking cases were reported as domestic, with only 15 percent involving victims from another region. Domestic trafficking tends to mirror international trafficking flows, with victims moving from poorer, often rural, areas to richer and more urban areas. An examination of cross-national trafficking reveals that victims tend to be from countries within the same region. Western and Southern Europe, North America, and the affluent countries of the Middle East are the only destinations with significant levels of detected victims trafficked from other regions (UNODC 2020).

Through these reports we can see that over the past fifteen years the number of detected victims has increased over time, becoming more equal among the sexes, with the share of adult women falling from 70 percent to less than 50 percent by 2018. Explaining why this split has become more equal over time, some scholars point to the shift from focusing solely on sex trafficking of women to other forms of trafficking and victims, as well as increases in awareness and training. Children account for about one-third of the detected victims of trafficking and are disproportionately linked with the broader issue of child labor in low-income countries. Sexual exploitation remains the most common motive for trafficking at 50 percent, with labor trafficking representing 38 percent among detected cases, 6 percent subjected to forced criminal activity, and more than 1 percent to begging. Smaller numbers were trafficked for forced marriages, organ removals, and other purposes. Domestic servitude, fishing, agriculture, and mining are industries in which labor trafficking has been well documented. Such sectors also lend themselves to workers being isolated, making abuses difficult to detect and punish. Direct physical violence is rarely used to recruit victims; instead, deception and targeting the victim's situation of need are used. After the recruitment phase, the use of violence is reported during the exploitation, alongside other means of control, such as confiscation of travel documents (UNODC 2020).

Another source of data at a global level is the Counter Trafficking Data Collaborative (CTDC). The CTDC is a dataset founded by the IOM with thousands of individual-level, anonymized entries about victims of human trafficking identified worldwide by counter-trafficking organizations. Because the data comes from identified cases of trafficking, it is important to keep in mind that the data may not be representative of the total victim population. As human trafficking is a crime intended to go undetected, identified cases are not a true random sample of the population. However, these cases do provide detailed data on the profiles, forms, and experiences of trafficking victims.

Data through 2021 shows that of the cases logged by the CTDC, 55 percent were categorized as sexual exploitation, 37 percent as labor exploitation, and the remaining 8 percent as other. Seventy-three percent of identified victims were female and 27 percent were male. The most frequently reported age category of the victims differs by type of exploitation, with ages nine to seventeen occurring most frequently for sexual exploitation and ages thirty to thirty-eight occurring most frequently for labor exploitation. The victims' relationship to their recruiter is far more likely to be an intimate partner, family member, or friend for victims of sexual exploitation, while for labor exploitation the *other* category is most frequent. The means of control used on victims also share some differences by type of exploitation. The top five means of control reported by victims of sexual exploitation in order are psychological abuse, threats, restriction of movement, physical abuse, and use of psychoactive substances. For victims of labor exploitation, the top five means of control reported are taking earnings, excessive working hours, psychological abuse, threats, and restriction of movement (CTDC 2021).

Qualitative research such as surveys and interviews conducted by researchers are another way in which we can gain detailed knowledge about the issue of trafficking. Reviews of the human trafficking literature have found that qualitative studies are more common, typically examining victims' exploitation and experiences with services (Russell 2018). Qualitative studies tend to focus on smaller units of study over national or cross-national studies. This is advantageous because qualitative and quantitative studies of cities or even small regions can provide valid numbers about the extent of the problem and richer information about the experiences of trafficking victims (Weitzer 2014). Such research can then be used to more effectively identify and target "hot spots" of trafficking for intervention efforts.

As one example, field work and respondent-driven sampling of undocumented Spanish-speaking migrant workers in San Diego led to 826 participant interviews. Among this sample, 31 percent experienced treatment that meets the legal definition of human trafficking, while 55 percent experienced various abusive labor practices (Zhang et al. 2014). The most frequently reported violations were unfair labor practices (45%), deceptive practices (28%), physical restriction (22%), and physical threats (15%). Construction work, food processing, and janitorial/cleaning were the top three industries migrant workers reported experiencing these abusive practices in. This reflects the findings of other research, that forced labor frequently involves migrants in industries where the cost of labor is the primary means of increasing a business's competitiveness (Zhang 2012). From their results, the authors then estimated the percentage of labor trafficking victims in the undocumented workforce of San Diego County to be between 26 and 35 percent (Zhang et al. 2014). While the authors note that such a local sample should not be generalized to the national level, studies like this are important in providing evidence that labor trafficking may be frequent among certain subpopulations or in particular industries.

There are also a variety of nongovernmental organizations (NGOs) working in the field of human trafficking, providing services to victims, training to law enforcement, outreach to potential victims, and more. Such organizations can also act as a source of data on human trafficking. These victim service providers can be a primary source of data on how victims are referred for services (i.e., from the police, a hospital, or other sources), the services victims sought and received, and demographic characteristics of the victims they serve.

In the United States, the National Human Trafficking Hotline, which receives federal funding, works to connect victims of human trafficking with the services and supports they need. Tips about potential situations of trafficking are reported to the appropriate authorities in certain cases. Between 2007, when the hotline began, and 2019, the hotline has received over 250,000 contacts about over sixty thousand distinct situations of trafficking. Among the suspected human trafficking cases being reported to the hotline, one study found that the majority involved direct contact with a potential victim (40.9%), followed by observation of suspicious activity (25.4%), victim self-report (24.2%), and indirect contact with a potential victim (11.9%). Approximately 7 percent of cases involved a victim in immediate need, with the most common request being for emergency shelter (Tillyer, Smith, and Tillyer 2023).

Statistics from the hotline can give us a general idea of the picture of human trafficking in the United States, though like official data, these only represent reported cases. Sex trafficking cases were more frequently reported to the hotline, making up 72 percent of all reports. Sex trafficking cases were more likely to involve female victims and minors, while labor trafficking cases were more likely to involve male victims and foreign nationals. However, labor trafficking cases involved greater numbers of victims, averaging 5.27 victims compared to 1.90 for sex trafficking cases (Tillyer, Smith, and Tillyer 2023).

RESPONDING TO HUMAN TRAFFICKING

Framing the Issue

To understand how governments respond to human trafficking, it is important to understand how the issue has been framed over time. Framing involves "a process of how politicians, policymakers relay their messages to attract media attention and put the best face on the events, how journalists construct messages under organizational guidelines and professional values, and how audience members interpret, think, and reassess those media messages" (Zhang 2000, 5). Media can thus not only influence the general public's understanding of human trafficking, but also shape the priorities of policies and laws (Sanford, Martínez, and Weitzer 2016).

When public interest in human trafficking as an issue first grew in the 1990s, it was discussed as a human rights issue, focusing primarily on the rights and needs of victims (Farrell and Fahy 2009). This framing of human trafficking focused on women and children who were being commercially sexually exploited. This is when stereotypes about human trafficking involving physical force and the underground industry of brothels emerged. Analysis of news coverage of human trafficking has consistently found a disproportionate focus on victims of sex trafficking, particularly women and children (Johnston, Friedman, and Sobel 2015; Marchionni 2012; Pajnik 2010; Sanford, Martínez, and Weitzer 2016).

The passing of both the TVPA in the United States and the United Nations Palermo Protocol enhanced public awareness of human trafficking as a criminal offense, prompting the media to take interest in this new crime. The narrative around human trafficking began to focus more on the progression of the act from beginning to end, including the recruitment, harboring, and transportation of individuals, rather than the conditions that make individuals vulnerable to human trafficking (Lee 2011). This shift in media framing of human trafficking redirected focus from framing human trafficking as a human rights issue to framing it as a crime and criminal justice problem. Media focused not on the human rights abuses experienced by the victims, but on the illicit and dangerous nature of human trafficking operations. Human trafficking was framed as a problem of organized crime, leading to a focus on trafficking being connected to foreign victims and crossing borders (Farrell and Fahy 2009). This is reflected in the fact that the Palermo Protocol itself is part of a larger protocol to the Convention against Transnational Organized Crime enforced by the United Nations Office on Drugs and Crime (Gallagher 2010). These changes importantly tapped into public attitudes about anti-immigration and transnational crime (Chuang 2006a; Farrell and Fahy 2009; Lee 2011), and calls for stricter border control policies were often portrayed as the solution to human trafficking (Pajnik 2010).

Although this shift in the framing of human trafficking as a problem of crime and justice helped draw more awareness, support, and funding for anti-trafficking efforts, it has also meant that such efforts have evolved from a criminal justice–focused perspective (Farrell and Fahy 2009; Hua 2011). Both the US TVPA and the UN Palermo Protocol outline a strategy for addressing human trafficking known as the 3P paradigm. The 3Ps are the framework used to combat trafficking and include prosecution of offenders, protection of victims, and prevention of the crime. This criminal justice framing means that the majority of anti-trafficking efforts have focused on prosecuting offenders, while protecting victims has received less attention (Chuang 2006a; Farrell and Fahy 2009). Furthermore, the prevention of human trafficking has not received as much attention at the government level. With governments focused primarily on treating human trafficking as a law-and-order problem, the underlying connections to migration, inequality, and violence are overlooked. As a result, anti-trafficking strategies have not focused on appropriate measures of prevention (Chuang 2006a; Shinkle 2007). Prevention efforts have largely been shortsighted, focusing on awareness campaigns, rather than addressing the root causes of human trafficking, such as economic policies, social inequalities, and conflicts (Chuang 2006a; Farrell and Fahy 2009).

Prosecution

As outlined by the US TVPA and the UN Palermo Protocol, the prosecution element involves the criminalization of human trafficking under law, government efforts toward investigating and prosecuting cases of human trafficking, and sufficient sentences for those convicted (Office to Monitor and Combat Trafficking in Persons 2022; UNODC 2009). In the past decade there has been an abundance of research on prosecution-related issues, including challenges in identifying victims, bias toward sex trafficking cases, and barriers to successful investigation and prosecution (Barrick et al. 2014; Farrell et al. 2016, 2020).

Between 2003 and 2013, all fifty US states criminalized the act of human trafficking (Farrell, Bouché, and Wolfe 2019). This is an important development toward increasing the identification, investigation, and prosecution of human trafficking cases as most criminal enforcement occurs at the local and state level, rather than the federal level (Barnhart 2009). Unfortunately, compared to their federal counterparts, municipal, county, and state law enforcement agencies face training and investigation deficits in identifying and responding to trafficking cases (Farrell, McDevitt, and Fahy 2010).

Sex trafficking cases are identified, investigated, and prosecuted at a higher rate than labor trafficking cases. This is not necessarily because there are significantly more sex trafficking cases. Instead, research shows a bias toward investigating sex trafficking cases (Farrell et al. 2020). Labor trafficking remains strikingly underenforced even by the statistics of the federal government itself (Barnhart 2009). This underidentification of labor trafficking victims compared to sex trafficking victims is likely due to a variety of factors, including definitional confusion between trafficking and smuggling, lack of awareness and prioritization of the issue among law enforcement, labor trafficking victims not coming into contact with the routine activities of police, and victims not coming forward due to being fearful of police and deportation (Barrick et al. 2014; Farrell et al. 2020). For example, with sex trafficking investigations, law enforcement are able to use traditional vice tactics, including undercover operations and stings. These methods are not useful for coming into contact with labor trafficking victims, who are often isolated at their workplace or private residence (Farrell et al. 2020; Peters 2013). For labor trafficking investigations, law enforcement is often dependent on tips from the general public or labor regulators, and such cases are often seen as the responsibility of federal authorities despite states having authority over labor trafficking cases as well (Barrick et al. 2014; Farrell et al. 2020; Farrell and Pfeffer 2014). Further complicating the issue, law enforcement may not believe labor trafficking to be a problem in their jurisdiction or may view labor trafficking victims differently from sex trafficking victims. Labor trafficking victims may not be viewed sympathetically, with law enforcement believing they wanted to come to the United States and therefore knew what they were getting into (Farrell and Pfeffer 2014; Peters 2013). Sex trafficking victims, on the other hand, are viewed through a moral lens, with their undocumented status being viewed as forced upon them (Peters 2013).

Protection

The protection element moves anti-trafficking efforts beyond just the identification of victims, also calling for comprehensive victim services, funding to government agencies or NGOs to provide those services, and legislative measures to ensure that victims are protected, including from deportation (Office to Monitor and Combat Trafficking in Persons 2022; UNODC 2009). However, funding for such assistance is often lacking (Nichols 2016). Further, services such as shelters may be limited to sex trafficking victims or women, excluding labor trafficking victims, men, and LGBTQ individuals (Heil and Nichols 2015).

One area where protection is lacking deals with the arrest of victims. Studies of law enforcement show that arrest of victims is commonplace and at times used as a measure to ensure victim cooperation (Barrick et al. 2021; Farrell et al. 2016). The prosecution of human trafficking cases is often heavily dependent on victim testimony, though the use of arrest and detention to secure that cooperation undercuts the idea that prosecution should not come at the cost of victim protections (Heinrich 2010). Making victim services conditional on such cooperation is also common (for more on this, see this chapter's policy box). One evaluation of a human trafficking task force in San Francisco found that police were conducting vice stings where individuals would be placed in handcuffs, questioned, and then given referrals for victim services, all without determining who was a sex worker and who was a trafficking victim. Minors were often sent to juvenile detention (Barrick et al. 2021). Such practices exacerbate the confusion between consenting sex workers and trafficking victims, and are likely to have detrimental effects on victim cooperation with law enforcement investigation (Barrick et al. 2021).

One way the TVPA works to protect victims of human trafficking is through T visas. T visas allow eligible foreign victims of human trafficking, and their families, to become temporary US residents eligible to become permanent residents after three years. These visas are intended to assist trafficking victims to stay in the United States as long as certain stipulations are met. To receive T visa status, you need to have been a victim of trafficking who would suffer extreme hardship if you were removed from the United States. Once approved, victims are eligible for federal benefits, such as Medicaid and food stamps, and are permitted to work legally in the United States. As a condition of the visa, victims are also required to comply with the investigation, unless they are a minor. The T visa status is limited to five thousand individuals each fiscal year. The spouse, children, or parents of a minor, in order to avoid extreme hardship, may also be given derivative T visa status (Pollock and Hollier 2010). In 2020, 2,058 T visa applications for victims of trafficking or their family members were approved, 1,289 were denied, and 3,246 are still pending, with the prior year's backlog carried over.

All victims of severe forms of trafficking are eligible to apply for T visas, though in practice, sex trafficking victims may be more likely to receive them than labor trafficking victims. Foreign migrant workers who have experienced labor trafficking may be fearful of cooperating with law enforcement, not only out of fear of retaliation from their trafficker but also because of experiences with corrupt or unreliable law enforcement in their home countries. Such individuals may also be reluctant to seek help due to the possibility of not qualifying for a T visa and thus risking deportation (Brennan 2008).

This fear of not qualifying is valid, as studies have shown that law enforcement often make value-laden judgments about who they endorse for visa eligibility. To be eligible, a T visa application must include an endorsement from the involved law enforcement agency. A study that involved interviews and fieldwork observations with law enforcement personnel showed they were often hesitant to endorse victims if the case did not fit with their notion of what trafficking looks like. The researcher states, "While many factors contributed to law enforcement's assessment of cases and their willingness to endorse victims (such as prosecutability, credibility of the victim, and availability of investigative resources), this was a key area where subjectivities around sex and 'sex trafficking' entered into decision-making.

Since law enforcement agents were less likely to investigate 'non-sex' cases, they were also less likely to endorse those victims" (Peters 2013, 247).

T visas are also criticized for the requirement that victims cooperate with the investigation and prosecution. Victim advocates and attorneys have observed that many trafficking victims do not wish to cooperate with law enforcement simply because it is not a priority for them (Pollock and Hollier 2010). In addition to fears of retaliation against themselves, they may fear retaliation against family members back in their home country. Other victims may not wish to cooperate due to the trauma of recounting their experiences of exploitation or facing their trafficker in court (Smith 2013). Language barriers and long processing times also act as barriers for potential T visa recipients.

Ultimately, T visas are underutilized, with many victims slipping through the cracks in the criminal justice system. This can be attributed to law enforcement's inability to identify or certify eligible victims, as well as victims being unwilling to report their trafficking or cooperate with authorities for a variety of reasons. Until changes are made, foreign victims will continue to be misidentified, most often as unauthorized migrants or as criminals, and face deportation. One alternative is to switch from a prosecution-first approach to a victim-centered, human rights approach. Rather than having criminalization and deportation as the default, placing services first would help victims begin to heal, which would lead to more successful prosecutions overall (Culkin 2015).

What other changes could be made to center protection of victims and victims' rights, especially during the process of prosecution?

Ultimately, while protections for victims do exist under the law, enforcement and criminalization remain the most common and well-funded anti-trafficking strategies. This is despite research that shows that victim protections do not have to take a backseat to prosecution, but can serve as a complementary aspect of anti-trafficking efforts (Farrell, Bouché, and Wolfe 2019; Heinrich 2010). Consider the fact that a recent study found that punitiveness is not the only predictor of effective arrests and prosecutions of traffickers, but so too was state investment in victim services (Farrell, Bouché, and Wolfe 2019). Funding such services can not only protect the interests of victims, perhaps leading to greater trust and cooperation with law enforcement, but also create a collaborative environment where law enforcement works directly with service providers.

Prevention

Finally, the prevention element is aimed at impeding human trafficking from a variety of angles. This includes information and programs designed to intervene in high-risk populations for victimization on the supply side, as well as those designed to end demand (Office to Monitor and Combat Trafficking in Persons 2022; Shinkle 2007). Awareness campaigns represent a common prevention method utilized within anti-trafficking programs (Bryant and Landman 2020; Shinkle 2007). Many awareness campaigns tend to be aimed at educating the general public, despite research that has shown that campaigns targeting at-risk groups or groups likely to come into contact with victims are more effective (Bryant and Landman 2020; Shinkle 2007; Szablewska and Kubacki 2018). Awareness campaigns may also be overly simplistic in their efforts to grab attention. This has the unintended effect of perpetuating stereotypes about human trafficking victims and mixing human trafficking with other issues, such as migration and prostitution (Szablewska and Kubacki 2018).

Prevention efforts also include public policies related to the root issues underlying trafficking victimization, including those around migration, education, employment, health, security, equality, and crime prevention (UNODC 2009). Such prevention efforts represent a long-term solution to reducing human trafficking, but governments have tended to focus instead on controlling migration, prostitution, and organized crime (Shinkle 2007). In the United States, prevention strategies focus on border interdiction, which often has the consequence of pushing undocumented migrants further underground, leaving them more vulnerable to traffickers (Chacón 2006). As a UNODC report on the implementation of the Palermo Protocol notes, "Prevention is one of the most important aspects of an effective anti-human trafficking response. However, not all prevention strategies are integrated into broader policies related to trafficking in persons and many lack evidence-based research and planning as well as impact evaluations" (UNODC 2009, 12). As has been noted in the literature, more research is critically needed in the area of anti-trafficking efforts, particularly program evaluations and outcome evaluations, in order to better assess what prevention efforts are effective (Bryant and Landman 2020; Szablewska and Kubacki 2018).

1. Explore myths, facts, and statistics of human trafficking from Polaris Project at https://polarisproject.org/myths-facts-and-statistics/.

2. Visit the Counter-Trafficking Data Collaborative website at https://www.ctdatacollaborative.org/. Explore the global dataset map to see trafficking flows between countries, as well as the characteristics of identified victims.

3. Look up the National Human Trafficking Hotline statistics for your state at https://humantraffickinghotline.org/states. Identify what types of trafficking are being reported in your state and how those trends have changed over time.

4. The Department of Justice (DOJ) Office for Victims of Crime provides a directory of crime victim services at https://ovc.ojp.gov/directory-crime-victim-services. Search the directory to compare the services available for labor trafficking and sex trafficking victims in your state.

CHAPTER DISCUSSION QUESTIONS

1. Google image search the term *human trafficking* and scroll through the results. What image of human trafficking are the results presenting? Are any stereotypes being reflected? How do you think media portrayals of human trafficking shape the average person's knowledge of the issue?

2. What are the differences between the concepts of human trafficking, smuggling, and migration? In what ways can they overlap?

3. Sex trafficking tends to be identified, investigated, and prosecuted at a higher rate, despite many scholars believing that labor trafficking is just as common. Discuss at least three reasons why this may occur.

4. Why is the T visa often criticized for requiring victim cooperation with law enforcement? What are some potential issues with this requirement?

TWO

Deterrence and Victimization Theories

CLASSICAL CRIMINOLOGY AND DETERRENCE

Before classical theory was developed, people believed that criminal activity was explained through a religious or spiritual cause. Criminals were believed to be sinners who were possessed by demons, and penitentiaries were constructed as places for people to repent for their sins (Hagan and Daigle 2020). This perspective dominated early explanations of crime until the Enlightenment in the seventeenth and eighteenth centuries.

The Enlightenment represented a major shift in the way people viewed the world and criminality. Enlightenment thinkers focused on observing and measuring behavior through a scientific approach. They believed that individuals have free will and make decisions based in rationality (Bohm and Vogel 2015). Within criminology, the Enlightenment led to the development of the classical school of criminological thought, which was the first modern approach to making sense of crime and criminality.

Cesare Beccaria (1738–1794) was an Italian philosopher of this time period who is often called the father of classical criminology. In his book *On Crimes and Punishment*, he wrote about the need to reform the criminal justice system, which he saw as arbitrary and cruel. Beccaria believed that punishment should be based on the degree of injury the offender caused, with a purpose of deterrence rather than retribution. In order for punishment to be effectively deterrent, it needed to be swift, certain, and severe enough to outweigh the personal benefits derived from crime (Beccaria 1963). By swift, Beccaria meant that the punishment should follow closely after the commission of the crime. Certainty refers to the likelihood that the offender would receive legal sanction for committing the crime. Finally, the severity of the punishment should be proportional to the seriousness of the crime.

For Beccaria, punishment could serve as both a general deterrent and a specific deterrent. General deterrence is aimed at society at large and is the idea that making examples of offenders by punishing them would discourage others from committing the same crime. Specific deterrence is aimed at the particular individual who committed the crime—by punishing them, they will be deterred from committing the crime again (Bohm and Vogel 2015).

Jeremy Bentham (1748–1832) borrowed from the ideas of Beccaria when he wrote *Introduction to the Principles of Morals and Legislation*, where he argued that the pain associated with crime commission must outweigh the pleasure derived from criminal activity. This approach has been termed the hedonistic calculus, or the idea that individuals weigh the potential benefits of an action against the potential costs (Schmalleger 2020).

Under the perspective of deterrence, crime is reduced by increasing the costs and decreasing the benefits for the commission of crimes. For those who do offend, their sentences work to deter both the specific individual from committing the same crime again in the future, as well as other individuals from committing that crime. However, these punishments only deter if individuals perceive that there is a high certainty that they will be caught and swiftly punished. Below, three areas of human trafficking that deterrence can be used to understand are explored, including the sentencing of traffickers, corporations using forced labor, and responding to sex trafficking by focusing on prostitution policy.

Deterrence, Sentencing, and Human Trafficking

Sentencing is one often-examined area of deterrence. To make the penalties for committing a crime deterrent, offenders must be convicted. Convictions are dependent on both prosecutions and police enforcement (Kara 2010a). Police enforcement is undermined by gaps in training and resources, reliance on reactive rather than proactive investigation techniques, and corruption (Farrell and Kane 2020). What human trafficking arrests are made may also not proceed to the prosecution stage (Kara 2010a). This may be due to uncertainty about the law and what evidence is required or relying on testimony from victims who may not wish to cooperate (Farrell and Kane 2020). Looking at federal cases from 2015, the most frequent reason US attorneys declined to prosecute was due to insufficient evidence (Motivans and Snyder

2018). State prosecutions reflect similar issues, with physical and corroborating evidence strongly predicting the prosecution of human trafficking cases (Farrell et al. 2016).

There are discrepancies in prosecution by type of case as well, with forced labor being more likely to be declined for prosecution than sex trafficking (Bouché, Farrell, and Wittmer 2015; Motivans and Snyder 2018). In addition to sex trafficking cases being more likely to be prosecuted, cases involving women and minors are also the most commonly prosecuted trafficking cases (Feehs and Currier Wheeler 2021). This may be the case due to increased awareness surrounding sex trafficking compared to labor trafficking (Bouché, Farrell, and Wittmer 2015). The low prosecution of forced labor cases has also been attributed to a lack of knowledge about the laws and limited understanding of how to properly apply them (Bouché, Farrell, and Wittmer 2015; Farrell et al. 2016). Sex trafficking cases that involve minors also have a lower evidentiary burden, as prosecutors do not have to prove force, fraud, or coercion (Santamaria 2021). In line with these issues, there is some evidence to suggest that it is not having harsh penalties in the law that works to deter, but increasing certainty by providing resources and support for investigators and prosecutors (Bouché, Farrell, and Wittmer 2015).

Before 2000, trafficking prosecutions were rare. Trafficking cases were difficult to establish, costly, and time consuming, with prosecutors piecing together various laws only to end up with a light sentence (Tiefenbrun 2006). With the passage of the TVPA in 2000, prosecutors now had a specific legal tool to bring forward human trafficking cases. With the sections added to the US Criminal Code by the TVPA, trafficking-related offenses could now carry lengthy prison terms related to trafficking, with enhanced penalties possible if the victim was underage (Santamaria 2021). Specifically, defendants convicted of sex trafficking under §1591 face a minimum of ten to fifteen years. Forced labor convictions under §1590 do not carry a mandatory minimum, but defendants may be sentenced to upward of twenty years (Feehs and Currier Wheeler 2021).

Looking at trends in both federal and state prosecutions of human trafficking, it is possible to discern the possibilities and limits of deterrence. Looking at twenty years of federal human trafficking prosecutions between 2000 and 2020, Feehs and Currier Wheeler (2021) found several trends. During this time period, over four thousand defendants were prosecuted in federal human trafficking cases since the enactment of the TVPA. At 93 percent, the majority of all federal prosecutions have been sex trafficking cases. In fact, more sex trafficking prosecutions were filed in 2020 alone than all forced labor prosecutions in twenty years. Sex trafficking cases are also significantly more likely to end in successful convictions compared to labor trafficking cases. In 2001, the average sentence in a trafficking case was just shy of five years at 59 months. By 2010, the average sentence was a bit over ten years at 128 months, and in 2020 the average sentence reached its highest point yet at 156 months, or thirteen years.

While all fifty US states have now criminalized human trafficking, penalties still vary widely from state to state (Farrell, Bouché, and Wolfe 2019). State laws may vary by who is defined as a trafficker, what is required to obtain a conviction, and the severity of the penalties (Teigen 2018). Prosecutors' lack of knowledge or experience with their state's trafficking laws can also lead to low prosecutions (Bouché, Farrell, and Wittmer 2015; Farrell et al. 2016). Because of this, it is common to see states make use of other types of charges to bring forward cases. A study of state prosecutions of human trafficking suspects across twelve US counties found that trafficking charges were only used in 20 percent of cases. State laws around the promotion or compelling of prostitution were often used instead (Farrell et al. 2016).

One of the main points deterrence-based theories make is that the punishment of traffickers would send a message to deter them as well as deter others. Deterrence theory would argue that the sentencing of traffickers needs to be sufficiently severe in order to be an effective deterrent. Overall, however, there is a lack of evidence that harsh sentences deter future offenders (Mollema and Terblanche 2017). Instead, it is often argued that effective investigation and enforcement is needed to better deter offenders. This is in line with research on trafficking prosecutions that has found that comprehensive laws with a support structure for their enforcement matters more than harsh criminal penalties (Bouché, Farrell, and Wittmer 2015). It is possible to envision how increases in funding, training, and education can be improved for police and prosecutors, leading to better enforcement and successful prosecutions of individual traffickers.

Corporations and Labor Trafficking in Supply Chains

One area that is in sore need of increased training and enforcement involves the prosecution of corporations involved in human trafficking. As corporations seek to cut costs and increase profits, forced labor is incentivized in their supply chains (Pierce 2010). Manufacturers, retailers, and service providers can all profit from the use of labor trafficking at various stages in their supply chains (Shavers 2012). Human trafficking can be found in any industry, though the risk is higher in industries that rely on low-skilled labor, industries that are seasonal in nature, and industries where the turnaround time for production is extremely short (U.S. Department of State 2015). Such industries include jobs that are "dirty, dangerous, and difficult . . . that are typically low-paying and undervalued by society and are often filled by socially marginalized groups including migrants, people with disabilities, or minorities" (U.S. Department of State 2015, 14). Since 2005 the U.S. Bureau of International Labor Affairs has produced a yearly report of goods from countries believed to be produced with forced labor or child labor. The 2020 report lists 156 goods from seventy-seven countries from agriculture, manufacturing, and mining industries. Some of the most frequent goods made with forced and/or child labor include bricks, gold, sugarcane, coffee, and garments (Bureau of International Labor Affairs 2020). It should be noted, however, that this list does not include goods or industries within the United States that use forced labor (Aronowitz 2019).

The 2008 reauthorization of the TVPA added language to allow for criminal and civil penalties for anyone who "'knowingly benefits, financially or by receiving anything of value, from participation in a venture which has engaged in the providing or obtaining of labor or services by means of force, threats, or abuse when the party knew or recklessly disregarded how the labor was obtained" (Ezell 2016, 502). States have also expanded their definitions of trafficking to allow businesses and corporations to be prosecuted (Teigen 2018). Such laws have created an avenue for businesses to face criminal penalties, fines, and even dissolution. The idea behind such laws is that by holding corporations liable for human trafficking they will be encouraged to eliminate trafficking from their supply chains and deter other corporations as well (Pierce 2010).

However, there are a number of barriers that halt the effective deterrence of labor trafficking. First, the language of the law can make prosecutions overly difficult. Prosecutors must establish that the defendant "knowingly" benefited or was in "reckless disregard" that forced labor was being used (Dryhurst 2012; Ezell 2016). One primary way corporations are able to avoid this liability is through subcontracting schemes (Bang 2013; Pierce 2010). Subcontracting occurs when an outside company or individual is used to fulfill contracts for services and labor. Subcontractors may perpetuate abuse against workers through actions like charging exorbitant fees, demanding excessive hours, or forcing individuals to work in hazardous conditions. Corporations are then able to claim ignorance and the subcontractor is held liable for exploitation rather than the company that employed the subcontractor. Many times, however, subcontractors are overseas, making a case difficult to bring in the United States, and those responsible simply disappear or reorganize (Bang 2013).

Second, industry regulation attempts have frequently relied on self-policing, which has provided mixed results (Aronowitz 2019). The idea of corporate social responsibility is often incorporated into industry regulation plans as a means to reduce trafficking in supply chains. Corporate social responsibility can be defined many ways but generally refers to the idea that businesses should incorporate social and environmental responsibilities into their business operations (Shavers 2012). Frequently this is accomplished through voluntary efforts by companies, such as providing awareness and training in relevant industries like hotels and trucking (see the policy box in this chapter). Two examples of industry-specific attempts at self-regulation include the Harkin-Engel Protocol and the Kimberley Process Certification Scheme.

The Harkin-Engel Protocol emerged after heavy media attention to the issue of child labor in the cocoa industry in 2000. In 2001, US Representative Eliot Engel introduced legislation that would create a federal labeling system to certify whether or not child slave labor had been used in certain cocoa products (Aronowitz 2019). Chocolate companies were strongly opposed to the regulation, which did not pass the Senate. Instead, a deal that would be named the Harkin-Engel Protocol was negotiated among major chocolate producers, such as Hershey, Nestlé, and Mars, that placed the responsibility of eliminating child labor from cocoa production in the hands of the corporations. Objectives and deadlines for each objective were set, and missed, in 2005, 2008, 2010, and 2020 (Whoriskey and Siegel 2019). Chocolate companies have turned to nonprofit groups like Fairtrade, Utz, and the Rainforest Alliance for help in labor certification labels, though some of the farms certified by these third parties continue to employ children (Aronowitz 2019). Monitoring systems are lacking, with sporadic and scheduled farm inspections making detection easily avoidable (Whoriskey and Siegel 2019).

The use of forced labor and child labor has also been linked to the mining of diamonds, frequently in countries linked to the production of blood, or conflict, diamonds. In 2003 the diamond industry established the Kimberley Process Certification Scheme, an international certification system designed to ensure that the diamonds that consumers were buying were conflict-free

(Baker 2015). Over a decade later, the process has not been successful, with loopholes unable to stop the flow of conflict diamonds. The process uses a very narrow definition of what qualifies as a conflict diamond, and applies only to rough diamonds. Once diamonds are cut and polished the scheme no longer applies to them (Global Witness 2013). Noncompliance has gone unchecked, with smuggling and money laundering contributing to the unaddressed issue of conflict diamonds reaching the market (Global Witness 2007). Ultimately monitoring efforts like the Harkin-Engel Protocol and Kimberley Scheme are difficult to implement, sustain, and assess in their effectiveness (Aronowitz 2019). There is often insufficient cooperation across agencies to ensure accountability, with independent monitors lacking the authority needed to enforce change (Aronowitz 2019).

However, corporations may not be willing to implement such monitoring on a voluntary basis, requiring government accountability instead. There have been some government efforts to regulate supply chains and hold businesses accountable. One example is the 2010 California Transparency in Supply Chains Act. The act requires companies doing business in California that have grossed over $100 million worldwide to make publicly available their efforts toward eliminating human trafficking in their supply chains. Specifically, companies must disclose the extent to which they verify the risks in their supply chains, complete supplier audits, certify that materials from their suppliers are produced in accordance with country laws, maintain internal accountability policies and procedures, and provide relevant training for employees and management (Pickles and Zhu 2013). A review of company compliance with the act found that of the 62 percent of eligible companies with a statement produced in accordance with the act, the majority lacked detail and verification (Ball et al. 2015). Companies frequently do not produce statements that address each of the five areas, focusing primarily on internal standards and training rather than independent audits (Aronowitz 2019). Further, the act has faced several criticisms, including moving responsibility from the purview of the state to corporations themselves and relying on corporate certification and audit systems that may be very weak (New 2015).

Third, there is a lack of both criminal and civil enforcement (Dryhurst 2012). Prosecutions of corporations for human trafficking remains dramatically low. Federal prosecutions have remained rare and focused on individual labor contractors instead of corporations and those higher up the supply chain (Dryhurst 2012; Pierce 2010). The same is true of European countries (Planitzer et al. 2018). Since the enactment of the TVPA in 2000, there have only been nine federal prosecutions against businesses and corporations, totaling less than 1 percent of all defendants (Feehs and Currier Wheeler 2021). The majority of these cases have been sex trafficking prosecutions related to hotels. This presents a stark contrast to civil suits, which frequently deal with forced labor lawsuits (Feehs and Currier Wheeler 2021). Civil suits against corporations have increased over time, although they are ultimately a slow and expensive way to seek accountability (Dryhurst 2012; Ezell 2016). Civil suits are also less effective as a deterrent because they provide no way to prevent trafficking in the first place (Ezell 2016). Further complicating the issue, research has found that the use of monetary sanctions in corporate cases has a limited deterrent effect (Planitzer and Katona 2017).

The near absence of prosecutions means that companies lack sufficient incentives to monitor trafficking in their supply chains (Dryhurst 2012). While eliminating labor trafficking and exploitation has no single or easy solution, steps can be taken to deter companies. Resources need to be purposefully directed toward investigating and prosecuting cases, with a focus on implementing long-term plans. The government's commitment to addressing trafficking violations can be shown through "relentless and high-profile prosecutions" that can act as a deterrent for the wider business community (Barrick et al. 2013).

Prostitution Policies and Sex Trafficking

There are several models of prostitution policy. First, there is the deterrence model, also known as the prohibitionist or criminalization model. Under this model, both the buying and selling of sex are criminalized. The underlying philosophy is the same as deterrence theory—by criminalizing both the selling and purchasing of sex, individuals will be deterred from the commercial sex industry, including sex traffickers. With the exception of a few counties in Nevada, this is the approach of the United States.

There are several limitations of this model. First, sex workers face high rates of violence and victimization (Nichols 2016). Research shows that criminalization creates an environment where offenders get away with harm and sex workers face increased risks of experiencing violence, exploitation, and trafficking (Albright and D'Adamo 2017a). Despite this victimization, many sex workers may not seek assistance or report the crimes committed against them. Instead, they face limited legal recourse as they themselves face arrest, stigma, and even harassment by law enforcement (Nichols 2016).

Under the criminalization model, sex workers fear judgment and arrest, eroding their trust in law enforcement, health care workers, and social service providers. They avoid disclosing their involvement in the commercial sex industry and whether they are involved by choice or not.

Aspects of harm reduction are also limited or nonexistent under the deterrence model. Harm reduction includes services that make sex work safer, with sex workers able to access help if needed. This approach includes things like "street outreach, safe shelter, social services to assist with exiting prostitution, substance abuse services, health screenings, and access to condoms and dental dams to prevent sexually transmitted infections as well as various forms of contraception" (Nichols 2016, 66). Providing such services is often seen as "pro-prostitution" under the deterrence model, and often organizations may face funding restrictions if they participate in such actions (Chuang 2010).

Further, research does not support the underlying philosophy of deterrence, with prostitution having high rates of recidivism (Nichols 2016). Sex workers who have been arrested and fined may face stigma from their record and have few options to pay the fines other than returning to sex work. A record for prostitution can limit employment opportunities, housing, access to benefits, and more. There are also issues of displacement to consider, as sex workers may move from place to place, including from street prostitution to indoor prostitution (Nichols 2016).

Displacement has also been a concern of the partial criminalization model. This model is a blend where the selling of sex is decriminalized, but the purchasing of sex and third-party involvement in the sex industry remains criminalized. The idea behind this model is to aim to eradicate prostitution and thereby sex trafficking, while also providing protections for sex workers themselves. However, the deterrence impact of this model is also questionable, with prostitution often pushed further underground. Official evaluations of the policy in Sweden have found that while street prostitution did appear to decrease, it is unknown what the impact has been on other forms of sex work and there is no reliable data on the numbers of sex workers before and after the implementation of the policy (Zeegers and Althoff 2015).

This blended model is often referred to as the Nordic model after Sweden. This model still faces many of the same challenges as the deterrence model. Sex workers report less trust in police and social service providers, along with feelings of vulnerability and stigmatization. In their efforts to remain secret and hidden from police, sex workers sacrifice an assessment of risk by moving into further isolated locations in order to secure their buyer and money

(Albright and D'Adamo 2017b; Nichols 2016). The criminalization of buyers may also mean that buyers are less willing to report any exploitation they have witnessed (Zeegers and Althoff 2015).

Two additional models include decriminalization and legalization. The goal of both models is to destigmatize sex work and provide protections for sex workers, though they differ slightly in their approach. The decriminalization model simply eliminates laws and enforcement around the selling or purchasing of sex. The legalization model does so as well, but the state remains involved in regulation, often requiring sex workers to have licenses, get regular health screenings, or work only in certain locations or zones (Nichols 2016). The legalization model is also referred to as the Dutch model, as it has been the Netherlands' approach to prostitution since 2000 (Zeegers and Althoff 2015). Under both models, sex trafficking remains criminalized as a separate offense from consensual sex work.

Decriminalization and legalization models have demonstrated evidence of improving the health, safety, and working conditions of sex workers (Lutnick and Cohan 2009). Harm reduction is an aspect found in both, though the quality of the services provided varies by country. Because sex workers are not criminalized, if they are victimized in the course of their work, they can seek legal recourse. Importantly, the Netherlands allows for both victims and clients to file anonymous reports, increasing the likelihood of undocumented individuals to report to police (Zeegers and Althoff 2015). Research does indicate that stigma does still exist in countries that have decriminalized or legalized prostitution, as sex workers still face higher rates of victimization compared to the general population (Nichols 2016). In countries with legalization models, sex workers also report still facing harassment from police regarding fees for licensing and working in the legal versus illegal zones.

Which model most effectively deters sex trafficking? Many view prostitution and trafficking as inherently linked and that, therefore, targeting prostitution will subsequently target sex trafficking. While forced prostitution and human trafficking do partially overlap, not all human trafficking is linked to the commercial sex industry. Some researchers claim that decriminalizing or legalizing sex work increases sex trafficking (Cho, Dreher, and Neumayer 2013; Jakobsson and Kotsadam 2013; Marinova and James 2012). Critics of such studies have found that these claims are frequently based on unsound methodological reasoning and bad data (Chuang 2010; Weitzer 2011, 2014, 2015b; Zeegers and Althoff 2015). These studies often use indicators that measure all forms of human trafficking together and make use of mere estimates rather than official counts of victims. It is also important to consider whether countries with legalized prostitution may simply be better at detecting sex trafficking. An official government evaluation conducted in Sweden could find no evidence that the ban on purchasing sex has deterred traffickers, while in the Netherlands an increase in reported victims was explained by brothel owners' increased awareness and willingness to report any "suspicious supply of women" to police (Zeegers and Althoff 2015).

Because of these issues, qualitative studies or smaller unit comparisons may provide more useful information about the on-the-ground impacts of policies on the lives of sex workers (Weitzer 2015b). For example, Harcourt et al. (2010) studied health and safety outcomes for sex workers in the cities of Perth (where prostitution is illegal), Sydney (where prostitution is decriminalized), and Melbourne (where prostitution is legalized and regulated). Melbourne was most likely to have in-room alarm systems, the use of security cameras, and access to free condoms, indicating that regulation has significant impacts on the safety and health of sex workers. Similarly, Cameron, Seager, and Shah (2021) found lower rates of sexually transmitted infections in a district of East Java, Indonesia, that decriminalized sex work compared to the neighboring districts where it remained criminalized. Interviews with sex workers show they also prefer a hybrid of legalization and decriminalization models to facilitate their ability to seek help and access services without facing the violence they see as rampant under criminalization models (Lutnick and Cohan 2009).

Ultimately the research on the link between prostitution policy and sex trafficking is limited, with complex questions frequently reduced to oversimplified findings. While an illegal market may certainly still occur in a legalization model—as sex workers avoid fees, licensing, or screenings—if consensual sex work is separated from sex trafficking, the findings are frequently unclear (Nichols 2016). It is likely that factors besides prostitution policy influence sex trafficking rates, such as the cost and ease of travel to the country, the number of vulnerable migrants in a location, and broader socioeconomic conditions linked to economic, gender, and racial inequalities (Chuang 2010; Nichols 2016).

RATIONAL CHOICE THEORY

Rational choice theory was developed by Cornish and Clarke in the late 1980s. It draws from the principles found in classical criminology, including the idea that humans are free-willed and rational. Rational choice theory is based on the idea that people make a cost-benefit analysis about whether or not to commit a crime. Risks are weighed against rewards. These rewards can include tangible and intangible benefits, such as money, excitement, revenge, or status. Risks include the risk of getting caught and punished, as well as other consequences, including shame or the loss of a job (Bohm and Vogel 2015).

Researchers have challenged the assumption that every individual weighs the costs and benefits the same and comes to the same decision (Schaffner 2014). Accounting for this, Cornish and Clarke (1986) do make several important distinctions from classical theory. They recognize that rationality is limited or bounded, meaning that people make decisions about their behavior, but these decisions are influenced by incomplete information, time, and ability. Further, not only will people have varying knowledge leading to different decisions, but they will also weigh the risks and rewards differently (Cornish and Clarke 1986).

Risks and Rewards in Human Trafficking

Rational choice theory can be used to understand traffickers' calculations of the potential risks and rewards involved in the crime. The primary benefit of trafficking is its profitability (Schaffner 2014). Interviews with former sex traffickers in Malaysia confirmed that a desire for money was their primary motivation for their involvement in trafficking (Mahalingam and Sidhu 2021). Profits from human trafficking are estimated to be USD$150 billion, with the majority of that coming from commercial sexual exploitation (ILO 2014). When looked at on an individual level, however, profits can vary greatly. Large criminal organizations make the highest incomes, while small-scale traffickers may earn little more than average wages (UNODC 2020). Still, the potential for high profits may outweigh any perceived costs. Beyond financial gain, other motivations for traffickers may include power and control (Kenyon and Schanz 2014).

Risks are minimized through low detection, arrest, and prosecution rates (Aronowitz, Theuermann, and Tyurykanova 2010). Comparing human trafficking with the similarly profitable drug and arms trafficking industries shows that human trafficking has a lower conviction rate (Wheaton, Schauer, and Galli 2010). Risks can also be reduced by exerting control over victims to avoid detection. Traffickers weigh risks and rewards in considering the level of control exerted over their victims. A study of domestic sex trafficking found that traffickers more frequently allow minor victims access to the internet and cell phones. This decision reflects a trade-off that the trafficker has calculated—victims are able to increase profits by assisting with posting advertisements and communicating with customers, but the trafficker's use of psychological coercion over the minor decreases the risk that they will get caught (Bouché and Shady 2017). Victims of any age may fear seeking out assistance due to threats made against themselves or their families, the criminalization of prostitution, or their status as an undocumented migrant (Aronowitz, Theuermann, and Tyurykanova 2010).

The issue of labor trafficking in sea fisheries can be used as an example. Researchers made use of satellite vessel monitoring data to study how vessels that use forced labor behave in identifiably different ways from other vessels. They found that between 14 percent and 26 percent of vessels were high risk for forced labor, accounting for fifty-seven thousand to one hundred thousand individuals (McDonald et al. 2021). The use of forced labor in Thailand's fishing industry specifically has been extensively documented (Human Rights Watch 2018; ILO 2013; Kara 2017). Many of the workers are migrants who are vulnerable to deception and coercion. Once aboard the fishing vessels, victims are subject to abuse, dangerous working conditions, withholding of pay and documents, and even death (Human Rights Watch 2018; Kara 2017). At sea the workers are isolated in remote locations for months or even years at a time. Risks are further decreased by Thailand's weak inspection regime, which is also subject to corruption (Human Rights Watch 2018; Kara 2017). The benefit for the employers lies in increased profits. One researcher summarizes it simply: "In the case of labor trafficking in sea fishing offenders choose to exploit cheap labor for sea fishery due to loopholes in migrant workers registration, weakness in law enforcement, and insufficient numbers of law enforcers and sea patrolling equipment. They calculate that their gains will outweigh the risks of being arrested and punished" (Jampawan 2018, 80).

Rational choice theory can also be used to understand how potential victims make decisions, evaluating the risks and benefits involved. Many victims may believe that the promises and offers made by recruiters and traffickers are the only options they will have. Victims may rationalize that even if their working situation ends up being worse than anticipated, they will still have the opportunity to make money (Kakar 2017). A study of women trafficked from Central and Eastern Europe to the Netherlands found two groups of women that reflect these circumstances (Vocks and Nijboer 2000). The group they called "deceived women" came from a poor financial background, were not afraid to take risks, and held unrealistic and overly optimistic expectations about life in another country. The group they called "exploited women" had previous experience working in prostitution, but lacked family ties and education, making the promise of work abroad a calculated risk for economic advancement. It is important to remember that rationality is limited—one's decisions are made based on what one believes to be true. Thus, victims in vulnerable situations are preyed upon by traffickers to make risky decisions based on false promises and offers.

By reducing potential profits and other rewards and increasing the risks and chance of punishment, rational choice theory would argue that traffickers can be deterred. Measures to reduce rewards can include focusing on financial investigations that track profits, seize assets, and impose harsh penalties on traffickers (Aronowitz, Theuermann, and Tyurykanova 2010). Other ways to reduce potential profits include demand reduction measures. For labor trafficking this can include consumer pressure and reputational risks for corporations to regulate their supply chains, though this shaming tactic may not change behavior (New 2015). End-demand approaches for sex trafficking show more promise, through programs that shame or educate johns about the risks of purchasing sex (Shively et al. 2012). Risks can be increased in a variety of ways, including campaigns to educate the public, training in industries that facilitate trafficking, improved passport controls, proactive investigation efforts, and resources to increase arrest and conviction rates (Aronowitz, Theuermann, and Tyurykanova 2010).

ROUTINE ACTIVITIES THEORY

Routine activities theory was first proposed by Cohen and Felson in 1979. Their theory assumes a rational, motivated offender like other deterrence-based theories. It differs, however, in its focus on how opportunities to commit crime come to be. Under routine activities theory, crime can only occur when three factors converge: the motivated offender, a suitable target, and an absence of capable guardianship. It is the daily routines of offenders and victims that lead to the convergence of these factors for crime in time and space (Cohen and Felson 1979).

Rational choice theory helps us understand the motivations of the offenders. Recruiters, transporters, traffickers, and other facilitators perceive the crime to generate a reward that outweighs the potential risks. Routine activities theory then explains how the opportunity for trafficking occurs. When these motivated offenders converge with suitable targets that lack capable guardianship, trafficking is possible.

Targets, Guardians, and Human Trafficking

Recall that the offender's behavior is not random, but the product of rational decision making. In that same way victimization is also not random, but rather, victims are targeted because they are vulnerable and easy to be recruited (Kakar 2017). Risk factors include living in a poverty-stricken area, having a dysfunctional family life, lacking education, having a history of abuse, being homeless, or having limited access to resources (Kakar 2017; Winterdyk 2020). Traffickers identify individuals who are desperate for opportunities, facing a crisis or emergency, or likely to be more compliant (Aronowitz, Theuermann, and Tyurykanova 2010). Interviews with former traffickers exemplify this, as they explained to researchers that they targeted young women in the Philippines and Indonesia who were seeking work in Malaysia. The women's age and economic background made them vulnerable to manipulation and deception (Mahalingam and Sidhu 2021).

Capable guardians include anyone who may come into contact with potential victims, such as police, immigration officials, health care workers, employees in the hospitality industry, and social service providers (Aronowitz, Theuermann, and Tyurykanova 2010). See this chapter's policy box for examples of ways in which training is being implemented in various industries to identify and prevent human trafficking. Environments that lack such capable guardians can facilitate the success of traffickers. This would include, for example, countries with unstable governments, and high levels of poverty, conflict, and statelessness (Stickle, Hickman, and White 2020). Other countries may have inadequate law enforcement personnel or resources that are further undermined by corruption (Mahalingam and Sidhu 2021).

Situational Crime Prevention

One of the strengths of routine activities theory is that it can be used to understand how a physical environment can be created that can deter crime. Situational crime prevention focuses not on the offender, who is assumed to be motivated, but on the opportunities to commit crime. By limiting those opportunities, crime can be prevented (Bohm and Vogel 2015). Common

One of the key elements from routine activities theory that can be altered to make crime easier or harder is the guardianship dimension. Guardians can be diverse, ranging from guard dogs to lights and cameras. Still, the presence and proximity of people often make them the most capable guardians (Hollis, Felson, and Welsh 2013). While law enforcement personnel may spring to mind as the typical presence that can act as a guardian against crime, the original authors of routine activities theory argued that ordinary citizens going about their everyday routines can also act as important guardians (Cohen and Felson 1979). Further, guardianship capability may matter more than guardianship credibility when it comes to effective crime prevention (Tilley 2014). One way that capable guardians against human trafficking are being created outside of law enforcement is through targeted training of populations likely to encounter trafficking victims.

One such population includes truckers. Truckers Against Trafficking (TAT) began its work in 2009 in order to bring awareness and training on domestic sex trafficking to the trucking industry. TAT offers videos and online resources for use in truck driving schools on how to identify, approach, and report potential victims they may encounter at truck stops (Aronowitz 2019). While there has been no systematic evaluation of its impact, TAT's 2020 report states that since their inception they have trained over one million individuals who have made over twenty-six hundred calls to the National Human Trafficking Hotline to report over seven hundred potential cases of human trafficking involving 1,296 victims (TAT 2020).

Another example can be found with airline personnel. Airline Ambassadors International worked closely with U.S. Customs and Border Protection to develop an industry-specific training. The Blue Lightning Initiative trains airline personnel on the indicators of human trafficking, including individuals traveling without luggage, avoiding eye contact or not being allowed to speak, and traveling with an older or much better dressed companion (AAI 2022). Training appears geared toward identifying minor victims of trafficking. The training is applicable to all airline industry personnel, not just flight attendants. In 2018, an American Airlines ticketing agent became suspicious of two teen girls traveling with one-way first-class tickets and called police. Investigation of the reported incident revealed they were traveling to meet with a suspected human trafficker who had promised them jobs in entertainment and modeling (KTRK 2018).

Finally, hospitals represent a new and growing avenue for trafficking awareness and training. Research shows that 50–88 percent of victims will seek health care services at some point while they are still being trafficked, with the majority visiting an emergency department (Armstrong et al. 2020). Because of this, health care systems and states are increasingly implementing training and policies around human trafficking. Warning signs may include delaying treatment, a pattern of injuries that doesn't make sense, reluctance to explain injuries, or coming in with someone who seems overbearing. However, training is still lacking in many health care settings and varies widely from site to site. For example, one study of hospital training in South Carolina found disparities in health care practitioners' recognition of potential labor trafficking victims (Armstrong et al. 2020), while another study of a health care system's trafficking protocol in the Midwest found that creating such a process can be taxing on the time and resources available to the staff, particularly when the training is made voluntary (Stoklosa et al. 2017).

Human trafficking awareness and victim identification training is increasingly being provided in professions outside of law enforcement. See the resources listed at the end of this chapter to learn about human trafficking awareness and training being provided to hotel staff. While such resources are important, many initiatives often tend to focus on sex trafficking cases. What industries might be targeted for training on labor trafficking? How might the signs of trafficking look different for potential labor trafficking victims?

methods of situational crime prevention include increasing the effort required to commit the crime, increasing the risks of getting caught, reducing potential rewards, reducing situations that can provoke criminal responses, and removing excuses that may allow the offender to claim ignorance (Clarke 2008). We can consider how these categories might be applied to human trafficking. The level of effort and risk required can be increased through regular inspection and monitoring of businesses where labor trafficking is known to occur. Rewards can be reduced through penalties for businesses found using forced labor, including fines, canceling business licenses, and dissolution of the company. Excuses can be removed by creating and enforcing training and eliminating legal loopholes around liability and subcontracting.

There has been some research on the applicability of situational crime prevention to human trafficking, with studies focusing primarily on commercial sexual exploitation in the hospitality industry. Research shows that hotels and motels play a significant role in facilitating sex trafficking (Kakar, Dressler, and Blakeman 2019). These are spaces where victims and offenders routinely interact, with the potential for guardianship from hotel managers and employees (Paraskevas and Brookes 2018). These environments can be amenable to trafficking when they allow traffickers, victims, and buyers to enter and exit from multiple locations, without being noticed, and are able to avoid interactions with employees (Hadjiyanni, Povlitzki, and Preble 2014; Kakar, Dressler, and Blakeman 2019). Studies have suggested implementing measures such as training for hotel managers and employees, increasing visibility between the front desk and parking lot, and requiring all guests to register (Hadjiyanni, Povlitzki, and Preble 2014; Paraskevas and Brookes 2018).

VICTIMIZATION THEORIES

While most traditional theories of crime seek to explain offending, victimization theories focus on the other side of the coin. When we examine factors that make potential victims vulnerable or appear as suitable targets to traffickers, we are not blaming the victim. Indeed, many of the factors that make them vulnerable are out of their control (Stickle, Hickman, and White 2020). Instead, it is about understanding how victimization is not random (Kakar 2017). For example, studies show that individuals with disabilities face higher rates of victimization, and this includes human trafficking (Nichols and Heil 2022). There are several factors that can contribute to a person with disabilities' risk or vulnerability of being trafficked that are both inherent and situational (Jagoe, Toh, and Wylie 2022). The inherent nature of visible, physical disabilities may make someone a target for trafficking, while situational vulnerabilities may include traffickers exploiting an individual's need for assistive devices, therapy, or other health care they cannot afford. Other inherent vulnerabilities include the use of deception to traffic persons with intellectual disabilities and mental disabilities (Jagoe, Toh, and Wylie 2022). While there is overall a lack of research on the relationship between disability and trafficking, several studies have focused on the sex trafficking of girls with disabilities (Nichols and Heil 2022). One study found that while girls with any disability reported higher rates of minor sex trafficking than girls without disabilities, those with severe physical disabilities or low cognitive abilities faced the highest rates (Franchino-Olsen et al. 2020). Yet another study of juvenile sex trafficking found disproportionate rates of girls with intellectual disabilities. They note that "complicating dynamics include victim lack of awareness of exploitation and its endangerments, the inability of victims to self-identify, and the ease with which traffickers can manipulate these youth" (Reid 2018, 125). There are several victimization theories that can be applied to understanding human trafficking, including victim precipitation theory, lifestyle theory, and deviant place theory.

Victim Precipitation Theory

Victim precipitation theory examines the ways that individuals can initiate events that lead to their victimization (von Hentig 1941). The theory considers the ways that individuals' relationships, personal characteristics, and surroundings play a role in precipitating their victimization. Victim precipitation is often distinguished into two categories. Active precipitation is when the victim knowingly provokes their victimization, while passive precipitation occurs when the victim unknowingly encourages the criminal action (Schmalleger 2020). Because victim precipitation theory is applied to violent victimization, it is well suited to examine human trafficking victimization as well.

Human trafficking often affects the most vulnerable in a society. Individuals who are desperate to improve their situation may deliberately seek out "opportunities, places, or persons that can facilitate their search and assist them in accomplishing their goals" (Kakar 2017, 109). Such individuals may accept risky migration decisions, but be defrauded or coerced into a situation of trafficking. One way to further examine this issue is through the overlap between migrant smuggling and risks of human trafficking.

As discussed in chapter 1, smuggling and human trafficking are definitionally two separate issues, though they do share overlap. Studies show that areas of high migration flows often see corresponding human trafficking flows as well (Akee et al. 2014; Mahmoud and Trebesch 2010). Areas that are experiencing high out-migration are more likely to be disadvantaged, with high economic disparities and weakened social institutions (Mahmoud and Trebesch 2010). The combined demand for labor with restrictive border controls in more affluent destination countries does not halt the flow of migration, but instead leads migrants to turn to alternative means, pushing both smuggling and trafficking further underground (Aronowitz 2001; Desyllas

2007). Individuals are then more willing to take risks in the migration process, with such risk-taking leaving them vulnerable to victimization. A migrant who has sought out such services may voluntarily enter into a contract with a smuggler. They may be willing to accept difficult, dirty, or dangerous job offers in order to leave their current conditions. A sex worker may consent to being smuggled into another country where the wages for prostitution are higher. Yet when such individuals are defrauded in their contracts about the work, have their pay and documents withheld, are not allowed to leave their work, and are otherwise exploited in transit or at their destination, they are also a victim of trafficking.

Research shows that individuals who are victimized by smugglers and traffickers are often among the most disadvantaged, with few economic prospects (Aronowitz 2001). Bangladesh faces widespread poverty, lack of employment options, and human rights abuses, leading many to seek work in other countries. A lack of legal channels means that many migrants turn to recruiting agencies to find illicit channels. To facilitate this labor migration, recruiting agencies rely on middlemen who are known locally as "dalal (broker) or adam babshahi or adam beapari (human trader)" (Joarder and Miller 2014, 142). A twenty-month study of undocumented Bangladeshi migrants who had returned to Bangladesh found that 81 percent qualified as trafficked for one or more experiences. This includes being given fraudulent documents, work contract violations, denial of wages, forced work, and harassment or assault. Many of these migrants had paid up-front fees to a broker or trafficker to facilitate their passage (Joarder and Miller 2014).

Lifestyle Theory

Lifestyle theory explores how victimization is related to your lifestyle. The theory has close connections to routine activities theory, in that it is through people's routine actions and behaviors that they increase or decrease their risk of victimization (Hindelang, Gottfredson, and Garofalo 1978). Lifestyles are influenced by demographic variables such as age, gender, and socioeconomic status, which can help explain variations in victimization rates. High-risk lifestyles for victimization can include drug users, the homeless, runaways, and sex workers (Kakar 2017). Applying the theory to human trafficking, a study of sex trafficking in South Africa found that, in particular, girls from socioeconomically disadvantaged backgrounds whose "routine activities and lifestyles include partying at nightclubs under the influence of alcohol and other substances are at the greatest risk of being trafficked for involuntary prostitution" (Lutya 2010, 94).

In the human trafficking literature, youth lifestyles consistently linked to vulnerability to victimization include runaways, welfare or justice involved youth, and LGBTQ youth (Hannan et al. 2017; Heil and Nichols 2015; Smolenski and Ingerman 2017; Wright et al. 2021). Many times, these risks may overlap. Research shows that traffickers may look for individuals to recruit in "juvenile detention centers and outside of courthouses, homeless shelters, and group homes as well as in schools, public parks, bus shelters, chat rooms, social media, and neighborhood streets" (Nichols 2016, 104).

Youth who are welfare and justice involved are likely to have a history of adverse experiences and vulnerabilities that leave them open to exploitation by traffickers. This includes a history of abuse, the trauma of home removal, disruptions to school attendance, and loss of personal supports. A study of domestic minor sex trafficking victims' relationship to their trafficker found that adolescents' welfare and juvenile justice involvement were significant predictors of both familial trafficking and stranger trafficking (Twis 2019). Because of their experiences, welfare and justice involved youth may become runaways or homeless. Congressional testimony presented by the National Center for Missing & Exploited Children attested that 67 percent of runaway youth who experienced sex trafficking were runaways from foster care homes (Hannan et al. 2017). Runaway and homeless youth may then be targeted by traffickers who offer support, love, material goods, or a better place to stay.

It is important to recognize that commercial sexual exploitation of these minors is not the only form of trafficking they may experience. A study by Wright et al. (2021) of 564 runaway and homeless youth in the metro-Atlanta area found that 40 percent had experienced some form of trafficking while homeless, with coerced labor (29.3%) and fraud (25.2%) occurring more frequently than sexual exploitation (15.6%). Their research is in line with other studies of US cities that have found estimated trafficking prevalence rates between 9.5 percent and 53.3 percent among homeless youth (Wright et al. 2021).

LGBTQ youth are overrepresented among runaway and homeless youth, increasing their vulnerability to trafficking (Smolenski and Ingerman 2017). LGBTQ youth can face increased bullying, harassment, and abuse from peers and family members. They may face barriers such as fear, stigma, and discrimination in trying to access services and shelter (Nichols 2016). Data from the national nonprofit Polaris Project found that 40 percent of homeless youth identify as LGBTQ, and that among these youth they were 7.4 times more likely to experience sexual violence than their heterosexual peers and 3 to 7 times more likely to engage in survival sex (Polaris Project 2016). Sex trafficking among LGBTQ youth is correlated through survival sex, which involves engaging in sex to meet basic needs such as food and shelter. However, if the individual is under eighteen it is still considered sex trafficking, even with the youth's consent and without the presence of a third party.

These lifestyles can also lead to repeat victimization. Prior victimization is a robust predictor of future victimization (Tseloni and Pease 2003). When lifestyles and routines place individuals in situations of continuing risk, there is an increase in the same type of victimization being repeated (de Vries and Farrell 2018). Over time, such individuals may even come to accept victimization as normal or inevitable. Such findings have also been found among human trafficking victimization. A study of labor trafficking victims found that individuals with a prior victimization of any type were 4.87 times more likely to experience victimization during the first trafficking stage of recruitment and 5.12 times more likely to experience victimization during transportation (de Vries and Farrell 2018). The study summarizes the connection between routines and repeat victimization as follows: "Labor-trafficked persons may have fallen prey to exploiters in the recruitment and transportation stage in part because of the traditional routines that brought them into contact with recruiters and transporters. Once in a trafficking situation, individuals continued to be near motivated offenders, were often socially isolated and had limited access to public services. As such, environmental conditions and routines can also explain the experience of repeat victimization of the same type during the employment" (de Vries and Farrell 2018, 636).

There are also certain conditions that increase victimization risk. In regard to trafficking vulnerability this can include employment in marginalized and unregulated industries or having an undocumented status (de Vries and Farrell 2018). Migrant domestic workers demonstrate these risks. Both globally and within the United States, domestic work remains the highest reported sector of labor exploitation (CTDC 2021; Polaris Project 2019). Domestic workers are vulnerable due to the conditions of their employment, with isolation, power imbalances, and historical and cultural biases all playing a role (Polaris Project 2019). Domestic workers are also excluded from protections under many US labor laws, including the National Labor Relations Act of 1935 and the Fair Labor Standards Act of 1938 (Polaris Project 2019). Many of the domestic workers in the United States are foreign-born women, who face additional language and cultural barriers. For example, while the National Human Trafficking Hotline does not have information about the visa status for a majority of trafficking cases reported, of those whose original visa status was known, 79 percent held A-3 and G-5 visas. A-3 visas are given to the employees of foreign diplomats or foreign government officials, while G-5 visas are given to employees working for international organizations like the United Nations or World Bank. Countries in Asia and Africa are the primary sources of domestic workers on A-3 and G-5 visas (Polaris Project 2019).

Deviant Place Theory

Deviant place theory is spatially oriented, focusing on how the environments people live, work, and interact in increase their risk of victimization (Stark 1987). Unlike the other victimization theories, deviant place theory does not emphasize how victims' personal characteristics, lifestyles, or actions may increase or decrease their chances of becoming victims. Instead, the theory centers on how people living in deviant places, places that are disorganized with high crime rates, have a higher probability of victimization.

In regard to human trafficking, community dynamics can play a role in vulnerability to victimization, increasing the likelihood of coming into contact with a trafficker. This can include factors such as "community poverty and unemployment, police corruption, and the presence of violence, crime, drug use, adult prostitution, and trafficking in the neighborhood" (Hannan et al. 2017, 111). Further, many victims are from marginalized populations who live in marginalized areas of communities (Kakar 2017). Recruiters may target these areas for potential victims, offering false promises of opportunity and a better life.

The Intersection of IPV and Human Trafficking

An area of victimization theory that has received much attention involves understanding intimate partner violence (IPV). Recently, research has started to explore the links between intimate partner violence and human trafficking. Some have suggested that the victimization theory of domestic violence can be used to at least partially understand human trafficking, particularly cases that involve the sexual exploitation of women (Bernat and Zhilina 2010). Further, frameworks initially developed to understand victims of domestic violence may also be useful in explaining why sex trafficking victims remain in situations of exploitation and may resist assisting law enforcement (Bernat and Zhilina 2010). Many times, cases of human trafficking have been mistakenly identified as solely cases of domestic violence at first. Consider the following 2011 federal case:

> In *United States v. Vianez,* the victim agreed to engage in commercial sex for the defendant in the hopes that he would "love her." She worked for Vianez for four years. Though she repeatedly tried to leave, Vianez physically abused her and forced her to continue working. Vianez beat the victim so severely that she had to undergo emergency surgery for her injuries. Hospital staff called the police, who arrested Vianez and initially charged him with domestic assault. He was later convicted of sex trafficking and related crimes, sentenced to 20 years in prison, and ordered to pay the victim restitution in the amount of $1,354,500 (Bessell 2018, 3–4).

There are several similarities between intimate partner violence and trafficking, including victimization risk factors like family dysfunction and a history of abuse, recruitment methods that exploit the relationship, and various physical and psychological means of control (Koegler et al. 2020). Other areas of overlap include grooming, the use of violence, secrecy and isolation, abuse and instability, and dominance and power (Roe-Sepowitz et al. 2014). While trafficking victims may be recruited by strangers, it is not uncommon to be recruited by someone they have a close personal relationship with, such as friends, family, and intimate partners. Data from the Counter Trafficking Data Collaborative shows that 21 percent of women were recruited by intimate partners compared to 2 percent of men. With regard to sex trafficking specifically, 35 percent of victims were recruited by an intimate partner (CTDC 2021).

The Duluth Power and Control Wheel is best known as a conceptual framework to understand how men use violence to exercise power and control in the relationship. The National Human Trafficking Hotline created an adapted model called the Human Trafficking Power and Control Wheel to explain traffickers' behaviors given the similarities they saw with batterers (Koegler et al. 2020). The modified wheel contains nine categories that link power and control to both sex and labor trafficking. These categories include coercion and threats, intimidation, isolation, using privilege, emotional abuse, economic abuse, physical abuse, sexual abuse, and denying, blaming, and minimizing. A study of trafficking cases that involved an intimate partner as the exploiter found an average of 2.7 types of abuse from the Human Trafficking Power and Control Wheel used in each case. The most frequently identified types of abuse included using privilege, economic abuse, physical abuse, isolation, and sexual abuse (Koegler et al. 2020). It is also important to note that it is not just sex trafficking from intimate partners that victims experience. Indeed, this study found that labor trafficking was experienced most frequently (Koegler et al. 2020).

CHAPTER RESOURCES

1. Watch the video "Sold in America: The Trafficking" by Newsy here: https://www.youtube.com/watch?v=Empxdrk7UuA. What are some risk factors for the commercial sexual exploitation of youth showcased in the video? This video focused on victims of commercial sexual exploitation, but what risk factors might matter for labor trafficking?

2. Review the Hospitality Toolkit from the DHS Blue Campaign on human trafficking and the hospitality industry here: https://www.dhs.gov/blue-campaign/hospitalityindustry. Discuss the ability of such training to create capable guardians to detect and deter trafficking. Does this training focus more on sex trafficking or is it applicable to potential labor trafficking victims as well? What other industries would such training be helpful for?

3. Visit the Human Trafficking Institute's state reports on federal prosecutions here: https://traffickinginstitute.org/state-reports/. View the 2020 report for your state to learn about the federal prosecutions for human trafficking in your state in 2020 and since the passage of the TVPA in 2000. Do the cases prosecuted in 2020 match up with the information reported to the National Human Trafficking Hotline for your state in 2020 (see resource 3 in chapter 1)? What are the twenty-year trends for prosecution in your state? How do they compare to another state?

CHAPTER DISCUSSION QUESTIONS

1. Which model of prostitution do you think is best and why? How effectively do you think each model is at deterring sex trafficking?

2. What are some of the various strategies for corporations to address labor trafficking in their supply chains? What are potential issues with these strategies?

3. When applying rational choice theory to human trafficking, what are some potential risks and potential benefits that traffickers might take into consideration?

4. What are some lifestyle and individual risk factors for human trafficking? How do victimization theories connect these risk factors to being a victim of human trafficking?

THREE

Pyschological Theories

PSYCHOLOGY AND HUMAN TRAFFICKING

Psychological perspectives can be used to understand both victims and offenders of human trafficking. This includes examining risk factors for victimization, the psychological impacts of trafficking on victims, and treatment options for survivors. Characteristics of traffickers can also be studied, including personality disorders and the grooming process (Beeson 2015). Various psychological theories and concepts can be extended from traditional studies of other forms of victimization to help understand the similarities to and differences from human trafficking victimization.

For example, traumagenic dynamics theory is traditionally used to understand the impacts of child sexual abuse. This theory looks at how such abuse impacts sexual development, creates distrust with adults, impedes healthy coping mechanisms, and leads to isolation. In the context of child sex trafficking, early sexual initiation may be coupled with running away, engaging in other risky behaviors that lead to revictimization, and isolation from potential help (Franchino-Olsen 2021a). Similarly, Biderman's theory of coercion was originally developed to understand how interrogators could manipulate prisoner behavior without having to resort to physical force (Baldwin, Fehrenbacher, and Eisenman 2015). Yet researchers have begun to look at how the theory can also be used to understand how traffickers maintain control over their victims. Biderman's theory includes eight methods of coercion: isolation, monopolization of perception, induced debt or exhaustion, threats, occasional indulgences, demonstration of omnipotence, degradation, and enforcing trivial demands. Interviews with women trafficked for domestic servitude and sex show that these domains also apply to the experiences of trafficking victims. Social isolation increases victims' dependence on their trafficker, dehumanizing techniques are combined with occasional demonstrations of kindness, and threats to report victims or harm their families are used to exercise control (Baldwin, Fehrenbacher, and Eisenman 2015).

Ultimately the experiences of trafficking victims place them at risk for both physical and psychological problems. Trauma impacts both psychosocial and neurobiological development. Psychological perspectives can thus be used to better understand the experiences of victims, the motivations of traffickers, and how to best provide services for survivors.

PSYCHOLOGY AND TRAFFICKERS

Psychopathy

While the majority of trafficking research has focused on victims, there has been some research on the characteristics of the offenders, generally documenting the demographics of traffickers. Even less is known about the personality traits and psychological processes of traffickers. There has been some research into the psychopathy of traffickers, primarily using the Hare Psychopathology Checklist (PCL-R), which consists of twenty traits and behaviors, such as superficial charm, lack of empathy, pathological lying, manipulativeness, impulsivity, and more (Beeson 2015). Prior research on psychopathy shows that compared to nonpsychopathic offenders, psychopaths tend to engage in criminal activity more frequently, demonstrate more violence, and have greater criminal versatility (Hargreaves-Cormany et al. 2022).

A study of 117 offenders engaged in the sex trafficking of juveniles between 1990 and 2011 found 75 percent of the sample scored high enough on the PCL-R to meet the criteria for psychopathy. The researchers determined two broad types of traffickers, those who were charismatic and manipulative or those who were aggressive and antisocial. The majority of the offenders also had violent criminal histories (Hargreaves-Cormany, Patterson, and Muirhead 2016). Another study of twenty-eight offenders arrested, charged, or convicted for domestic sex trafficking found a similar rate of psychopathy, with 79 percent of offenders scoring in the high or very high range of the PCL-R (Gotch 2016). Finally, a Canadian study of twenty-two pimps found the offenders had higher overall scores for psychopathy compared to other incarcerated offenders, particularly in the areas of superficial emotional responses, lack of empathy, cunning and manipulativeness, and failure to accept responsibility for actions (Spidel et al. 2006).

Given that research on trafficking victimization frequently highlights tactics of coercion, manipulation, or deception, it is perhaps not surprising to find high rates of psychopathy among traffickers. Indeed, a common strategy used by sex traffickers is to manipulate the victim under the guise of an emotional attachment, gradually increasing the level of control and violence in the relationship. While there have been no studies to date on psychopathy among labor traffickers, similarities to sex trafficking in regard to the use of deception, manipulation, and control lead to a tentative assumption that psychopathic traits may also be found (Hargreaves-Cormany et al. 2022).

Grooming

Psychological perspectives can also provide insight into the grooming process used by traffickers. Much of the literature on grooming has focused on child sexual abuse, but in recent decades scholars have begun to examine the grooming tactics used by child sex traffickers (Winters et al. 2022). Grooming processes typically capitalize on a victim's existing vulnerabilities, including emotional and physical needs. The goal is to isolate a victim, instill a sense of trust and loyalty, and create a relationship with a power imbalance that is used to control (Beeson 2015). There are also many similarities with the process of trauma-coerced attachment, including alternating between punishments and rewards (Reid and Jones 2011).

One study of forty-three cases of sexually exploited girls found that their traffickers used various tactics to coerce and control them, including romancing them with gifts and affection and gaining their trust by helping them from a difficult situation. Once enmeshed in sex trafficking, shame, blackmail, isolation, and intimidation were used to control the victims (Reid 2016). Another study found considerable overlap between the stages of child sexual grooming and child sex trafficking (Winters et al. 2022). At stage one, victims are selected based on vulnerabilities related to their psychological and emotional state, environment, or family stability. Many of these vulnerabilities were discussed in relation to victimization theories in chapter 2. At stage two, traffickers gain access by establishing relationships and isolating the child. Stage three involves deepening that trust and cooperation, often through tangible and intangible rewards and gifts. In stage four, desensitization tactics are used to prepare the victim for commercial sexual encounters. Finally, stage five involves coercive tactics and violence to maintain the abuse and control.

The growth of the internet and digital technologies also present new means to identify and groom potential trafficking victims, with social media sites being a major facilitator (O'Brien and Li 2020). Specifically, research has found that social media platforms are more likely to be used in the grooming and recruitment of domestic minor sex trafficking victims who are fifteen or younger (Bouché 2015; Wells, Mitchell, and Ji 2012). The National Human Trafficking Hotline has recorded recruitment on sites such as "Facebook, Instagram, Snapchat, Kik, Meetme.com, WhatsApp, and dating sites/apps like Plenty of Fish, Tinder, and Grindr" (Anthony 2018, 18). Online recruitment may entail the development of an intimate relationship or deception through a false job advertisement. Online grooming is not limited to sex trafficking, either, with sites like Craigslist and Facebook being linked to labor trafficking and social media used to connect organ brokers and organ trafficking victims (Anthony 2018; Fraser 2016).

TRAUMA AND TRAFFICKING VICTIMS

Human trafficking has been studied in relation to the short- and long-term impacts on victims. Research shows that trafficking represents a unique form of trauma when compared with other forms of violent victimization (Gerassi and Nichols 2018). There is an array of physical and psychological effects that victims may experience. Psychologically these include anxiety and depression, PTSD, suicidal ideation, dissociation, impulse control, and other effects stemming from trauma (Gerassi and Nichols 2018). Related issues may include alcohol and substance abuse, self-harm, detachment or withdrawal, anger, and aggression. Complex trauma and C-PTSD are also prevalent among survivors, referring to the individual's exposure to chronic or cumulative trauma (Hopper 2017a). Physically, trafficking survivors report many symptoms that may have psychological contributors, such as headaches, dizziness, nausea, problems sleeping, and somatic complaints (Hopper 2017a). Other physical symptoms relevant to sex trafficking victims may include communicable diseases, reproductive health impacts, and malnutrition, while labor trafficking victims may report environmental and industry specific occupational risks, overcrowded and unsanitary living environments, and chronic pain (Macias-Konstantopoulos and Ma, 2017).

While much of the research on trauma and human trafficking has focused on survivors of sex trafficking, there is evidence to suggest similar outcomes for survivors of labor trafficking. A study of sixty-six sex trafficking and sixty-five labor trafficking survivors found that 71 percent of respondents met the diagnostic criteria for depression and 61 percent met the diagnostic criteria for PTSD, with no significant differences by type of trafficking victimization (Hopper and Gonzalez 2018). Sex trafficking survivors, however, were more likely to suffer from C-PTSD and more likely to report symptoms of dissociation, affect dysregulation, impulsivity, mistrust and avoidance in relationships, and revictimization (Hopper and Gonzalez 2018). Psychological perspectives about these issues can help researchers and service providers better understand the traumatic experiences of trafficking victims and provide appropriate treatment.

Trauma-Coerced Attachment

Trauma-coerced attachment can be defined as "a powerful emotional dependency on the abusive partner and a shift in world- and self-view, which can result in feelings of gratitude or loyalty toward the abuser and denial or minimization of the coercion and abuse" (Doychak and Raghavan 2020, 339). This creates a paradoxical situation where victims who are experiencing abuse and control also hold feelings such as love or admiration toward their abuser. Trauma-coerced attachment is now used over the term trauma bonding to mark the deliberate use of control in the relationship and unidirectional trauma.

Not every human trafficking victim will experience trauma-coerced attachment. One study of sex trafficking survivors found that the women had varied experiences, ranging from no attachment, to mild and moderate, to severe attachment. Those with no attachment reported negative and fear-based emotions toward their traffickers, while those with mild attachment reported some positive feelings but held no illusions about the abusive nature of the relationship. Women with moderate attachment also held no illusions about the nature of their relationships with their trafficker, but reported feelings of warmth and gratefulness toward their trafficker as well. Finally, those with the most severe attachment reported idolization of the trafficker and unwavering loyalty (Doychak and Raghavan 2020).

Research shows that defining features of trauma-coerced attachment include the use of control tactics, exploitation of power in the relationship, alternating between rewards and punishment, and victim internationalization of the trafficker's view (Casassa, Knight, and Mengo 2022; Doychak and Raghavan 2020; Sanchez, Speck, and Patrician 2019). Victim vulnerabilities are exploited by the trafficker in order to coercively control them and develop an attachment. Victims experience manipulation, isolation, degradation, physical and sexual violence, and more. At the same time, positive behavior is displayed intermittently by the trafficker, including tangible gifts or affection and intimacy. In combination with isolation, this can alter the victim's perspective, leading to dependency on the trafficker and an adoption of the abuser's view. This trauma-coerced attachment can ultimately lead the victim to take responsibility for the abuser's crimes, protect them, and even seek to return to them (Chambers et al. 2022).

Victim-Offender Overlap

One way that human trafficking is unique from other crimes is the ways in which victims may find themselves in the role of offender, something referred to as victim-offender overlap. As discussed in previous chapters, victims of human trafficking face criminalization for prostitution and immigration violations. These victims are often misidentified and treated as offenders rather than victims.

Juvenile victims of sex trafficking also frequently face criminalization, despite federal law that states that any minor participating in sex work is a victim. Safe harbor laws have been enacted at the state level across the United States in order to protect commercially exploited youth by decriminalizing juvenile prostitution and diverting youth away from the justice system and into services (Mehlman-Orozco 2015). In practice, however, many juveniles are still being arrested and/or detained in juvenile detention facilities (Finklea, Fernandes-Alcantara, and Siskin 2015). An analysis of data from four states before and after the passing of their safe harbor laws suggested a trend of increases in arrests of juveniles for prostitution rather than the expected decline (Mehlman-Orozco 2015).

A growing form of human trafficking includes trafficking for the purpose of forced criminality. This includes using force, fraud, or coercion in the recruitment, harboring, reception, or transfer of a person for the purpose of forcing them to commit crime (Rodríguez-López 2020). Globally, 6 percent of all detected victims were subjected to forced criminal activity, ranging from petty crimes such as shoplifting and pickpocketing to more serious crimes related to drug trafficking (UNODC 2020). Other documented forced crimes include begging, fraud, and even being forced to recruit other victims (Aronowitz and Chmaitilly 2020). Perhaps even more so than traditional forms of human trafficking, victims of trafficking for forced criminality are not frequently identified as such, and instead are arrested and prosecuted.

Victim-offender overlap can occur at various stages of the trafficking process and within various types of exploitation. Schloenhardt and Markey-Towler (2016) categorize the crimes human trafficking victims may commit into three types. Status offenses include those that are a direct result of the individual's status in the place they have been trafficked through or to. This category includes migration-related offenses. Consequential offenses are those that occur because the victim was under duress, either forced or coerced by the trafficker to do the offenses. This category includes many crimes, such as drug-related offenses, prostitution-related offenses, property crimes, and violent crimes. Finally, liberation offenses are the crimes that occur while the victim is trying to flee their situation, perhaps involving the use of violence against their trafficker. It is possible to consider how these categories map onto the case of Cyntoia Brown, discussed in this chapter's policy box.

Ultimately, the victim-offender overlap has long-term consequences for survivors of human trafficking. Experiences of arrest and conviction during their trafficking experience can expose them to further trauma and revictimization, create a distrust of law enforcement, and hinder their ability to leave their trafficker. A 2015 survey of 130 survivors of human trafficking found that 90.8 percent reported being arrested, with 40 percent being arrested over nine times (Jacobs and Richard 2016). Victims were arrested for crimes related to prostitution, drug sales and possession, and other crimes, and about 50 percent were convicted of at least one crime as a juvenile. The majority of respondents reported that these arrests and convictions created long-term impacts on their lives, including barriers to accessing employment, housing, food stamps, and financial and educational loans, and being able to keep their children. While there are laws in place for trafficking victims to have such convictions vacated, many reported that the process was too expensive, time-consuming, and difficult to complete (Jacobs and Richard 2016).

Cyntoia Brown was a victim of domestic minor sex trafficking who, at the age of sixteen, was sentenced to life in prison for the murder and robbery of Johnny Allen. The forty-three-year-old Allen had picked up Brown for sex and was shot after Brown believed he was reaching for a gun. Running away from a troubled and abusive home life, Cyntoia met and began using drugs with a man known as "Cut Throat." At her trial, Brown testified that the twenty-four-year-old "was nice to her at first, but subsequently, he began to verbally and physically abuse her as well as sexually assaulting her and forcing her to prostitute herself" (Rodriguez 2021, 462). In 2017, over a decade after her conviction, the hashtag #freecyntoiabrown began to trend after celebrities such as Rihanna and Kim Kardashian brought attention to the case. After several years of high-profile media attention, Tennessee governor Bill Haslam commuted Brown's sentence and she was released in 2019 after serving fifteen years (Rodriguez 2021).

While Cyntoia Brown has been one of the most well-known cases of human trafficking victims being criminalized, there are many other cases that have not received such attention. Shamere McKenzie was subjected to complex trauma and sexual abuse from a young age. Still, she went on to attend college on an athletic scholarship, majoring in criminal justice. After losing her scholarship due to an injury, she met a man who offered to help her find a way to pay for her college. McKenzie had seen the man as a potential boyfriend, but she now recognizes that he was grooming her with flattery, love, and attention to earn her trust. He soon began forcing her to prostitute herself, and she experienced regular beatings, rapes, and threats (Hamilton 2019). McKenzie's trafficker later used her to transport other girls across state lines, eventually leading to her arrest. McKenzie faced state charges for prostitution and federal charges for transporting minors across state lines for illegal purposes. She pled guilty and was sentenced to five years of probation, two hundred hours of community service, and the requirement to register as a sex offender (End Slavery Now 2015). How do both of these cases demonstrate victim-offender overlap?

McKenzie was later able to access a program for victims of sex trafficking, where she received both counseling and housing. However, the cases of both Brown and McKenzie highlight the failures of the criminal justice system to recognize those being trafficked as victims rather than offenders. The criminalization of trafficking victims occurs at multiple levels. At the individual level, criminalizing and stigmatizing language is used in the courtroom. A study of commercially sexually exploited girls in the juvenile justice system found that court personnel perpetuated myths and victim-blaming ideologies, frequently framing the girls as juvenile delinquents rather than victims of exploitation (Anderson, England, and Davidson 2017). A similar Australian study of judges' remarks found a tendency to classify women as either victim or offender, without attending to the nuance of overlap. Instead, labels of *deserving* versus *undeserving* victims and language that the victims "should have known better" were used to criminalize victims (Baxter 2020). At the structural level, trafficking laws emphasize prosecution over the protection of victims' rights. Altogether, this means that the victim-offender overlap remains unrecognized, trauma goes untreated, and many victims continue through the system as defendants. What knowledge could you share with criminal justice practitioners to prevent this pervasive problem?

RESPONDING TO TRAFFICKING SURVIVORS

The Unique Needs of Trafficking Survivors

Trafficking survivors are often placed in services that were originally created for survivors of domestic or sexual violence. While these populations certainly share some overlap, human trafficking survivors also have many unique needs that may require different approaches to treatment or additional services. Service providers have informed researchers that trafficking survivors' needs are often more extreme and enduring compared to similar victim populations that they serve (Duncan and DeHart 2019).

The needs of trafficking survivors can often be divided into immediate and acute needs versus long-term and ongoing needs. The short-term needs may include basic necessities for survival such as food, water, shelter, urgent medical care, and crisis intervention. Long-term needs may include permanent housing, therapy and mental health treatment, substance abuse treatment, legal aid, and job or educational assistance (Duncan and DeHart 2019; Gerassi and Nichols 2018).

In order to help meet these needs, a trauma-informed approach should be taken with the services and interventions provided to trafficking victims. US agencies have noted the importance of using a trauma-informed approach in anti-trafficking efforts (Hopper 2017b). Despite this, surveys of anti-trafficking providers have found that most respondents feel well informed about trauma-informed care but lack concrete examples and knowledge of how to incorporate such practices into their organizational activities (Chakoian, Sethi, and Santos 2021). Interviews with women who were sex trafficking survivors in the Midwest revealed that they felt that many of the professionals they encountered were not trained in trauma-informed psychological care. They reported that criminal justice officials such as judges and law enforcement, health care professionals, and other service providers often lacked a full awareness of how trauma impacted survivors' decisions and behavioral responses, leading them to feel distrusted, alienated, and blamed (Rajaram and Tidball 2018).

SAMHSA's guidance for a trauma-informed approach emphasizes six key principles: safety; trustworthiness and transparency; peer support; collaboration and mutuality; empowerment, voice, and choice; and cultural, historical, and gender considerations. Overall the framework is about recognizing the symptoms of trauma and avoiding revictimization by working to empower victims by creating an environment where they can feel safe, trust is fostered, unique needs are addressed, and individual choices are respected (Lewis-O'Connor and Alpert 2017).

One aspect that service providers can struggle with is trusting survivors to make decisions about their own safety rather than penalizing them for not following strict rules. A survey of anti-trafficking providers found that many times when individuals were concerned about a survivor's safety, they would force a particular choice rather than help the survivor identify their best options. This was often in response to providers' frustration over survivors returning to their traffickers, not seeking certain services, or choosing to sleep on the street rather than return to a home or shelter where they felt unsafe (Chakoian, Sethi, and Santos 2021). Consider the story of trafficking survivor Li, as told by the researcher who interviewed her: "When Li rejected a housing option, for example, providers felt reluctant to continue working with her. I explored Li's reasons for declining the housing referral. She explained that the unit was too far from her community, with which she had just started to reconnect. Li wanted to stay close to important social resources. . . . The isolation was magnified at the shelter where she felt misunderstood, struggled to understand the rules, and felt that the staff assumed her English was much better than it was" (Contreras, Kallivayalil, and Herman 2017, 44). Those who come into contact and work with human trafficking survivors need to make use of a trauma-informed approach to understand the psychological impacts of trafficking and respond by centering the needs and autonomy of each individual survivor. The ability to make decisions and choices, even if they differ from the providers' preferences, are particularly important in encouraging the development of autonomy, something that has often been denied to survivors during their victimization.

Specific recommendations for organizations taking a trauma-informed approach include the use of survivor mentorship and peer-support models, prioritizing a survivor-centered approach rather than a one-size-fits-all model, allowing survivors autonomy and control, and collaboration across organizations to provide comprehensive and long-term care (Gerassi and Nichols 2018). It is also important to reduce barriers to care for survivors, including their inability to access services due to a lack of documents or insurance, language barriers, and impediments due to child care, transportation, or finances (Hopper 2017a).

CHAPTER RESOURCES

1. As discussed in the chapter, many survivors of human trafficking also have a criminal record. States across the United States have attempted to provide relief by giving trafficking victims a path to clear their criminal records. The Polaris Project grades what is and isn't working for each state's laws, as well as offering steps for improvement. Check out your state's full report card here: https://polarisproject.org/grading-criminal-record-relief-laws-for-survivors-of-human-trafficking/.

2. Visit the Florida State University National Toolkit to read about how law enforcement officers can take a trauma-informed approach to human trafficking victims, including trauma-informed care and trauma-informed language: https://nationaltoolkit.csw.fsu.edu/leo/part-3/victims-and-trauma/. What might trauma-informed care and trauma-informed language look like for other professions who work

with human trafficking survivors? Consider health care personnel, social workers, and more.

1. What are parts of the grooming process? How might these aspects look different for a victim encountering a trafficker in person versus online?
2. What is trauma-coerced attachment and how can it be used to control trafficking victims?
3. What do we mean when we talk of victim-offender overlap? What are the three categories of crimes that human trafficking victims may fall into according to Schloenhardt and Markey-Towler (2016)?
4. Beyond the ones discussed in the chapter, what might be some short-term and long-term needs of human trafficking survivors?

FOUR

Social Structure Theories

This chapter explores a variety of social structure theories and the relationship that structural variables share with human trafficking. Social structure theories consider the role an individual's location within the structures of society plays in crime. The social structure is made up of social institutions, including things like the government, education, the family, religion, schools, the economy, law, and more. These theories explain crime through reference to these economic, social, and political institutions of society, often highlighting how the organization or structure of society creates environments conducive to crime. There are three primary social structure theories that will be discussed in this chapter: social disorganization theory, strain theories, and subcultural theories.

SOCIAL DISORGANIZATION THEORY

Social disorganization theory differs from other theories due to its focus on space and the environment. Originating from the University of Chicago in the 1920s and 1930s, the theory explores how the environments we find ourselves in can either encourage or prohibit criminal behavior. Research using social disorganization theory frequently focuses on studying crime in spaces such as neighborhoods, schools, and cities.

In the 1920s, sociologists Robert Park and Ernest Burgess took an ecological approach to the study of crime and deviance in cities. They argued that cities are environments with people and activities clustered into particular areas. As cities grow and change over time, people and their activities disperse away from the center of the city toward the suburbs. Their concentric zone model stated that cities take the form of five concentric rings, with areas of social and physical deterioration concentrated near the city center and more prosperous areas located toward the city's edge. This model was used to explain the existence of social problems such as unemployment and crime in specific Chicago districts (Park and Burgess 1925).

Criminologists Shaw and McKay would take this idea of crime being concentrated in certain areas to map and study boys' delinquency. They collected data on over eight thousand boys in Chicago between 1927 and 1933 and mapped their home addresses using this idea of zones.

Much like Park and Burgess had proposed, they found that delinquency was not randomly distributed, but instead was highest in the zone closest to the central business district, declining as you move outward. They called this high-crime zone the "zone in transition" and reasoned that there were three factors contributing to the crime. First, this zone was often where the most disadvantaged could be found, people living in poverty, with little to no education, who were in need of work. Second, this zone was in transition due to the high rate of population turnover. This constant changing meant that people were not really invested in working to change the neighborhood because they moved in and move out quickly. Those who did remain were often in poverty and unable to contribute to making changes. Finally, high racial and ethnic heterogeneity meant you had immigrants from a variety of different backgrounds, which acts as a barrier for a community to come together and work to change things (Shaw and McKay 1942).

Social disorganization theory fell out of favor over social process theories (see chapter 5) until some influential works tested the theory and showed that it had validity. One of the most influential of those was research by Sampson and Groves in 1989. Their model of social disorganization expanded the causal explanation of the theory by adding mediating factors.

The relationship between social disorganization—things like poverty, racial and ethnic heterogeneity, population turnover, family disruption, and urbanization—and crime was mediated by other neighborhood factors. Sampson and Groves (1989) argued that neighborhoods that experienced social disorganization would, as a result, also have sparse networks, unsupervised youth, and low organizational participation, which would then lead to crime and delinquency. Socially disorganized communities would not have the connections and friendships to help monitor and protect against crime and delinquency—particularly coming from youth.

Social Disorganization and Human Trafficking

Many of the factors identified by social disorganization theory are also factors that researchers have linked to human trafficking. Studies have shown that traffickers often target communities where there are high levels of poverty and unemployment and low levels of educational attainment (Eargle and Doucet 2021). Within these environments these structural conditions may lead to a decreased level of formal and informal social control, impacting the social order and collective efficacy of a community and allowing human trafficking to flourish (Diaz, Huff-Corzine, and Corzine 2022).

Rapid urbanization and densely populated areas have also been associated with human trafficking. These issues may have particularly impacted rapidly globalizing countries, where both formal and informal controls may weaken, including those in West Africa, such as Nigeria (Aransiola and Zarowsky 2014; Sawadogo 2012). In Turkey, a rapid increase in the population density, urban population, industrialization, and movement of goods and people occurred between 1980 and 2000. Turkey experienced both changes in the labor force and an influx of migrants from the defunct Soviet Union, and research found an associated increase in sex trafficking in Turkish communities characterized by poverty, heterogeneity, mobility, urbanization, and family disruption (Karakuş and Başıbüyük 2010).

A study of fifty-three countries confirmed that the rapid social changes and displacements associated with globalization increase social disorganization. Specifically, a country's level of poverty and urbanization and total population had a statistically significant impact on the cross-national distribution of human trafficking, even when controlling for inequality and proportion of younger population (Karakuş and McGarrell 2011). Racial and ethnic heterogeneity, measured as the percentage of foreign born, residential mobility, and family disruption did not have a significant impact in this study. Other researchers have focused on trade openness rather than economic development, arguing that rapid growth in trade can weaken social controls. One study of forty-three countries found that nations experiencing such transitions are vulnerable to human trafficking, as trade openness outpaces the ability of the government to develop effective political and legal institutions of control (Jiang and LaFree 2017).

But many times, social disorganization theory is examined at a smaller unit than the nation level, such as states, counties, cities, or neighborhoods. In a quantitative study of all US states, Eargle and Doucet (2021) found that resource disadvantage (consisting of poverty, unemployment, high school dropout rates, percentage of female-headed households, and the Gini inequality index) and residential instability were both significant in their effect on human trafficking. Their urban diversity factor consisting of the foreign-born, Hispanic, undocumented immigrant, and urban population was not found to be significant. This is perhaps due to the fact that their study examined all fifty states, where there is a wide variety in the demographics of the population.

Some studies have applied social disorganization theory to examine other issues of human trafficking, such as arrests or the development of task forces. These studies have had mixed results. One study of Florida counties examined the impact of sociodemographics, tourism measures, police officers, and task force presence. The only statistically significant predictor of human trafficking arrest was the presence of a dedicated task force, where membership in a task force increased the odds of counties reporting a human trafficking arrest by a factor of thirty-nine times (Huff-Corzine et al. 2017). A more recent study of Florida counties between 2013 and 2017 found more complex results (Diaz, Huff-Corzine, and Corzine 2022). Counties with higher levels of residential instability and greater numbers of police agencies but lower levels of concentrated disadvantage and drug arrests were associated with higher numbers of human trafficking arrests. More specifically, for every one unit increase in the residential instability index, there was a 158 percent increase in the number of human trafficking arrests, while a one unit increase in the concentrated disadvantage index was associated with a 70 percent decrease in the number of human trafficking arrests. The researchers hypothesize that the positive impact of residential instability could be related to the high levels of tourism in Florida, creating a more transient population. The negative effect of concentrated disadvantage could be due to the focus on arrests as the outcome. This could be an indicator of where commercial sex act transactions are more likely to take place, such as higher income areas, rather than where potential victims are coming from.

A study of 168 large, municipal police departments across the United States further illuminates the complicated relationship between social disorganization variables and policing outcomes. The study measured social disorganization using five indicators: residential instability, racial heterogeneity, family disruption, poverty, and unemployment. Social disorganization and organizational size were the only variables to have a statistically significant impact on whether or not agencies have a human trafficking unit (Jurek and King 2020).

That is, communities with larger agencies and less social disorganization were more likely to have specialized human trafficking units. Explaining this, the authors posit that communities experiencing high levels of social disorganization may not have the resources and capital to push for a human trafficking unit or may simply be focused on addressing more visible types of crime and disorder (Jurek and King 2020). Ultimately, more research is needed to test the relationship between social disorganization theory and human trafficking, tease out the mechanisms related to social controls, and examine how variables like residential instability and racial/ethnic heterogeneity relate.

Environments of Risk

While not explicit tests of social disorganization theory, some general environmental risk factors have been identified by human trafficking research. These include factors related to various social problems. For example, residing in high-crime communities, areas with high levels of poverty, police corruption, and the presence of prostitution in the neighborhood have all been connected to juvenile involvement in commercial sexual exploitation (Mitchell, Finkelhor, and Wolak 2010; Reid 2012). Areas with high demand for sexual services are also associated with sex trafficking, including the presence of tourism, military bases, and truck stops. Community risk factors may differ by region as well, with armed conflict, political instability, and forced migration being identified risk factors for trafficking in Mexico (Reid 2012).

Similar community dynamics may also influence labor trafficking, as migrants seek opportunity elsewhere. Their home environments place them at risk for trafficking throughout the migration process. In interviews with migrant farmworkers at risk for trafficking, the majority identified some form of violence that they were fleeing by coming to the United States (Norwood 2020). A study of labor trafficking among migrant farmworkers in North Carolina found certain county characteristics were connected to trafficking victimization. Counties with large and stable Hispanic populations reported less victimization than those counties that had experienced a more recent influx of Hispanic residents. Trafficking and abuse was also less common in counties with large percentages of the labor force employed in agriculture, suggesting that larger commercial farms may be subjected to increased oversight. Finally, for undocumented workers specifically, living in a labor camp was associated with increased likelihood of trafficking victimization, likely due to their isolated work environment (Barrick et al. 2013).

Stemming from social disorganization theory's focus on space and the environment, some researchers have begun to examine the spatial distribution of human trafficking, and in particular sex trafficking. As with other crimes, human trafficking is not distributed randomly in space. Instead, the social and physical environment can hinder or facilitate human trafficking occurrences. Sex trafficking studies show that there are several areas where cases may cluster, including areas where prostitution laws are not heavily enforced, cheaper hotels/motels, areas with brothels and/or massage parlors, and major interstate truck stops (Mletzko, Summers, and Arnio 2018).

Existing research also shows that sex trafficking cases frequently tend to cluster along major interstate highways. For example, in Ohio, major interstates, the presence of military bases, proximity to Canada, and water transit routes have all been identified as important facilitators of trafficking (Chohaney 2016; Davis 2006). Interviews with police, legal personnel, and service providers in St. Louis all reiterated that interstate circuits are commonly used to move victims from city to city (Nichols and Heil 2015). There are several explanations for this observation, including that highways offer both easy access and escape, offer anonymity, draw in a new consumer base, and allow traffickers to isolate their victims from their known communities in order to prevent them from seeking out help (Nichols 2016). Studies also show that sexually oriented businesses, such as illicit massage parlors, and low-cost motels and hotels tend to spatially cluster with prostitution activity, with some researchers finding a similar pattern for sex trafficking as well (Bouché and Crotty 2018; Chin et al. 2015; Crotty and Bouché 2018).

One study examined the spatial distribution of sex trafficking cases between 2013 and 2015 at the census block group level in Austin, Texas. Researchers found that cases were concentrated in certain census block groups, with just 4 percent accounting for 30 percent of all sex trafficking cases. Analysis showed that high volumes of sex trafficking cases were explained by proximity to major intersections of I-35, presence of more motels or sexually oriented businesses, and higher levels of concentrated disadvantage (Mletzko, Summers, and Arnio 2018). Proximity to a truck stop, residential instability, and racial/ethnic heterogeneity were not significant predictors. As with several other studies discussed already, the outcome used in this study dealt with sex trafficking offenses known to the police. These offenses are frequently identified at the transaction stage. Other social disorganization variables may have more of an impact at the recruitment stage, which is not captured by such studies.

The study of Austin demonstrates a common method of spatial analysis, which is identifying areas that depart from the average distribution of crimes, also known as hot spot analysis. Makin and Bye (2018) also performed one such study, mapping online queries to identify interest in massage parlors and strip clubs. They recognize that licit markets such as strip clubs and massage parlors are separate from both prostitution and sex trafficking, but argue they share important overlap. They find several "interest corridors" along major interstates across the United States, including I-20 from San Antonio to Atlanta and I-85/95 from Atlanta to New York. Further analysis found a weak but statistically significant relationship between interest in adult services postings on Backpage.com and incidents of sex-based offenses (Makin and Bye 2018).

Displacement

When one thinks about the spatial environments of human trafficking, displacement should also be considered. Displacement refers to the "relocation of a crime from one place, time, target, offense, tactic, or offender to another as a result of some crime-prevention initiative" (Guerette and Bowers 2009, 1333). Heavy policing of hot-spot areas can lead to such displacement. This effect has been seen with human trafficking as well. Recall that in chapter 2, various prostitution policy models were associated with the displacement of sex work, creating issues with the safety of sex workers and the ability of police to investigate possible trafficking cases.

This issue was reflected in a study of Cyprus, Greece, where enforcement efforts around prostitution and sex trafficking altered the characteristics of sexual exploitation cases. Both prostitution-related and trafficking offenses shifted from being native traffickers working out of cabarets and pubs year-round to foreign perpetrators working out of private residences with seasonal patterns (Constantinou 2016). Displacement has also been studied in relation to the online environment (refer to the policy box in this chapter).

Special Cases: Boomtowns

There are also special cases that can be used to study the issues associated with social disorganization theory and environmental patterns of trafficking.

The 2010 shutdown of Craigslist's erotic services section led to the emergence of similar websites hosting sexual advertisements, with Backpage quickly becoming the most popular (Nhan and Bowen 2020). In response to the growth of such websites, and concerns about how they were being used to host trafficking, the US SESTA-FOSTA Act was enacted in 2018. The Stop Enabling Sex Traffickers Act (SESTA) and Allow States and Victims to Fight Online Sex Trafficking Act (FOSTA) were enacted with the idea of stopping online sex trafficking by allowing civil and criminal liability for websites such as Craigslist and Backpage.

Supporters of the law claimed the law would "decimate" online sex trafficking, claims that conflated all sexual advertising with sex trafficking. Yet more than two years after its passage, only one prosecution and a handful of lawsuits have been brought, and an investigation showed that the number of online sexual advertisements has not significantly decreased (Albert et al. 2020; Burnitis 2019).

It is true that the internet facilitates sex trafficking, from grooming and recruitment to the selling of sexual services. However, websites are also prime resources for investigators and prosecutors to identify traffickers, rescue victims, and build successful cases. Prior to the passage of SESTA-FOSTA, it was estimated that 25–33 percent of sex trafficking cases were uncovered through web searchers and online stings (Heil and Nichols 2014). Targeting these websites as part of an anti-trafficking effort, however, has had several negative consequences.

First, elimination of websites such as Backpage simply leads to displacement. Scholars had previously warned that traffickers would simply change where they advertised and the known code words used in advertisements (Heil and Nichols 2014). Backpage was seized and shut down in 2018 following the passage of the law. Immediately, there was a decrease in the number of sexual advertisements; however, within a few months the number increased as new websites took the place of Backpage (Burnitis 2019). The law has made it more difficult for law enforcement and prosecutors to successfully identify both traffickers and victims. Law enforcement enjoyed cooperation with Backpage as a US-based website, and they were able to subpoena ads from the website for evidence. Following the new law, agencies across the United States have reported their investigations have become more difficult, as new, foreign-based websites have no obligation to cooperate with US law enforcement. The darknet is also increasingly being used, where user identities are protected by encrypted protocols and relays, making monitoring and identification by police all but impossible (Nhan and Bowen 2020).

Second, critics of the law have pointed out how it has the potential to harm both sex workers and trafficking victims (Burnitis 2019). As websites change their terms of service, sex workers have been pushed onto the street to work, increasing their exposure to violence in several ways. Online advertising allows sex workers to screen potential clients, reduces their reliance on third-party managers such as pimps, and allows information sharing, such as blacklists of bad clients (Albert et al. 2020). When these safety features are removed, it endangers not only consensual sex workers, but also trafficking victims who are forced to sell sexual services.

In March 2022, several US representatives and senators reintroduced the SAFE SEX Workers Study Act. The bill previously failed in 2020, but would direct the Department of Health and Human Services to conduct the first federal study on the impact of SESTA-FOSTA. As politicians and researchers alike begin to study the long-term impacts of this bill, criminologists will want to follow the results closely.

Thinking about digital environments and online "displacement," what can be done to address sex trafficking online while taking into consideration the negatives from legislation like SESTA-FOSTA?

One such recent example of this phenomenon is oil boomtowns. When we think about boomtowns, the California gold rush may come to mind—communities experiencing rapid growth and change due to sudden wealth. Between 2008 and 2014, the Bakken region experienced such a boom with rapidly expanding oil production, primarily in North Dakota but also in Montana (Conway 2020). With these dramatic changes, communities often experience reduced formal and informal social controls, which in turn increases disorder and crime.

Rural communities that experience "boom and bust" cycles due to resource extraction often experience rapid population growth and economic expansion, which leads to stress on infrastructure services, law enforcement, and more. In the Bakken oil region specifically, media and scholarship have reported increases in drug crimes, assaults, drunk driving, prostitution, and sex trafficking (Junod et al. 2017; Ruddell and Britto 2020). One study identified a surge in online sex advertising in Minot, North Dakota, likely associated with the dramatic population increase from work in the oil sands (Dubrawski et al. 2015).

As for crime, communities in the Bakken region of both Montana and North Dakota have reported significant increases in gender-based violence. A Bureau of Justice Statistics report found that between 2006 and 2012 the rate of serious violent crime increased 38 percent in the Bakken region, with female violent victimization increasing by 18 percent. The number of reported statutory rapes, the type of crime that increased the most for female victims, was up 53 percent (Martin et al. 2019). Arrests related to sex trafficking have also increased in North Dakota, likely due to the demand from male workers for purchasing sex (Nichols 2016). Ruddell and Britto (2020, 204) identified five community factors about the Bakken boomtowns that facilitate crimes against women, including "(a) precarious housing arrangements; (b) the social isolation of women; (c) lack of domestic violence shelters and other social supports for survivors; (d) a workplace culture in the oilfields supportive of substance abuse and hyper-masculinity; and (e) the inability of boomtown justice systems to respond to these crimes in an effective or timely manner."

These community risk factors are further exacerbated by the fact that the Bakken region contains several Indian reservations. A large portion of the Bakken oil fields are encompassed by the Fort Berthold Indian reservation, which has reported an increase in violent crime and the sex trafficking of Indigenous women associated with the oil workers living in temporary camps (Finn et al. 2017). It is known that American Indian and Alaska Natives (AI/AN) experience higher rates of violence than other races in the United States (Hagen and Whittemore 2017). Indigenous women in particular are more than twice as likely to experience violent crimes than all other women (Finn et al. 2017). AI/AN communities also experience high rates of poverty, isolation, homeless and runaway youth, child welfare involvement, substance abuse, and historical trauma (Roetzel, Petro, and Ramstad 2019). These factors all leave Indigenous populations at an increased vulnerability to human trafficking (Tribal Insights Brief 2016). It is estimated that Native Americans experience higher rates of trafficking compared to the rest of the population (Roetzel, Petro, and Ramstad 2019; Shanley and Jordan 2017). These cases are often complicated by jurisdictional issues around the prosecution of non-Natives on tribal land (Finn et al. 2017). All of these factors make boomtowns such as the ones in the Bakken region a prime site to explore connections between the community environment and crime.

In his 1897 book on suicide, Émile Durkheim challenged the traditional idea of suicide as an individual, personal act. Durkheim introduced the idea that there are social influences on suicide rates, which allows us to explain why suicide rates may vary by country and community. Part of this explanation was his concept of anomie. Durkheim's definition of anomie refers to a state of normlessness where society fails to effectively regulate the expectations or behaviors of its members. It's a state or condition of individuals or society characterized by the breakdown or absence of social norms and values (Durkheim 1951).

In the 1930s a sociologist named Robert Merton developed strain theory, which built from Durkheim's concept of anomie. Specifically, Merton argued that anomie results from strained differences in the cultural goals we are socialized to strive for and achieve, and the legitimate means to go about achieving those goals. The problem, Merton argued, is that there are structural impediments that mean everyone does not have the same opportunities for success, despite the fact that we are all socialized into desiring this success. Scholars should consider how a lack of education and jobs can lead to strain that can lead to crime as an alternative means of achieving. Based on these two things, cultural goals and legitimate or institutionalized means of achieving these goals, Merton devised a typology that has five adaptations. Most people are conformists, accepting the cultural goals and legitimate means of achieving those goals. Others are innovators, seeking alternative means. Ritualists do not take any chances, following the means but not actively pursuing cultural goals. Retreatists drop out of society, not pursuing cultural goals or employing legitimate means. Finally, rebels seek to substitute new goals and new means (Merton 1938).

Robert Agnew's general strain theory expanded on previous theories by agreeing that strain can result from the failure to achieve these culturally valued goals, but stating that strain can also result from other things, like negative relationships. Agnew's theory focused on asking what circumstances lead an individual to deviant behavior. Besides strain from failing to achieve goals, Agnew thought three types of negative relations could also lead to strain and subsequently crime. The first is a relationship that prevents or threatens to prevent achievement of valued goals. The second is the removal of or threat to remove positive stimuli. The third is the presentation of or threat to present negative stimuli. The negative affect, and especially anger and frustration, that can result from these relations can promote the desire to correct or rectify the situation, making crime a possible option. Agnew also identified specific types of strain that are most likely to lead to crime. These include high amounts of strain, strain that is seen as unjust, strain associated with low self-control, and strain that creates more pressure or incentives for criminal coping. Agnew argued that not all individuals respond to these strains with crime. Most people cope in legal and conforming ways through behavioral, cognitive, and emotional coping (Agnew 1992).

Robert Merton once said that a cardinal American virtue, ambition, causes a cardinal American vice, crime. The last strain theory mentioned in this section explains that. Messner and Rosenfeld's institutional anomie theory argues that the cultural and structural organization of American society contributes to crime. They specifically focus on the United States in their theory, but it has been applied to other Western industrialized nations as well. They argue that the American Dream is what sets up our expectations, the goals we are to pursue. The American Dream also embodies many of the basic value commitments of our culture, specifically, achievement, individualism, universalism, and the fetishism of money. Structurally, the institutions in our society are not balanced, and specifically, economic institutions dominate over noneconomic institutions, meaning the economy dominates over other things like the polity, family, and education. They argue that economic dominance manifests itself in three ways: the devaluation of noneconomic institutional functions and roles, requiring noneconomic institutions to accommodate to the demands of the economy, and economic norms penetrating into other noneconomic institutions. Taken together, there is a culturally intense pressure for monetary success with a weak emphasis on how you get there, or the means. Structurally, controls are weakened as noneconomic institutions like the family and school are unable to socialize values, beliefs, and commitments beyond economic ones. There is weakening of social support, social controls, and prosocial socialization, which contributes to crime (Messner and Rosenfeld 2013).

Globalization, Strain, and Human Trafficking

The globalization of nations is a process that links strain and human trafficking. Globalization refers to the processes that help or hinder the cross-national movement of people, goods, and information (Ritzer 2010). The ideologies that surround globalization tend to emphasize individualism and competitiveness alongside free markets and trade (Mishra 2015). This has the impact of exacerbating the existing inequalities so often associated with poverty and exploitation, often increasing inequalities both within and between nations (Chuang 2006a; Zhang 2007). Globalization is linked to human trafficking through these inequalities and their associated strains (Lee 2011). In addition to social and economic changes, globalization has created cultural change as well. The spread of global media and the internet has led to an influx of messages that promise better opportunities elsewhere (Cameron and Newman 2008; Chuang 2006a). Altogether these shifts create a structural environment that increases strain and a cultural environment that fosters expectations for better outcomes. Together, this can increase the vulnerability of individuals seeking a better life to traffickers and exploitation.

Globalization and strain theory can be used to understand the increase in trafficking in former Soviet states. After the collapse of the Soviet Union, Central and Eastern European countries began the shift toward a free-market capitalist economy. This shift was fraught with high inflation, high unemployment rates, and a loss of social safety nets, with women often facing worse outcomes. Coupled with an "idealized imagination of the 'Rich Western Countries,'" many women experienced strain due to a disconnect between expectations and opportunities (Vocks and Nijboer 2000, 384). At the same time, traffickers began to originate from these countries as opportunities were blocked and they turned to illegitimate means for economic achievement (Choi 2010). Thus, economic motivations play a role in both the origination of victims and traffickers.

This desire for a better life is often used by traffickers during the recruitment process. A study of foreign labor trafficking victims in the United States found that a desire for opportunity in order to support their family was a primary motivation for leaving their home country (Owens et al. 2014). An idealized vision of the United States as a land of opportunity was echoed in their interviews, with one respondent stating, "You know, when we hear 'America' back in my country . . . to come here you have big opportunity; you can give everything to your family that they need. So I take the chance" (Owens et al. 2014, 46). While this study focused on labor trafficking, similar sentiments can be found in all forms of trafficking, as traffickers exploit the poverty and desperation of potential victims. Organ trafficking and child trafficking through intercountry adoption represent two unique forms of trafficking that exemplify these issues.

Poverty and Organ Trafficking. It is first important to clarify terminology when referring to trafficking in persons for organ removal and organ trafficking. Although both are used interchangeably here, and do frequently overlap, there are important distinctions. Trafficking in persons for organ removal includes situations in which an individual is subjected to organ removal through force, fraud, or coercion. Organ trafficking involves a donor being paid, falsely claiming to be giving their organ out of altruism, or otherwise violating the national laws of organ transplantation (Bruckmüller 2020). The former is a crime against the person, while the latter is a crime against the organ. Compared to other forms of trafficking, organ trafficking makes up only about 1 percent of cases worldwide (UNODC 2020). Still, estimates of transplants that involve trafficking range from 10 to 20 percent, with kidneys and livers being the most trafficked organs (Nichols 2017).

Organ trafficking victims are frequently young men, around thirty years old, poor, and not well educated. Low education plays a role in the problem of informed consent, as many victims are not aware of the dangers and risks involved, or their rights as a donor (Bruckmüller 2020). The root causes of these individuals' vulnerability include extreme poverty, lack of employment prospects, and belonging to marginalized groups (Stickle, Hickman, and White 2020). Interviews with survivors in India found that 98 percent resorted to selling a kidney in response to increased economic strain, with the hope of eliminating debt and overcoming poverty (Budiani-Saberi et al. 2014). Similar reasons were found with interviews of male survivors from Pakistan, as selling an organ appeared to be one of the only options to pay off loans and provide for their families (Yousaf and Purkayastha 2015).

As with other forms of trafficking, organ trafficking can involve force, fraud, or coercion. Donors may agree to sell an organ but not receive the agreed upon payment or medical care (Bruckmüller 2020). Deception is often used during recruitment, with potential victims being told that the surgery is painless or risk free. False medical information is relayed, including promises that the removed kidney will regrow or that a second kidney is not necessary to begin with (Kakar 2017).

The Promise of a Better Life and Intercountry Adoption Trafficking. Actress Angelina Jolie adopted her son Maddox from Cambodia in 2002. Two years later, a woman involved in the adoption pled guilty for her role in potentially hundreds of illegal adoptions (Turner 2014). In the past several decades, domestic adoptions have decreased. Correspondingly, the numbers of intercountry adoptions have increased in all Western countries (Loibl 2020). International adoptions largely flow from low-income countries in the Global South and postcommunist Eastern Europe to wealthy nations in the Global North. Frequently, countries that have experienced war, natural disaster, or extreme poverty are attractive source countries for adoption. Scholars have argued that the global orphan crisis is largely an inflated Western myth, and that instead many of these children have at least one living parent or live in alternative traditional family forms, such as being raised in an extended family network (Loibl 2020).

Many international adoption agencies allow potential parents to fill out a checklist with preferences of the child's age, gender, health, and origin. This can create pressure to meet Western demand and generate the desired adoptable children encouraging opportunities for criminal networks to intercede (Loibl 2020; Meier 2008). While kidnapping and abduction is one tactic, deception and fraud are also frequently used to have individuals relinquish their parental rights. Scouts are often sent out as recruiters, targeting impoverished and vulnerable families. Coercion may be used by telling the parents that the child should have the opportunity for a better life than their own, demonstrating psychological pressure that is often combined with financial reward (Loibl 2020).

Deception is also used to obtain consent for the adoption. Parents are often provided false information about the process, including that their child is only leaving temporarily, will be provided educational opportunities, and will remain in contact through letters and payments, or that they will be allowed to join their child in the Western country once they are grown (Heil 2017; Loibl 2020). Whatever the method, parents are frequently misled that they are not severing parental rights but merely providing a better life for their child and perhaps themselves (Smolin 2006). For example, in a study of seventy-three birth mothers from the Marshall Islands, 82 percent reported a misunderstanding of the permanency of adoption, believing their child would return to them at eighteen. The study found that their extreme poverty, lack of family support, and cultural misunderstandings about adoption led to their exploitation by recruiters (Roby and Matsumura 2002).

The finances involved in intercountry adoption contribute to the trafficking of children as well (Heil 2017). Adoption agencies request financial contributions from the adopting parents. What seem like reasonable costs from a Western perspective incentivize orphanage directors, government officials, and others to continue to provide adoptable children, even if through illegal means (Gibbons 2017; Loibl 2020). Orphanages also frequently pay per-child fees to individuals who "find" children, which can further incentivize obtaining children through any means necessary (Meier 2008). While there is often a large economic difference between the sending and receiving countries in intercountry adoptions, some adoption schemes have become large criminal enterprises. Operation Broken Hearts was a large-scale US investigation into child trafficking through adoption from Cambodia. Those involved in the criminal enterprise had received USD$8 million from adoptive parents, which they used to fund their own lavish lifestyle. Adoptable babies were generated through recruiters and buyers who frequently used deception to obtain children. Parents were told that their child would attend a nice school and be raised by a rich family, and that they could visit whenever they liked. Small payments and some rice were often given to the families up front (Maskew 2005). In regard to both organ trafficking and adoption trafficking, it is often the most vulnerable who are targeted, with traffickers promising solutions to their strains, in the form of fraud and coercion.

General Strain Theory and Commercial Sexual Exploitation

Agnew's general strain theory has been studied in relation to sex trafficking and commercial sexual exploitation, with support found for the theory. Much of this research finds pathways to sex trafficking through caregiver strains, child maltreatment, or an unstable home life. Caregiver strains linked to an increased likelihood of child sexual exploitation include substance use, emotional and mental health problems, arrests, domestic problems, and family violence (Franchino-Olsen 2021b). Professionals working with at-risk youth reported in one survey that compromised parenting and lack of home stability are the most commonly seen vulnerability factors for minor sex trafficking victimization. Other high-risk factors mentioned included material need, developmental issues, mental health, and a history of abuse or neglect (Cole and Sprang 2015). Youth cope with the negative emotional states caused by such an environment by running away, using substances, or associating with delinquent peers. These risk-taking behaviors make youth vulnerable to trafficking by placing them in a position where others can exploit them or where they engage in sex work to meet their basic needs (Franchino-Olsen 2021a).

One study examined the relationship between caregiver strain, child maltreatment, and vulnerability to commercial sexual exploitation using a sample of 174 women, 12 percent of whom had experienced prostitution as a minor (Reid 2011). The researcher hypothesized that a pathway to sexual exploitation exists through caregiver strain, which results in child maltreatment. Maltreatment as a strain that is considered unjust or high in magnitude can result in disappointment and frustration that can prompt various behavioral responses, including those linked to heightened vulnerability. The study found that those who reported higher levels of strain experienced by their mothers also experienced higher levels of child maltreatment. These children ran away at higher rates, initiated drug or alcohol use earlier, and were more likely to report sexual denigration, or self-blaming and self-denigrating attitudes after sexual abuse. These dysfunctional coping behaviors were risk-inflating and were related to minor involvement in prostitution (Reid 2011).

A similar study examined the link between childhood maltreatment and trafficking victimization, but accounted for differences by gender. For girls, emotional and physical neglect by the caregiver and exposure to family violence resulted in the child seeking attention and support outside of the family, increasing their vulnerability to victimization. Similarly for boys, both sexual and emotional abuse were predictive of human trafficking. In their case, emotional abuse rather than neglect can lead to social alienation and withdrawal, linking to trafficking victimization (Reid et al. 2017).

Finally, a study examined data from over a thousand serious youth offenders in which about 8 percent of boys and girls reported commercial sexual exploitation (Reid and Piquero 2016). Testing the strain reactive pathway between caregiver strain and youth commercial sexual exploitation, the researchers found that for both boys and girls caregiver strain was associated with poor nurturing, which was associated with greater negative psychosocial emotions, increased running away, and earlier substance use and initiation of sexual relationships. For boys, it was the negative psychosocial emotion and earlier initiation of sexual relationships that was significantly related to commercial sexual exploitation, while girls' vulnerability was predicted by earlier substance use. These researchers suggest that prevention and early intervention targeted toward strained families can help reduce commercial sexual exploitation by avoiding the risky coping behaviors that stemmed from poor nurturing. This includes efforts such as parenting classes, substance use treatment, intimate partner violence assistance, and more (Reid and Piquero 2016).

Some scholars have used the idea of weakened social institutions from institutional anomie theory to explore vulnerability in relation to sex trafficking. A study of trafficking in St. Louis showed that weakened social institutions, such as the family, education, and facets of the economic system, expose individuals to social environments that are conducive to trafficking victimization (Heil and Nichols 2015). In regard to the family, an unstable home life, abuse, neglect, and child welfare or juvenile justice involvement increase the likelihood of runaways, exposing individuals to sex trafficking by getting involved with a boyfriend-as-pimp or engaging in survival sex (Heil and Nichols 2015). Schools with high dropout and truancy rates, low academic performance, and high student and teacher mobility reflect a weakened institution. Truancy, dropping out, and low educational levels are all linked to sex trafficking victimization (Heil and Nichols 2015; Nichols 2016). Finally, economic conditions such as poverty and a lack of social safety nets, including substance treatment, job and educational services, mental health assistance, and more, exacerbate sex trafficking vulnerability (Heil and Nichols 2015).

More formal applications of institutional anomie theory have explored the linkages between migration and human trafficking. In a study of human trafficking in five post-Soviet countries, institutional anomie theory highlighted how the transition from a centrally planned economy to a capitalist free market caused a host of rapid social and economic changes connected to women's vulnerability to trafficking (Hupp Williamson 2017). Following the collapse of the Soviet Union, crime levels increased as controls weakened and individualism was emphasized with new economic reforms (Passas and Agnew 1997). The process of privatization that happened in these post-Soviet states frequently led to heightened inequalities as elites concentrated the wealth. Throughout the transition there was a focus on economic institutions without regard to social and cultural institutions as well. This meant that social protections previously provided disappeared and gender inequalities were exacerbated. These issues ultimately influenced the decision of many women to seek migration, increasing their vulnerability to trafficking victimization (Hupp Williamson 2017).

Comparative and historical analysis was used to examine how economic policies in Cambodia, Bolivia, and The Gambia strengthened economic institutions while correspondingly weakening noneconomic institutions, creating an environment conducive to migration and trafficking (Hupp

Williamson 2022). Historically, policies stemming from organizations such as the International Monetary Fund and World Bank worked to structure nations' economies in accordance with neoliberal ideology. However, the promises of prosperity were often not realized, as social safety nets were weakened and inequalities increased. In Cambodia, neoliberal economic policies increased income inequality and gender inequality in education and employment. These conditions contributed to a high rate of irregular migration to neighboring countries such as Thailand or Malaysia, leaving undocumented labor migrants vulnerable to abuse and exploitation. In Bolivia, the government's continued prioritization of foreign investments from transnational corporations in their natural resources has exacerbated corruption and victimization of Indigenous populations. In Gambia, market reforms did not address economic hardships, political instability, and attacks on individual rights. This environment led many young people to seek migration "the back way" through Africa and into Europe, again leaving them vulnerable to traffickers. In each of these countries, trafficking vulnerabilities were exacerbated by policies that prioritized economic dominance over noneconomic institutions. Migration to seek opportunity elsewhere then made individuals vulnerable to the human trafficking flows that were occurring alongside migratory flows (Hupp Williamson 2022).

SUBCULTURAL THEORY

Subcultural theories concentrate their focus on cultural deviance, or how one's socialization can reflect norms and values that are in conflict with the law, conventional customs, or morality. Early formations of subcultural theory, such as Miller's focal concerns theory and Wolfgang and Ferracuti's subculture of violence theory, have been criticized for an excessive focus on the lower class and largely unsupportive results (Bohm and Vogel 2015). Differential opportunity theory was later developed by Cloward and Ohlin (1960). The theory builds off strain theories and social learning theories to argue that crime is learned, but not everyone has the same opportunities to learn the skills for different types of crime. This theory focuses on opportunity structures to explain crime and criminality. Cloward and Ohlin argue there are legitimate opportunity structures, which we see from strain theory, but there are also illegitimate opportunity structures that may be available. According to differential opportunity theory, everyone wants economic success, but lower-class youth do not have the same economic opportunities. They realize they are set up for failure by the system and form subcultures as a solution.

The types of subcultures that can form are based on the opportunities, legitimate or illegitimate, that are available to individuals. Based on whether or not illegitimate opportunity structures are available, Cloward and Ohlin argue that three types of delinquent subcultures can emerge. The first is criminal subcultures, which provide illegitimate opportunity structures. Often associated with gangs and organized crime, these illegitimate opportunity structures provide a way for individuals to make money. Next are conflict and retreatist subcultures. In each of these types, both legitimate and illegitimate opportunities are unavailable to individuals. This can lead to anger and frustration and the formation of violent gangs as part of conflict subcultures. These subcultures are often found in neighborhoods that are socially disorganized with crime and violence. What distinguishes conflict subcultures from criminal subcultures is that the crime is mostly individualistic, petty, and does not provide much money. Finally, retreatist subcultures develop among what they termed double failures, or those who cannot find legitimate or illegitimate subcultures. Having no place in a criminal or conflict subculture, such individuals may withdraw from society, often turning to drugs or alcohol, similar to Merton's concept of retreatists (Cloward & Ohlin 1960).

The subcultural/cultural deviance perspective has often been studied in relation to crime committed by organized groups, criminal networks, and gangs. Each of these can also be examined in relation to their involvement in human trafficking.

Organized Crime and Trafficking

The UN Palermo Protocol on human trafficking is part of a larger Convention against Transnational Organized Crime. Article 2 of that convention defines an organized criminal group as a "structured group of three or more persons, existing for a period of time and acting in concert with the aim of committing one or more serious crimes or offences established in accordance with this Convention, in order to obtain, directly or indirectly, a financial or other material benefit" (UN 2000b). That the largest international instrument on human trafficking is included under a convention on organized crime highlights how interconnected the relationship between these two phenomena is typically viewed. Human trafficking is frequently described as one of the fastest growing areas of organized crime, where sophisticated underground criminal networks are involved in undermining countries' stability (de Vries, Jose, and Farrell 2020). Media reports also tend to perpetuate stereotypes about the massive profits of successful global organized crime rings involved in heinous acts such as sex trafficking (Goździak 2015; Urban and Arends 2018; Viuhko 2018). This is despite the fact that there is a lack of clear evidence about the relationship between organized crime and human trafficking (Lee 2011). Research does not show a clear-cut consensus about the extent of organized criminal groups' involvement in human trafficking (Tripp and McMahon-Howard 2016). Much of this research lacks sound methodology and empirical evidence or is significantly dated (Tripp and McMahon-Howard 2016; Vermeulen, Van Damme, and De Bondt 2010).

One frequent differentiation between traffickers involves distinguishing between individual traffickers, small groups of loosely organized networks, and more traditional highly structured criminal enterprises (Aronowitz 2009). Loose networks tend to be more flexible and adaptable due to their decentralized structure and subgroup specialization (Farr 2004; Shelley 2010). These networks may be structured according to their various functions, with little contact between the different individuals involved (Vermeulen, Van Damme, and De Bondt 2010). By comparison, pyramid-shaped, well-organized groups tend to control every stage of the trafficking process and are likely to be involved in other criminal activities as well (Aronowitz and Veldhuizen 2021). The UNODC makes a similar distinction between individual traffickers who work on their own, opportunistic traffickers who work as a duo, business/enterprise types of organized criminal groups that involve three or more traffickers working together, and governance types of organized criminal groups that control an area with fear and violence and may be involved in multiple illicit markets (UNODC 2020).

Other scholars have attempted to differentiate types of organized crime by region. Aronowitz and Veldhuizen (2021) and Shelley (2010) distinguish between post-Soviet organized crime groups that focus on short-term profits through the sex trafficking of women, Chinese and Thai traffickers that function more as a structured business focused on long-term profits, US-Mexico border traffickers that focus on volume, Balkan crime groups that use violence and force in their opportunistic trafficking of women, and the trafficking of women out of West Africa that involves physical violence and psychological means of control.

Some researchers have argued that it is a myth that most trafficking organizations are highly sophisticated, instead claiming that such operations tend toward loosely organized entrepreneurial networks over highly structured, hierarchical crime groups (Aronowitz and Veldhuizen 2021). Empirical studies of the evidence for organized crime involvement frequently make use of official data through court case documents. An examination of twenty-four federal trafficking cases indicted in the metropolitan area of Atlanta between 2000 and 2013 revealed the majority of cases contained no significant relationship between organized crime and human trafficking (Tripp and McMahon-Howard 2016). Instead, only eight cases contained evidence of organized criminal networks and only one evidence of an organized criminal syndicate. Most of these were international sex trafficking cases, while domestic cases were carried out by only one or two offenders. A partial replication of this study in Missouri of twenty-six human trafficking cases found that only one case involved a criminal network and two involved an organized, hierarchical group (Urban and Arends 2018).

A study of eleven cases in Finland found that perpetrators of trafficking were rarely members of organized crime groups, but instead small networks of individuals that were opportunistic in their involvement and often connected to the victim as an acquaintance, relative, or partner (Viuhko 2018). Similarly, a study of 114 federal cases of sexual exploitation in Australia found only 19 involved organized criminal syndicates, which varied greatly in the extent of their organization (Langhorn 2018).

Bouché (2017) examined 862 federal prosecutions of human trafficking between 2000 and 2015 and found 58 percent exhibited some evidence of organized criminal group involvement. These cases were further divided into the following group types: mom and pop groups (35%), crime rings (33%), illegal enterprises (26%), gangs (6%), and cartels/mafias/syndicates (0%). The UNODC asserts that when organized criminal groups are involved in human trafficking cases, more victims tend to be trafficked for longer periods across greater distances than cases that do not involve organized crime. Their 2020 report on global cases of human trafficking found an average number of 2.5 victims for individual and opportunistic traffickers compared to an average of 11.5 victims for organized criminal groups (UNODC 2020). This also appears to be the case for Bouché's research in the United States. Mom and pop groups include small-to-medium groups of family and friends that strongly identify with the group involved in trafficking, with an average of 17.6 victims and 5.3 defendants per case. Crime rings are also small-to-medium groups but have low self-identification with the group, with an average of 7 victims and 5.3 defendants. Local or national gangs were found to have an average of 8.8 victims per case with 14.5 defendants. These numbers pale compared to illegal enterprise groups, whose high sophistication averaged 65.7 victims and 7 defendants per case (Bouché 2017).

Interviews are another way to examine organized crime involvement in human trafficking. Using interviews with victims, police, judges, and non-profit workers in Bulgaria, Petrunov (2014) identified several types of sex traffickers. This included lone traffickers who often exploited a woman they had an existing relationship with, independent traffickers who coordinated the destination exploitation for two to five women, collaborative groups of traffickers who were each in charge of one to seven women, and large hierarchical organizations that managed more than one hundred sex workers and were also involved in human trafficking. In the United States, interviews with convicted sex traffickers found that 57 percent operated alone with no organizational ties, and the involvement of criminal enterprises frequently centered on other crimes (e.g., drug trafficking) rather than human trafficking (Shively et al. 2016).

From all of this evidence, perhaps one of the only discernable conclusions is that there is a large amount of diversity in both the types of traffickers and the structure of organized crime involvement (Vermeulen, Van Damme, and De Bondt 2010). Traffickers and their organizations are highly varied, differing in the complexity of their organization, the number of victims involved, and the size and scope of their operation (Aronowitz 2009; Aronowitz and Veldhuizen 2021). Varying definitions of organized crime and what constitutes an organized criminal group only further complicate the evidence (Turner and Kelly 2009).

Gangs and Trafficking

In their 2015 report, the National Gang Intelligence Center in the U.S. Department of Justice reported that gangs were increasingly becoming involved in human trafficking, and in particular, sex trafficking. Surveys and reporting from federal, state, local, and tribal law enforcement agencies confirmed this. For example, Fairfax County in Virginia reported that 20 percent of the leads for their human trafficking unit were gang related (National Gang Intelligence Center 2015). It is important to note that gangs are also frequently involved with sex work such as prostitution, which can make it difficult to separate gang-run prostitution from gang-involved sex trafficking (Lugo 2020).

As with studies of organized crime's involvement with human trafficking, many studies of gang involvement make use of official court cases, with one study using court cases to highlight how gangs become involved in sex trafficking. The authors note that the command structure, organized division of labor, enforced loyalty, and willingness to use violence within gangs enable them to easily shift to involvement in sex trafficking. Gang members then exploit attraction to wealth, offer up romantic relationships, supply drugs, and use the threat of violence and indebtedness to recruit victims and maintain control (Frank and Terwilliger 2015).

Another researcher made use of federal indictments from twenty gang network cases in the United States between 1981 and 2017 (Lugo 2020). They found that gang practices did differ along ethnic and cultural lines. Black gang indictments demonstrated a flat, loose network structure with cooperative behavior between cliques. Hispanic gangs such as MS-13 tended to be more hierarchical with strict rules, with those involved in carrying out sex trafficking paying taxes up the command structure. White gangs such as Hell's Angels were highly regimented and extremely violent. Another study of gang sex trafficking in California found that skinhead gangs were frequently involved in sex trafficking within massage parlors, escort services, and strip clubs (Carpenter and Gates 2016). Hispanic gangs were frequently involved in prostitution and pimping, though they were less likely to identify it as a top money-making activity compared to Black gangs.

Such gangs may have different "rules of the game" that apply not only to the men who are gang members but the women involved in sexual exploitation as well. Rules for women working as prostitutes in Black gangs may include not accepting Black clients due to the possibility they are from a rival gang (Lugo 2020). These rules often work to exert control over the women. Consider the following about the Outlaws Motorcycle Club:

> Armed guards watch the clubhouse around the clock, and a witness has testified that the clubhouse is stocked with weapons and explosives. Women cannot join the Outlaws but may either be a member's "old lady," effectively his property, or belong to the entire group. Gang members often have more than one old lady, with the highest-ranking female members responsible for training new recruits. Most of the women are forced to generate income for the Outlaws by working as nude dancers or through commercial sex acts. The Outlaws also use female gang members to transport drugs to gang members in prison. Because

the Outlaws control the flow of money and drugs to the women, the women find themselves dependent on the gang and unable to leave. Punishment for misbehavior ranges from beatings to gang rape (Lederer 2011, 7).

Human trafficking research on gang involvement may also make use of other qualitative methods, such as surveys, interviews, and fieldwork. A three-year study of gang involvement in sex trafficking in San Diego County, California, made use of several such methods, including surveys with identified prostitutes, intake forms with sex trafficking survivors, arrest records, focus groups at schools, and interviews with gang members (Carpenter and Gates 2016). The researchers discovered 110 gangs involved in sex trafficking, ranging from cliques that were only loosely affiliated with gangs for protection to highly organized and even transnational criminal networks. They found that gang involvement in sex trafficking was about equally split between gang-directed sex trafficking and undirected gang member involvement in sex trafficking. Four broad profiles of sex-trafficking facilitators were identified through interviews with gang members. These included the enforcer-contractor (67% of cases) who reported sharing revenue between themselves and those involved in the commercial sex work; the traditional facilitators (28%) who generally self-identified as pimps and kept most or all of the money made; the viscous-violent facilitator (4%) who used extreme physical and psychological tactics to control women and enforce quotas; and organized trafficking groups (1%) that involved more clandestine, closed networks run by a core group (Carpenter and Gates 2016).

This study stands in contrast to another study of sex trafficking completed in neighboring Tijuana, Mexico. In Tijuana, Zhang (2010) found that neither organized crime nor street gangs had infiltrated the commercial sex industry. Such groups remained focused on drug trafficking and smuggling. The difference could be due to Tijuana's regulation of prostitution as a legal business, leading to a high presence of police officers and low tolerance for disruption of business in the red-light district.

Making use of eighteen years of research and over four hundred interviews in El Salvador, Honduras, and Guatemala, Boerman and Golob (2021) highlight just how gangs are able to coerce victims and maintain control. Gangs such as MS-13 and factions of Barrio 18 use the control and violence they exert over an area to force young people into committing crimes. Youth may be forced to traffic drugs or firearms, spy on rival gangs, smuggle contraband, and work in domestic or sexual servitude. Indeed, many gangs specifically target vulnerable juveniles for recruitment, including targeting them to engage in prostitution on behalf of the gang (National Gang Intelligence Center 2015). Female gang members may be initiated via a "sex-in" or a gang rape. Once in the gang, they may be expected to prostitute for the gang (Lugo 2020). Focus groups with school staff in California identified a wide range of factors tied to a student's risk for sex trafficking, including being lonely and isolated, living in poverty, being in special education, experiencing previous sexual abuse, runaways and homelessness, and drug addiction (Carpenter and Gates 2016).

Less commonly studied is gang involvement in forced criminality. As opposed to many other cases of human trafficking that involve fraud, gangs may be more likely to rely on coercion and force (Boerman and Golob 2021). Consider the case of Jaysson:

> Jaysson was left in the care of an uncle after his mother migrated to the U.S. His mother was sending money to the uncle but he was squandering it and not only failing to care for Jaysson, but also abusing him and periodically throwing him out of the house and forcing him to live on the street. 7 MS13 members began offering Jaysson food and a place to stay in return for doing simple favors for them. They later began subjecting him to beatings and demanding that he engage in criminal activity on behalf of the gang, telling him that they "owned him." After learning of MS13's involvement in serious crime, including the murder of a police officer, members of the gang began monitoring Jaysson constantly and warning him that if he disclosed information about their activities, they would kill him. Jaysson was eventually taken in by missionaries and cut all ties to MS13 but members of the gang encountered him later and demanded that he repay his "debt" for the care they had provided him in the past. Specifically, they demanded he sell drugs to students in the school he was attending; provide intelligence on the Barrio 18, which controlled the area around the school; and assist in the extortion of school staff. Jaysson refused and members of the gang told him that he would always be "MS13 property" and if he refused, he would be killed. With assistance from the missionaries who had taken him in, Jaysson fled the country but states that he knows MS13 will kill him if he ever returns and is located (Boerman and Golob 2021, 247).

Unfortunately, many law enforcement and state officials are unable or unwilling to differentiate between gang members and individuals coerced into service to the gang, including forced criminality. Many times, such youth are victimized not only by gangs, but also by their governments as they are viewed as criminals rather than victims (Boerman and Golob 2021).

1. Watch the *W5* news report on exposing child sex tourism in the Dominican Republic here: https://www.youtube.com/watch?v= p65lqLercz4. After you watch the video, what are some environmental factors from social disorganization theory you can identify that contribute to the problem? Institutional anomie theory considers the impact of weakened social institutions; do you see any of those in the video? If you were going to create policies or programs to address this issue, what could be done about it on both the demand side and the supply side?

2. Visit the UNODC SHERLOC Case Law Database here: https:// sherloc.unodc.org/cld/v3/sherloc/cldb/index.html?lng=en. Select the Crime Type of Trafficking in Persons. Further filter the results by also selecting the additional criteria of the Crime Type of Participation in an Organized Criminal Group. Select several cases to read about. How was organized crime involved in each case? What elements of force, fraud, and/or coercion were present related to the trafficking?

CHAPTER DISCUSSION QUESTIONS

1. What are some areas that might be "hot spots" for both sex and labor trafficking?

2. What is displacement and what problems might it create when policing human trafficking?

3. Some individuals argue that we already sell things like eggs and sperm, so why not organs? They argue that legalizing and regulating the sale of organs will make the process safer and help eliminate exploitation. Opponents argue that such policies would only institutionalize harm for marginalized populations. Research the arguments for and against legalizing the sale of organs and have a class debate on how this would impact trafficking in persons for the purpose of organ removal.

4. Summarize the evidence for and against organized criminal involvement in human trafficking. What about the evidence for gang involvement?

FIVE

Social Process Theories

This chapter explores a variety of social process theories and the relationship that social interactions and socialization share with human trafficking. Social process theories are theories that consider the impact of external influences on behavior. These theories explain crime through reference to the process of socialization, often highlighting how external groups such as the family or peers influence behavior. There are four primary social process theories that will be discussed in this chapter: social control theory, learning theories, neutralization theory, and labeling theory. It is important to note that the literature reviewed in this chapter focuses primarily on sex trafficking. From control and learning theories, researchers have examined the relationships between family, peers, and sex trafficking victimization. Moral crusades and moral panics from labeling theory have primarily centered around controlling prostitution and concern over trafficking. There is a lack of literature applying the concepts from these theories to the issue of labor trafficking, something future researchers should consider.

SOCIAL CONTROL THEORY

In *Causes of Delinquency*, Travis Hirschi argued that crime is not a response to learned behavior, stimuli, or strains. Instead, he said criminality is a given and it is the absence of criminality that needs to be explained. We need to ask not why people are criminal but why do people conform? For Hirschi (2009), the reasons people do not engage in crime is because of their social bonds to conformity. For this reason, his social control theory is sometimes referred to as social bond theory. There are four components to social bonds:

attachment, commitment, involvement, and belief. Attachment operates as the emotional bond—we care about conformity through other's opinions and reactions to our behaviors. Commitment is the rational bond and involves individuals rationally weighing the costs and benefits of nonconforming behavior. Involvement deals with involvement in conformist activities, leaving little time for deviance and crime. Finally, belief entails an understanding of and agreement with the rules and norms that influence conformity (Hirschi 2009). While few studies have directly tested the applicability of social control theory to human trafficking, many aspects of the theory can be found throughout the literature. This includes, in particular, the role of the family as a source of attachment and provider of economic, social, and emotional support (Vocks and Nijboer 2000).

Family Environments and Parental Relationships

A review of human trafficking studies published between 2000 and 2011 found a wide variety of social control mechanisms connected with both risk factors and juvenile involvement in sex trafficking (Reid 2012). This includes a dysfunctional upbringing, such as childhood abuse, caregiver drug or alcohol abuse, or being abandoned or thrown out of the home. The author argues that such things are indicators of weak social bonds at a critical point in the transition from childhood to young adulthood and increase the likelihood of becoming entrapped in prostitution at a young age (Reid 2012). This argument is supported by other studies, which have frequently relied on information from minors involved in prostitution.

Analyzing the stories of thirty-seven sex trafficking survivors, Rosenblatt (2014) found that family division, lack of family support, and exposure to drugs, prostitution, and abuse in the home were factors that played a role in the recruitment of youth into sex trafficking. Another study of 158 adolescent prostitutes living in a halfway house compared their experiences to high school girls. Those in the halfway house had more dysfunctional families and negative parental rearing compared to the control group. Quantitative analysis found that the variables of parental care and maternal protection contributed to adolescent prostitution through the variable of neuroticism (Lung et al. 2004). Interviewing adult female sex workers, Potter, Martin, and Romans (1999) found that women who described having negative parental relationships that were less caring and highly controlling were more likely to become involved in prostitution as juveniles.

While many of these studies focus on family environment measures such as family structure and family dysfunction, McNeal and Walker (2016) delved deeper into aspects of parental relationships. Parental attachment, intimacy of communication, and parental involvement in activities and school are measures included in their study of juveniles exchanging sex for drugs or money. They found that in addition to sex, age, delinquency, and substance use, a juvenile's family structure and parental involvement in school were significant predictors related to exchange of sex for drugs or money.

Factors related to family dysfunction and attachment are risk factors for juvenile sex trafficking because offenders use their vulnerability to their advantage. A study of survivors of juvenile sex trafficking found themes of insecure attachment, a need to belong, and a desire for love and attention (Hargreaves-Cormany and Patterson 2016). Other prominent elements included conflict with their family, financial strain, and involvement of child protective services in the household. Interviews with six women who had worked in prostitution as minors revealed that their desire for love and acceptance as children was directly related to their vulnerability to recruitment (Cecchet and Thoburn 2014).

Parents and Schools as Protective Factors

In addition to negative parental relationships, studies also point to the important role that school plays, with poor school performance and lack of school involvement also being connected to trafficking vulnerability (Reid 2012). At the same time, parents and schools may also act as protective factors against juvenile recruitment into prostitution. In a study comparing youth who have sold sex versus those who have not, the author found that being happy at school and feeling connected to school were significantly associated with lower likelihood of selling sex (Kaestle 2012). In another study, interviews with survivors of domestic minor sex trafficking (DMST) highlight the role of positive early relationships. Specifically, survivors emphasized that "learning self-worth, interpersonal boundaries, and sexual limit-setting were not only important in mitigating risk for DMST victimization but also important to be taught during early interpersonal relationship with a caregiver, family member, or trusted community partner" (O'Brien 2018, 7).

Social control theory can thus show how social supports such as parents, school connections, and attachment to mentors can work as protective factors. This has implications for policies that target at-risk youth, including training for school teachers, programs that target victims of abuse and homelessness, and peer mentorship. One study in particular cited such interpersonal relationships as key to fostering resiliency, encouraging reintegration, and protecting survivors from returning to their pimps or traffickers (O'Brien 2018). These relationships were found in staff working at safe houses, mental health providers, and survivor-to-survivor mentorships.

LEARNING THEORIES

Learning theories such as Sutherland's differential association theory and Burgess and Acker's social learning theory argue that criminal behavior comes about through processes of socialization and learning. These theories argue that criminal behavior can be learned the same way we would learn any other sort of social behavior. Sutherland (1947) argues that a person's associations can expose them to both criminal and noncriminal patterns of behavior. Associations vary in regard to aspects such as their frequency, duration, priority, and intensity (Sutherland 1947). Burgess and Akers (1966) build on differential association theory by adding in principles of operant conditioning, such as modeling or imitation. Specifically, they argue that the introduction of positive stimuli or removal of aversive stimuli can be seen in both positive and negative reinforcement, encouraging behavior to continue (Burgess and Akers 1966). From learning theory, researchers can understand the important role family and peers often play in the trafficking of minors.

Familial Trafficking

Familial trafficking includes cases where there is a familial relationship between the victim and the trafficker. According to global CTDC data, 14 percent of all human trafficking cases in their database involve a familial relationship between a victim and their recruiter. This percentage increases to 45 percent when looking at cases that involve children (CTDC 2021). Specific to the United States, a review of studies found ranges from 3 percent to 44 percent of trafficking cases reportedly involving family members (Raphael 2020). Studies have found that the age at first exploitation of victims in family-involved cases is on average lower than those involving nonfamily perpetrators (Edwards, Middleton, and Cole 2022; Reid, Huard, and Haskell 2015), that familial victims are less likely to be using substances than nonfamilial victims (Edwards, Middleton, and Cole 2022; Twis 2019), and that those trafficked by family members are less likely to report running away (Reid, Huard, and Haskell 2015).

When studying predictors of the type of relationship between victims and their trafficker, Twis (2019) found that child welfare involvement was a significant predictor of familial traffickers for domestic minor victims of sex trafficking. Specifically, DMST victims trafficked by a family member were 11 percent more likely to have child welfare involvement and 647 percent less likely to be involved in the juvenile justice system than youth trafficked by a stranger (Twis 2019). Studies show victims of family-facilitated juvenile sex trafficking were also more likely to come from home environments of domestic violence, sexual and physical abuse, and neglect or abandonment (Reid, Huard, and Haskell 2015; Sprang and Cole 2018).

Exploring the child's relationship with their family member, one study found that the most common familial trafficker was the child's biological mother, making up 66 percent of family-facilitated trafficking cases in their sample, followed by the biological father, stepfather/mother's boyfriend, and uncle (Allert 2022). This finding is consistent with other studies, which have also found that the mother-daughter relationship was the most commonly reported type of trafficker-victim relationship (Reid, Huard, and Haskell 2015; Sprang and Cole 2018).

In cases of familial trafficking, the caregiver frequently uses threats, intimidation, and parental authority to control the victim (Sprang and Cole 2018). This authority and dependency that the caregiver holds over the child acts as a barrier to coming forward or disclosing victimization. Children may also not understand that they are being groomed or exploited (Reid, Huard, and Haskell 2015). In fact, one study found that familial trafficking cases were more likely to be reported by anonymous, nonrelative community members compared to nonfamilial cases, which were reported by community professionals and law enforcement, indicating a lack of understanding of the dynamics involved in family-facilitated trafficking (Edwards, Middleton, and Cole 2022).

Motivations for family-controlled trafficking include monetary financial gain, frequently to support a drug habit (Cole 2018; Raphael 2020; Reid, Huard, and Haskell 2015). Other motivations may include parents who are involved in the sex trade industry, either as facilitators or victims themselves (Raphael 2020). These motivations are reflected in the story of Jean, a child survivor of commercial sexual exploitation in Nevada, who speaks about her mother's involvement in the sex trade: "She's the one that introduced me to the life when I was 13. . . . Then she had a drug dealer that lived right next door. He was my mom's drug dealer. . . . My mom just, in other words, sold me to him for drugs, so he was a pimp. . . . My mom knew everything that was goin' on, but didn't do anything" (Reed et al. 2019, 6). For such individuals, prostitution as a way of life may be normalized, or even glamourized (Gerassi and Nichols 2018; Kennedy et al. 2007).

Intergenerational prostitution refers to cases that involve entering prostitution through family members and has been described as a common pathway for minors entering prostitution. In one study of adolescent females involved in prostitution, 43 percent of the sample reported prostitution as common in their neighborhoods and that they simply saw it as a way to make money (Oselin 2014). A woman named Beverly describes her entry into prostitution as occurring through socialization with those already in the trade, including her father, where she learned the values, beliefs, and behaviors of the sex trade. Beverly and others in the study also describe the way they viewed the lifestyle as glamourous as adolescents. Jacqueline stated, "After my father died we were so poor and in that area that's all you see are prostitutes and pimps. The girls are wearing nice clothes and making money, that's what I wanted too, so that's how it started for me" (Oselin 2014, 29). It is ultimately these intimate social networks and early exposure to prostitution, including values, attitudes, and beliefs that are encouraged and reinforced by others, that are connected to underage individuals entering prostitution (Oselin 2014).

Peer Influences

One way that traffickers normalize prostitution is through peer influence and peer recruitment (Baird and Connolly 2021; Reid 2016). Traffickers may use another girl to act as a friend and set up a double date that will involve exchanging sex for money (Reid 2016), or themselves befriend potential victims, leading them to believe it is a mutually beneficial relationship (O'Brien and Li 2020; Twis, Kirschner, and Greenwood 2021). Overall, recruitment by friends is common among trafficking victims, with CTDC data reporting that 18 percent of all cases involved recruitment by a friend (CTDC 2021). A review of twenty-three studies of human trafficking found that friends are the second-most-common recruiter relationship reported after romantic relationship (Baird and Connolly 2021).

Interviews with over three hundred CSEC-involved youth, 53 percent of whom reported recruitment via friends, highlighted the ways friends modeled the behaviors of sex work (Curtis et al. 2008). While in some cases youth reported feeling pressured to join, many reported a fascination with the lifestyle or saw it as a way to meet economic needs. One girl who began prostituting at age fourteen describes her entry:

> One of my best friends used to do it. When I was 14, I used to hang out with her all the time. Then, after like 3 months, I wondered how she would get her money, 'cause she didn't work or anything. So one day, she brought me with her to her friend's house. She always used to bring me with her, but she never showed me. She'd go into a room and come out, and we had pot to smoke and she'd have money and stuff. And she would be, like, her friend gave it to her. Then one day she was like, "Come in the room with me," and she wanted me to sit and watch. I felt really weird. So, I'm not on the bed, I'm in the corner on the chair, watching. And I was like, "Oh wow, this is what she does, how she gets her money. It all makes sense now" (Curtis et al. 2008, 52).

Examining young people who trade sex, Lutnick (2016) found that friends can connect clients to each other, share knowledge about working in the sex trade, and recruit each other to act as a third party or pimp. Other studies have similar findings, with peers acting as a role model in a variety of ways, such as teaching others how to set up an online profile and how much to charge, and showing youth how to stay safe (Dank et al. 2015; Reed et al. 2019).

In addition to playing a role in recruitment, peer influences also matter in regard to youths' decision to remain in the sex trade. With extensive networks made up of other CSEC-involved youth, some report feeling obligated to help their peers and remain in the life due to the emotional and financial support those peers provide (Curtis et al. 2008). Understanding these issues can help shape the response to juveniles involved in the sex trade, including the need to take into account a survivor's environment, personal networks and behaviors, and beliefs and cognitions. Responses influenced by learning theories may take into account the role of positive role models and relationships, peer-to-peer mentorship, and cognitive therapies that address coping skills and self-views (Hargreaves-Cormany and Patterson 2016).

TECHNIQUES OF NEUTRALIZATION

In their attempts to expand upon Sutherland's work and understand how individuals come to learn and accept criminal definitions, Sykes and Matza identified various techniques of neutralization. Offenders were still aware of societal norms and mores of conformity, but these neutralizations "free" them to commit crime by acting as justifications or rationalizations for their behavior (Sykes and Matza 1957). Sykes and Matza specifically identified five common techniques of neutralization. These include denial of responsibility, denial of injury, denial of the victim, condemnation of the condemners, and appeals to higher loyalties. The applicability of these neutralizations to those involved in human trafficking is reviewed below.

Traffickers' Techniques of Neutralization

As discussed previously, familial involvement and community exposure matter for victim recruitment. Yet studies have also shown that those same factors act as entry points for pimps and traffickers (Dank et al. 2016). From seventy-three interviews with individuals charged with pimping or trafficking, Dank et al. (2016) found that 32 percent reported family member involvement in the sex trade impacted their entry decision. As with victims, the normalization of prostitution as a means to earn income occurred during childhood. For 18 percent of the offenders, mentorship by other pimps influenced their entry, with the glamourization of the lifestyle acting as a compelling force. Interviews with convicted traffickers highlight money as their primary motivation, with some also claiming pressure from family or friends (Shively et al. 2016). While these studies highlight the pathways to becoming a trafficker, others highlight how traffickers neutralize or rationalize their actions.

Interviews with forty-six convicted traffickers, forty-five of whom were convicted for sex trafficking, revealed they were quick to offer justifications for their behaviors. These included claims that the victims were engaging in prostitution voluntarily, that they were just trying to help them, that minors had lied about their age, or that while psychological coercion may have occurred, they never used physical force. Such claims can be seen as fitting with many of Sykes and Matza's techniques of neutralization, including denial of the victim and denial of injury. This is in line with other research that has shown that traffickers distinguish between women who are "forced" to prostitute and "ones that choose," as well as claims that violence is a natural part of the sex trade (Troshynski and Blank 2019).

Studies have sought to apply Sykes and Matza's techniques directly, with strong results. Denial of responsibility is seen when traffickers claim it was the only way for them to make money (Aronowitz, Theuermann, and

Tyurykanova 2010; Shively et al. 2016). Others minimize their role in trafficking. For example, a trafficker who facilitated the entry of women into Greece claimed, "I have no responsibility if anything bad happens to the girls. I do not do anything. . . . What responsibility should I have . . . I just get the papers" (Antonopoulos and Winterdyk 2005, 143).

Denial of the victim is used to dehumanize victims, particularly victims of sex trafficking (Copley 2014). Distinctions about who is or is not a victim may be made along lines of deception and country of origin. Women may have known they were going to work as a prostitute, and although they did not know the extent of exploitation they would face, because there was no initial deception, they "had it coming" (Antonopoulos and Winterdyk 2005). Traffickers may also claim that the victim has been helped by the trafficker, as they now have better living conditions than in their home country (Antonopoulos and Winterdyk 2005; Aronowitz, Theuermann, and Tyurykanova 2010).

Sex traffickers also make use of the denial of injury neutralization. Similar to denial of the victim, traffickers may claim that they are assisting victims in finding a means of survival and improving their overall financial position (Aronowitz, Theuermann, and Tyurykanova 2010; Copley 2014). One pimp of minor girls stated, "I helped girls who no one else would. I picked up throwaways and runaways and dressed them up and taught them how to survive" (Raphael and Myers-Powell 2010, 5).

When condemning the condemners, traffickers may justify their actions by highlighting corrupt or complacent government (Aronowitz, Theuermann, and Tyurykanova 2010; Copley 2014). One trafficker stated, "Everyone is bribed. Do you know anyone, who is not bribed? . . . And the police not only take money, but they also have sex for free, and have drinks for free. And they do not come alone; they always come with company" (Antonopoulos and Winterdyk 2005, 145). Traffickers may also claim that purchasing sex is normal and that trafficked women are just another commodity in the illicit economy (Antonopoulos and Winterdyk 2005).

Researchers have not found evidence of appeals to higher loyalties in studies with traffickers (Antonopoulos and Winterdyk 2005; Copley 2014). Still, some hypothesize that this neutralization may be found within trafficking networks organized around family ties or friendships (Aronowitz, Theuermann, and Tyurykanova 2010). Indeed, a study of internal child sex trafficking cases in the United Kingdom found that 96 percent of offenders were linked to at least one other offender—typically through their everyday life as friends, neighbors, relatives, or colleagues. Further, 89 percent of the offenders co-offended in a trafficking activity with one or more codefendants (Cockbain and Wortley 2015). Certainly, appeals to higher loyalty may play a role in some trafficking networks.

LABELING THEORIES

Labeling theories originated with the perspective of symbolic interactionism. Under this perspective, people interact through shared symbols that give meaning to social interaction. Society is essentially played out through these daily interactions between people. Labeling theory takes this symbolic interaction approach and looks at the way that social reactions influence behavior. Labeling theorists examine the social meaning of labels, how those labels are understood, and how they impact the individuals to whom they are applied. The impact of the stigma of a criminal record is one aspect often studied by labeling theorists. In regard to human trafficking, the movement around ending demand for purchased sex focuses on the label of the john and how stigma can be used to both shame and redirect future behavior (see the policy box in this chapter).

Moral Crusades and Moral Panics

When studying labeling it is important to understand where the rules that are enforced come from (Becker 1963). Moral crusades and moral panics are two ways we can understand this process. Becker (1963) identified a moral entrepreneur as a crusader who identifies an evil that must be suppressed through the introduction of specific rules. The implementation of such laws can often differ in practice from their intention, as we see with legislation on sex trafficking and prostitution.

Reactions are crucial to the concept of moral panics as well, where the reactions of the media, law enforcement, politicians, action groups, and the general public are out of proportion to the reality of the issue. Goode and Ben-Yehuda (1994) identify five important elements of a moral panic, including a heightened level of concern over the issue, hostility toward the stereotyped villains, widespread consensus that the problem is real and serious, exaggerated figures and disproportionate concern, and volatility where the concern seemingly emerges from nowhere and can just as suddenly fade from

In *Crime, Shame and Reintegration*, John Braithwaite highlights how reintegrative shaming can be used within society to control crime. With reintegrative shaming, there is a separation of the behavior from the offender, so that the focus shifts from the offender as a whole to simply the offender's behavior. When shaming is reintegrative, others care about seeing the successful reincorporation of the individual back into society (Braithwaite 1989). Shaming that is disintegrative, or stigmatizing, occurs when the offender is pushed away from society and efforts of forgiveness and inclusion are not made. This type of shaming is also likely to lead to recidivism.

John schools are programs that focus on men who purchase sex, with the aim of ending demand for commercial sex. The first john school was started in San Francisco in 1995, with one study identifying at least fifty-eight US cities that have implemented similar programs (Berger 2012; Shively et al. 2012). The majority of john schools are structured as diversion programs, where successful completion results in the dismissal of charges. Schools vary in the number of sessions and fines an individual must complete, but all involve discussing the "health and legal consequences for johns if they were to continue engaging in commercial sex, and the negative impact of prostitution on prostituted women and girls and communities. . . . Other curriculum components include discussions of healthy relationships, anger management, sexual addiction, pimping and pandering, human trafficking, and johns' vulnerability to criminal victimization while engaged in commercial sex" (Shively et al. 2012, 62). While the structure of john schools can vary from city to city, many of these programs make use of elements of reintegrative shaming.

Advocates of john schools claim that any embarrassment or shame felt by participants is natural to the program but that these schools can ultimately help johns avoid the stigma associated with a criminal charge (Berger 2012). John schools focus on shaming the behavior and the potential harms of the behavior of purchasing sex, with the aim that offenders will come to reject that wrongdoing rather than their entire self (Valenzuela 2016). Some programs also incorporate the stories and experiences of former sex workers, with the aim that offenders gain empathy toward those impacted by their behavior. Additionally, advocates claim such programs could act as a deterrent and reduce recidivism, as one San Francisco john school was found to reduce recidivism by over 40 percent (Shively et al. 2008).

Still, critics contend that there have not been many formal evaluations of john schools, and some of the evidence is mixed. Further, surveys about changes in johns' attitudes toward prostitution may be skewed by social desirability bias, where johns are simply aware of what the "correct" answers should be (Berger 2012).

Interviews with participants of the Nashville John School highlight this complicated picture, with half of the sample experiencing feelings of shame, guilt, and regret that were induced by the reintegrative shaming and shame management tactics of the program (Valenzuela 2016). This included approaching the topic of purchasing sex from the perspective of potential harms to the johns and having a former sex worker speak about her exploitation, explaining how "demand" harmed her without making explicit accusations. However, others exhibited embarrassment or unresolved shame, not viewing prostitution as immoral or harmful or claiming that their arrest was unjust (Valenzuela 2016). Ultimately, more research is needed on the effectiveness of john schools and john shaming. Further, end-demand efforts should expand beyond the purchase of sex to include addressing the demand for cheap and exploitative labor in all sectors (Berger 2012).

How do john schools and the principles of reintegrative shaming reflect the concepts of labeling theory?

public awareness. These elements can be seen in the way that unfounded concerns about human trafficking in relation to specific events, such as major sporting events, give rise to media panic and changes in policing, often to the detriment of immigrants and sex workers.

The Crusade against Sex Work. As discussed in chapter 1, the history of human trafficking has roots in the panic of White slavery in the 1800s. The campaigns against White slavery reflected fears and anxieties over national identity, increasing migration, and women's autonomy (Doezema 2000). Researchers have argued that many of these same concerns are reflected in modern human trafficking ideology, with the panic leading to an emphasis on controlling immigrant populations and eliminating sex work (Kempadoo 2007).

The crusade against human trafficking has often taken a moralistic tone, led primarily by a coalition of the religious right and abolitionist feminists, both of whom seek the elimination of all sex work (Brennan 2017; Weitzer 2020). This includes groups such as Focus on the Family, Concerned Women for America, the International Justice Mission, Shared Hope International, the Coalition Against Trafficking in Women, and the Protection Project (Weitzer 2010). In their crusade, groups such as these repeat unverifiable claims, including that prostitution is intrinsically evil and linked with sex trafficking, and a problem of great magnitude. This is despite a lack of evidence that the majority of sex workers are trafficking victims and the fact that the hidden nature of human trafficking that makes estimates difficult to verify (Weitzer 2007). Sex workers are also portrayed with a lack of agency where there is no voluntary migration, misrepresenting the often-complex processes of choice involved in the stories of many trafficking victims. Those involved in the process represent the folk devils. Customers and traffickers are portrayed as evil sexual predators, with sweeping generalizations about their characteristics and motivations (Weitzer 2007). According to Brennan (2017, 484) this messaging gained traction because "women working in brothels fit the public imagination of trafficked victims, while men picking fruits and vegetables failed to stir similar outrage."

Such groups were very influential during the Bush administration, with success in influencing policy around human trafficking (Brennan 2017). Signaling government acceptance of the crusade's message, such organizations have been granted consultative access and funding, entered into formal collaborations with government agencies, and taken lead roles in drafting legislation (Weitzer 2007). The result has been a perpetuation of the ideal victim and offender stereotypes. The panic over sexual slavery creates division between the "ideal innocents" and "illegal immigrants," leaving men and labor exploitation out of the discussion (Brennan 2008; Chapkis 2003). Weitzer (2020) argues that the success of this crusade is further reflected in political speeches and government reports, which conflate all forms of sex work with trafficking, facing little counter-discourse from those who argue otherwise. A misguided focus on linking transnational migration and organized crime to human trafficking also narrows representation of the problem. Rather than focusing on socioeconomic conditions, migration policies, or state safety nets, responses emphasize increased border control, restrictions on women's movement, and an abolition of sex work (Kempadoo 2007; Weitzer 2007).

Sporting Events and Moral Panics. Moral panics related to human trafficking have frequently been connected with large sporting events, such as the World

Cup, Super Bowl, and Olympics. These panics often begin with what one author called "zombie data," unverified estimates that thousands of women will be trafficked for sex, repeated over and over in media stories leading up to such events (Brennan 2017). In the panic around the 2006 FIFA World Cup, women's rights groups, faith-based organizations, and political officials all repeated claims that young, naïve, foreign women would be trafficked into Germany for the event. Media reported that up to forty thousand women would be trafficked (Hennig et al. 2007). However, crackdowns on prostitution and raids on sex workers found only five cases of trafficking with some connection to the World Cup (Dagistanli and Milivojevic 2013; Hennig et al. 2007).

Comparable claims have been made about the Super Bowl being an event that attracts sex traffickers due to the influx of tourism. One study found that 76 percent of print media between 2010 and 2016 reported a link between the Super Bowl and sex trafficking (Martin and Hill 2019). These claims have been largely anecdotal, with little supporting evidence (Miller, Kennedy, and Dubrawski 2016). While not a measure of sex trafficking, the volume of escort advertisements around this annual sporting event has been examined by researchers, who found no significant changes in the days leading up to a Super Bowl (Dubrawski et al. 2015). A similar study of the 2010 World Cup in South Africa found no major increase in female sex worker advertisements and no major changes in sex worker demographics (Richter and Delva 2011).

Such panics around these events often serve to increase police contact with sex workers, leading to harassment, arrest, and even deportation (Dagistanli and Milivojevic 2013; Richter and Delva 2011). Focusing on law-and-order responses by increasing brothel raids and prostitution crackdowns reinforces stereotypes around immigration, sex work, and sex trafficking, while overlooking labor trafficking (Dagistanli and Milivojevic 2013). Further, anti-trafficking organizations have reported that such panics can make their work more difficult by conflating sex work with trafficking and causing hype around a specific event that disappears quickly from public awareness, particularly when inflated figures turn out to be unfounded (Hennig et al. 2007).

CHAPTER RESOURCES

1. Visit the National Center on Safe Supportive Learning Environments (NCSSLE) guide on human trafficking in schools here: https:// safesupportivelearning.ed.gov/human-trafficking-americas-schools.

Learn about the recommendations to prevent trafficking in schools at each of the three tiers. Search for a human trafficking school curriculum to learn more. Examples include A21, Project STARFISH, Not a Number by Love146, and the Prevention Project. How does this program reflect the policies and protocols recommended by the NCSSLE?

2. Read the Everyday Sociology blog about moral panics in 2020: https://www.everydaysociologyblog.com/2020/11/moral-panics-in-2020.html. For further reading, check out news articles about the Pizzagate and Wayfairgate trafficking conspiracy theories. What elements of a moral panic can you identify in these conspiracies? How might social media enable the spread of such misplaced panics?

CHAPTER DISCUSSION QUESTIONS

1. What role do peers play in the recruitment process of juvenile sex trafficking?

2. Discuss how each of the techniques of neutralization can be applied to traffickers.

3. What are the primary claims moral crusaders have made about human trafficking? What impact has this had on policy around human trafficking?

SIX

Critical Perspectives

This chapter explores a variety of critical perspectives and their relationship to human trafficking. Critical theories are diverse but are united in the fact that they consider the impact of social structures, inequality, and power. These theories highlight the role these aspects play in defining who and what is criminal. Various critical theories and perspectives will be discussed in this chapter, including cultural criminology, conflict theories, feminist and queer criminology, and critical race theory and intersectionality.

CULTURAL CRIMINOLOGY

Cultural criminology situates crime and punishment squarely within the cultural, examining their public and private displays, messages, and meanings (Muzzatti and Smith 2018). Drawing heavily from a symbolic interactionist perspective, cultural criminology critiques the process by which things and people come to be defined as victims and criminals. This includes the role of the media in constructing the reality of crime, with cultural criminology being known for making use of a wide variety of methodologies to examine the content and discourse of various media forms (Muzzatti and Smith 2018).

Media Representation

Representations of human trafficking are found throughout the news media, pop culture, government reports, and awareness campaigns. These depictions are important to understand because they not only influence the general public's understanding, but also have a substantial impact on research, funding, and laws (Albright and D'Adamo 2017b). Among the general public, media portrayals of human trafficking have shaped incorrect beliefs about what human trafficking looks like. A survey administered to a representative sample of two thousand Americans found that 92 percent of respondents believed human trafficking victims are almost always female, 71 percent believed trafficking was just another word for smuggling, 62 percent believed trafficking always requires physical violence, and 59 percent believed trafficking requires movement across borders (Bouché, Farrell, and Wittmer 2015). These incorrect and stereotypical beliefs are also found to be held by law enforcement and government officials, whose perceptions of human trafficking are also influenced by the media (Farrell, Pfeffer, and Bright 2015). These inaccurate beliefs are perpetuated by media portrayals that simplify and distort narratives of human trafficking. Frequently, this includes conflating trafficking with other concepts such as smuggling and prostitution, with a skewed focus on sex trafficking and the sex trade (Gregoriou and Ras 2018). Stories often focus on the most sensational and egregious cases of trafficking, which represent only a small minority of cases (Albright and D'Adamo 2017b).

Additionally, media reporting tends to ignore the structural causes that make people vulnerable to victimization, influencing public opinion and policy (Gregoriou and Ras 2018). One analysis of over two decades of news articles found that criminal activity was cited as the cause of human trafficking twice as much as socioeconomic and political causes, such as poverty, conflict, corruption, and discrimination (Gulati 2011). Instead, media coverage frequently focuses on the criminal justice side of the issue—the investigation, discovery, and rescue of victims (Albright and D'Adamo 2017b). Media stories that approach trafficking from this crime framing are also less likely to suggest remedies, such as legislation and awareness, to address the problem (Johnston, Friedman, and Sobel 2015). When solutions are put forth, they are likely to simply suggest stricter law enforcement, rather than policies that address the root causes of trafficking (Gulati 2011). Further, a lack of coverage of survivors rebuilding their lives after trafficking can lead to a lack of policies and resources that address the long-term needs of victims (Albright and D'Adamo 2017a).

Victims and Villains

Media representations of human trafficking have consistently stereotyped what both victims and villains look like, contributing to the idea of both the "ideal victim" and the "ideal offender." The concept of the ideal victim was first described by Christie (1986) and involved a weak and blameless victim taken advantage of by an evil stranger (Hoyle, Bosworth, and Dempsey 2011). These elements are reflected in the construction of the ideal trafficking victim. The ideal trafficking victim is a victim of sex trafficking, female, and young. She also lacks agency, with victims not choosing to participate in sex work, and therefore being helpless and blameless (Rodríguez-López 2018). Such portrayals evoke more outrage and sympathy than the story of an illegal migrant or prostitute who finds herself in a trafficking situation. These stereotypes are recreated in a variety of media, from fictional movies to government reports.

For example, the Trafficking in Persons (TIP) reports, discussed in this chapter's policy box, focus on victim narratives and images that fit this ideal narrative. Trafficking victims are depicted as young, female, innocent, and weak. The TIP reports overrepresent this victim type as being deceived into sex work. Blamelessness is reflected in 360 of the 361 victim narratives presented in the reports, with victims being kidnapped or sold rather than participating in risky and illegal migration schemes (Wilson and O'Brien 2016). An idealized scenario is repeated: "A young, foreign girl believing that migration to the industrialised world will improve her socioeconomic conditions; yet, the message is that this belief is naïve and misguided, as she is instead brutally coerced into the commercial sex industry" (Wilson and O'Brien 2016, 39).

The 2007 and 2010 Hollywood films *Trade* and *Taken* also reflect many of these stereotypes. Both films use a rescue narrative to tell the story of a young girl kidnapped and sold into sexual slavery only to be rescued by their heroic savior. Race and nationality play into the roles of victim, offender, and rescuer (Baker 2014). In *Trade,* the victim's brother is assisted by a White, Texan cop in rescuing his sister from Russian and Mexican traffickers. In *Taken,* a White former CIA operative rescues his daughter from Albanian and Arab traffickers. *Taken* grossed over $145 million at the box office, with two sequels being released in later years. While such portrayals can mobilize public concern about the issue of sex trafficking, they obscure the more common reality of what trafficking looks like, including deeper causes such as globalization, inequality, and discrimination (Baker 2014).

These narrow constructions often do not reflect the lived experiences of trafficking victims. The ideal victim lacks agency and is portrayed as totally blameless. In reality, many trafficking victims may play an active role in the trafficking and may be unwilling to testify against their trafficker (Boggiani 2015). Many victims may have crossed borders as voluntary migrants only to be later exploited, thus not fitting into the narrow conception of a naïve and passive victim taken against their will.

Nor does the concept of the "ideal offender" reflect the reality of traffickers. Traffickers are stereotyped as male foreigners with no known relationship to their victims who use physical force to control them (Raby and Chazal 2022). Instead, studies show that traffickers are often known to the victim, as employers, friends, relatives, or intimate partners (Viuhko 2018). Rather than evil figures enmeshed in organized crime rings, offenders often come from a similar background as victims. One study of traffickers in Vietnam shows that much like their victims, traffickers were poor, ethnic minorities with few educational or income opportunities (Le and Wyndham 2022).

The consequences of these stereotypes are far-reaching, as misrepresentation impacts everything from awareness of the issue to policy and responses (Gregoriou and Ras 2018). Framing the issue as a crime and justice problem obscures the structural factors that leave individuals vulnerable to trafficking in the first place. By using a simplified victim and villain narrative, human trafficking is reduced to an individual problem remedied by law enforcement and charity (Raby and Chazal 2022). This isolation overlooks the complex role that factors like poverty, discrimination, and demand for cheap labor all play (Albright and D'Adamo 2017b; Gregoriou and Ras 2018).

Beyond the public, law enforcement officers, prosecutors, judges, and service providers also fall victim to trafficking stereotypes and use these distorted images of trafficking to make decisions (Austin and Farrell 2017). A narrow view of sex trafficking diverts resources from labor trafficking and leads to an underidentification of legitimate victims (Wilson and O'Brien 2016). Migrants and sex workers experiencing exploitation face criminalization rather than help (Boggiani 2015; Wilson and O'Brien 2016). A victim hierarchy is created that separates victims into simplistic categories of good and bad, deserving and undeserving, or slave and migrant (Boukli and Renz 2019). One researcher describes the hierarchy as ranging from "'ideal victims' such as young girls abducted from an orphanage and trafficked into prostitution, down to women already working in the sex industry who are persuaded that the money could be better if they migrate to another country, and then find themselves trapped in unacceptable conditions or in debt bondage" (Hoyle, Bosworth, and Dempsey 2011, 315). This hierarchy can result in some victims being offered less or even no support compared to those ideal victims (Gregoriou and Ras 2018; Jones and Kingshott 2016). Research shows that criminal justice personnel may also be less sympathetic or more reluctant to treat someone as a victim if they do not fit the ideal victim construction (Farrell, McDevitt, and Fahy 2010; Farrell, Owens, and McDevitt 2014).

Conflict theories take a structural approach to criminology, emphasizing the larger social and economic conditions that help us understand crime. Conflict theories rest on the assumption that society is characterized by conflict and competition between groups, such as the rich and the poor (Bohm and Vogel 2015). This includes studying things such as how socioeconomic class impacts the application of the law and interaction with the criminal justice system (Matthews 2011). Conflict theorists emphasize the role of power in these interactions and how stratification and hierarchical relationships lead some groups to be able to dominate over others (Bohm and Vogel 2015).

In the study of human trafficking, this perspective highlights the role of vulnerability and power differentials. For example, economic inequality is widely accepted as one of the key factors that places individuals at risk of human trafficking. Research has consistently shown that measures of poverty (such as the head-count ratio of poverty based on a two-US-dollars-per-day poverty line) and income inequality are connected to human trafficking flows (Bales 2007; Cho 2015; Rao and Presenti 2012). Economic deprivation and insecurity can exacerbate vulnerability and make migration for work or other economic opportunities the most viable option (Chuang 2006a; Surtees 2008). Risky migration decisions linked to trafficking victimization go hand-in-hand with economic-based disparities such as poverty and blocked job or educational opportunities (Bales 2004; Cameron and Newman 2008; Farr 2004; Jac-Kucharski 2012; Mishra 2015; Outshoorn 2015; Truong 2003; Zhang 2007). Traffickers can ultimately exploit these vulnerable populations by deceiving individuals with promises of jobs or education (Cameron and Newman 2008; Hughes 2000). Conditions of poverty not only drive trafficking flows from poor to wealthier countries, but also from rural to urban areas within countries (Aronowitz 2017).

Globalization, Inequality, and Trafficking

Unequal economic development is a central feature of globalization, with growing inequalities both between and within countries (Chuang 2006a;

Shelley 2010). These inequalities are exacerbated by neoliberal global economic policies found in structural adjustment programs, economic restructuring, and other policies stemming from international economic institutions such as the IMF and World Bank (Cameron and Newman 2008; Hupp Williamson 2022; Lee 2011; Shelley 2010; Stone 2005; Truong 2006). These international financial institutions impose debt and massive restructuring under the guise of development and growth, though these decisions skew toward the interests of transnational companies based in "the most empowered countries" (Rothe and Friedrichs 2015) and often have the negative outcome of cuts in social programs and increased poverty among women and children (Hupp Williamson 2022; Shelley 2010; Truong 2006).

Around the world, structural adjustment programs in countries such as Nigeria, Russia, Argentina, Thailand, Indonesia, Cambodia, Bolivia, and Gambia have ultimately been associated with increased human trafficking (Shelley 2010). Comparative and historical analysis showcases how this happens using the case studies of Cambodia, Bolivia, and Gambia (Hupp Williamson 2022). In Cambodia, IMF and World Bank policies heavily shaped local policy and created a government dependent on external aid. An emphasis on market liberalization and privatization meant that social programs were weakened and income and gender inequality increased. Individuals sought out job opportunities in Thailand and Malaysia, but strict migration policies have left these individuals vulnerable to abuse and exploitation. In Bolivia, transnational corporate investment and foreign involvement in extractive industries has come at the cost of protecting the rights of the Indigenous people and the environment. Neoliberal economic reforms intended to stabilize Gambia's economy have not been successful, with economic hardships, harsh political restrictions, and growing social inequality driving many young people to seek migration into Europe. High rejection rates for visa applicants from West Africa means that many Gambians must cross through northern Africa and across the Mediterranean Sea, a route that often involves trafficking.

Globalization has facilitated trafficking by creating a mismatch between demand for cheap and unskilled labor and migration policies that limit the flow of people to meet that demand, leading many to make risky migration decisions that leave them vulnerable (Cameron and Newman 2008). Positioned in this light, it is possible to see why human trafficking research has identified a strong relationship between migration flows and human trafficking flows (Akee et al. 2014; Akee et al. 2010; Mahmoud and Trebesch

2010; Skeldon 2002). Chuang (2006a, 138) emphasizes that "more often than not, trafficking is labour migration gone horribly wrong in our globalized economy." In fact, what often begins as voluntary migration can turn into a situation of exploitation both during movement and at the end destination (Mo 2018; Petrunov 2014).

A Problem for the Criminal Justice System?

It is in this blurry boundary between migration and trafficking that many anti-trafficking responses actually work as a carceral practice of migration control. The emphasis that human trafficking policies place on criminal justice priorities rather than things such as human rights has resulted in policies of tighter border controls and greater policing of immigrants (Kempadoo 2007). For example, if nations seen as source or transit countries of human trafficking wish to receive financial development aid, they are often required to adopt policy that involves policing their borders to prevent migrants from "leaving their shores and troubling" the destination country (FitzGerald 2016). This is also reflected in the United States' annual tier ranking of countries in the Trafficking in Persons Reports, where the threat of economic sanctioning for countries that fail to pass has resulted in the passage of stiff anti-prostitution laws, border tightening, and restrictions on migrant travel (Bernstein 2012; Chuang 2010). The consequence of these policies has meant increased criminalization of marginalized populations and a focus on eliminating prostitution, rather than on properly identifying and protecting trafficking victims (Bernstein 2010; Chapkis 2005; Chuang 2006b).

These outcomes stem from an emphasis of human trafficking as a problem for the criminal justice system, to the exclusion of other efforts, such as human rights approaches (Chuang 2006b; Jones and Kingshott 2016). The excessive focus on criminalization is even reflected in the UN Palermo Protocol, which places human trafficking as an issue within the larger convention on transnational organized crime. Country obligations under this international protocol are organized around the three Ps: prosecution of the offender, protection of the victim, and prevention of the crime. However, the strongest terms are tied to prosecution as obligations, with substantially weaker terms tied to aspiration for protection and prevention. While it is *mandatory* that countries adopt legislation criminalizing human trafficking, it is only required that countries *endeavor* to take measures to prevent

Since 2001, the U.S. State Department's Trafficking in Persons (TIP) reports have annually ranked countries on their compliance with US standards of human trafficking, emphasizing aspects of offender prosecution, victim protection, and crime prevention. Countries are ranked according to whether they "(1) fully comply with the minimum standards (Tier 1); (2) do not yet fully comply but are making significant efforts to do so (Tier 2); or (3) are not making significant efforts to comply (Tier 3)" (Chuang 2006b, 453). Countries may also be placed on a Tier 2 Watchlist, indicating that these countries should be carefully evaluated the following year. Countries ranked on Tier 3 may be subject to sanctions, including the withdrawal of certain forms of financial assistance, if significant efforts are not made to come into compliance within ninety days (Chuang 2006b).

Applying a critical lens illuminates the many potential pitfalls of the TIP reports. First, the criteria for placing countries on the tiers has been criticized as vague and inconsistent. Rankings and sanctions have not been consistently applied, leading to charges of political bias. Countries such as Saudi Arabia, Indonesia, and South Korea have been given tier upgrades despite a lack of improvement, with many citing their economic and political ally relationship with the United States as the true reason for the tier change (Chuang 2006b; Weber, O'Regan, and Rosen 2019; Weiss 2012). Conversely, of the dozens of countries placed on Tier 3, the small number sanctioned tend to be countries with strained US relations (Chuang 2006b). The United States itself was not ranked until 2010, when it was observed that a Tier 1 ranking was given despite the United States not meeting its own standards. For example, the 2018 TIP report emphasizes the risks of family separation policies. Despite a Tier 1 ranking, the Trump administration enacted a zero tolerance separation policy for migrant parents and their children (Weber, O'Regan, and Rosen 2019).

Second, the reports rely on second-hand data, creating country profiles using a compilation of government and NGO reports that are not always fully cited (Gallagher 2011). This creates questions about the quality and reliability of these sources. The collection of this data can be further undermined by governments and organizations seeking to downplay their trafficking problems to avoid sanctions (Chuang 2006b).

Third, an emphasis on sex trafficking and prosecution has been criticized by human rights organizations. The reports tend to weigh efforts to combat sex trafficking greater than those aimed at other forms of trafficking (Chuang 2006b). Data from law enforcement is given primacy over other measures of vulnerability and prevalence (Weber, O'Regan, and Rosen 2019). The consequence of such things is that the TIP reports reproduce stereotypes about trafficking, including that trafficking is the result of victims being powerless to their traffickers, obscuring the role of larger structural conditions (Merry 2016; Wilson and O'Brien 2016). Such depictions reinforce the idea that trafficking must be tackled solely through law-and-order and foreign policy responses. These policy implications then justify the criminalization of sex workers and immigrants, and the arrest and detention of trafficking victims, and divert resources and identification away from labor trafficking (Merry 2016; Wilson and O'Brien 2016).

Finally, the very effectiveness of these reports has been called into question. One researcher notes that compliance by creating certain laws and policies is not the same thing as effectively carrying out such measures (Gallagher 2011). A longitudinal study of rankings found that, overall, country tier rankings have not improved over time and funds have not been allocated appropriately based on the tier system's recommendations (Wooditch 2011). Further, the emphasis on externally imposed standards means that when governments do craft anti-trafficking policy, they may overlook country-specific issues and ignore local NGO recommendations, focusing instead on only meeting the TIP minimum compliance standards (Chuang 2006b).

How do the TIP rankings reflect the ideas of conflict theory and inequalities between countries? Do they emphasize criminal justice approaches over other solutions to trafficking?

trafficking and *consider* implementing measures to protect and provide for victims (Todres 2009).

Scholars have drawn parallels between human and drug trafficking. Similar language is used—it is a war, a problem we must combat, an issue of law and order, one solved with increased arrests (Swenstein and Mogulescu 2016). Yet much like the war on drugs, this "war" on human trafficking leads to several issues. An emphasis on prosecution leads to a reliance on the arrests of low-level offenders, while perpetrators of more serious offenses remain free. Stings are often aimed at women engaging in sex work, consensually and otherwise, or the johns who purchase sex (Swenstein and Mogulescu 2016). Women of color and migrants in particular are criminalized for their survival strategies, including prostitution (Bernstein 2010, 2012). In their attempts to keep up with these pressures, prosecutions in countries with underdeveloped justice systems may also violate fair and safe standards (Gallagher 2016).

On the other side, victims may be compelled to cooperate with criminal justice officials throughout the prosecution in order to receive assistance, leading to further trauma (D'Adamo 2016). Criminalization extends to victims, in what one scholar calls carceral protectionism (Musto 2016). This refers to the "arrest to assist" model, where the arrest and detention of victims is seen as necessary for their safety by law enforcement and service providers. This is reflected in the growth of special human trafficking–related courts across the United States (Kulig and Butler 2019; Musto 2016). While these courts can vary widely in their structure, they generally target trafficking victims involved in the commercial sex trade, though they may include all individuals regardless of this history. Eligibility criteria may exclude those with violent or felony offenses, trans or nonbinary individuals, and trafficking victims forced to commit nonprostitution-related crimes (Kendis 2019). Victim-defendants who successfully complete the program may have their charges dismissed or expunged (Kulig and Butler 2019). While these courts are considered an alternative to traditional sentencing, many involved still spend time in jail as a consequence of wait times for openings at treatment facilities or noncompliance with program requirements, exacerbating the trauma of victims (Kendis 2019). The treatment in these programs tends to emphasize commercial sex involvement as an individual problem tied to trauma and addiction, ignoring the role of structural barriers such as homelessness, poverty, gender and LGBTQ discrimination, and more (Kulig and Butler 2019). The fact that expunging a criminal record is a difficult and expensive legal process, tied with lack of programming aimed at housing and employment, can make it difficult for many victim-defendants to successfully leave the life, facing further stigma from their criminal record if they fail to complete the program (Gruber, Cohen, and Mogulescu 2016; Musto 2016).

Prioritizing prosecution to the detriment of protection and prevention prevents meaningful change. Prosecutions of individuals alone cannot solve the problem. While these actions do hold offenders accountable for the consequences of trafficking, they do not address the conditions that give rise to it. There is a need to place trafficking in a broader perspective and view it as a problem of migration, poverty, and discrimination (Chuang 2006a). This includes tackling issues connected to inequality, migration laws, labor regulations, homophobia, racism, and sexism (Swenstein and Mogulescu 2016; Thiemann 2016). It is only by addressing the larger structural issues that create vulnerability to exploitation that victimization can truly be reduced.

Alternative Forms of Justice. Alternatives to retributive justice focused on prosecution and incarceration are just beginning to be explored within research on human trafficking. One important aspect of this is to understand what survivors' perceptions of justice are. One such study addressed this by exploring survivors' experiences and the potential for alternative forms of justice. Interviews from eighty survivors of both sex and labor trafficking across the United States showed that the majority of survivors felt that retributive justice focused on incarceration was not the best form of justice (Husseman et al. 2018). Incarceration was criticized by survivors for not being rehabilitative for traffickers, potentially even exposing traffickers to further criminal behavior or normalizing attitudes around trafficking. With 72 percent of sex trafficking survivors and 16 percent of labor trafficking survivors having prior involvement with the criminal justice system as a defendant, many survivors were hesitant to pursue traditional criminal justice remedies. Concerns included unfamiliarity with the law and criminal justice system, immigration concerns, negative prior experiences with law enforcement, and criminalization for prostitution or drug use during their trafficking (Husseman et al. 2018).

Instead, survivors emphasized their vision of justice through their own autonomy and empowerment in moving beyond their victimization and through anti-trafficking prevention efforts. Three alternatives to retributive justice highlight how these goals can be achieved, including procedural justice, restorative justice, and transitional justice. Procedural justice emphasizes the process of achieving justice rather than the outcome of a case, with survivors being involved in decisions and having the opportunity to participate in the process where they wish (Husseman et al. 2018). Under this model, it is important that survivors feel they have the opportunity to voice their stories, without having to repeatedly share their stories over and over. Survivors in the study felt they were involved in decisions related to the services they received, which was empowering, but felt less involved in decisions related to the criminal justice case. This was particularly true when charges were used against survivors to pressure them into cooperating with the investigation (Husseman et al. 2018).

A study of law enforcement working in a specialized human trafficking unit in Canada highlights how procedural justice can be incorporated to the benefit of survivors. The training these officers received allowed them to better understand the victims' trauma, use compassion to build rapport, remain flexible with victims' needs to build trust, and use transparent communication (Ballucci and Stathakis 2022). Interviews with the officers highlighted how conviction was not the ultimate measure of success for cases. Instead, officers pointed toward factors such as victims leaving their trafficking situation, acknowledging their trauma, receiving the necessary supports, and reintegrating into society. A by-product of these victim-centered investigations was that it allowed the officers to build a stronger case through the evidence they gathered (Ballucci and Stathakis 2022).

Restorative justice focuses not on conviction and incarceration, but on addressing the harm that has occurred between the offender, victim, and broader community. Pathways to healing are emphasized, including victim confrontation of the offender, apologies, and the payment of reparations (Husseman et al. 2018). In their interviews with survivors, Husseman et al. (2018) found that desires for these forms of justice frequently differed by type of victimization. Labor trafficking survivors more frequently expressed the desire to confront their trafficker, while sex trafficking survivors more frequently wished for reparations, and both sex and labor trafficking survivors were divided in their desire for an apology from their trafficker. One researcher notes that while the number of human trafficking victims who wish to engage in measures of restorative justice is likely to be small, practices such as victim-offender dialogue can still be empowering and healing. The ability to confront their trafficker in an environment outside of a courtroom can allow victims to have a sense of control in sharing their stories (Patritti 2010).

Finally, transitional justice looks at the larger community role in responding to crimes, including provision of services and advocacy and prevention efforts. For survivors, this model emphasizes things such as reforms, education and awareness, and survivor-led change. One such example includes survivor mentorship and leadership in community service organizations related to human trafficking (Husseman et al. 2018).

FEMINIST AND QUEER CRIMINOLOGY

Feminist theory in criminology has been described as a broad set of perspectives linked to different assumptions about the origins of gender inequality, including liberal, radical, Marxist, socialist, and Black feminist thought

(Daly and Chesney-Lind 1988; Renzetti 2011). Feminist theory examines gender as a social construct that organizes life and structures institutions in society. This includes the ways that gender constructs such as masculinity and femininity are not equal, but exist within a patriarchal society where men dominate women (Renzetti 2011). In criminology, feminist thought can be used to study women as offenders, women's victimization, the ability of traditional theories of crime to explain women and crime, masculinity and men's involvement in crime, and gender differences in treatment under the criminal justice system (Daly and Chesney-Lind 1988).

Gender Inequality

One of the principles of feminist criminology includes the ways that gender inequality connects to crime and victimization as well as intersects with other inequalities (Renzetti 2011). The everyday lives of women and girls are impacted by disadvantage and discrimination stemming from sociocultural beliefs and practices that reinforce the patriarchy. Typically this is seen in high rates of poverty, disadvantage in educational opportunities, and discrimination in employment, but can also include various forms of sexual and physical violence against women (Burke, Amaya, and Dillon 2020). These factors are consistently connected to women's vulnerability to trafficking victimization (Burke, Amaya, and Dillon 2020; Shelley 2010).

Large-scale, quantitative studies have looked at the links between measures of gender inequality and human trafficking. Rao and Presenti (2012) found that the male-to-female income ratio and male-to-female life expectancy ratio are both positively and significantly correlated to human trafficking incidences. Often, such studies have employed the number of legal cases and prosecutions as a measure of human trafficking. For example, Cameron et al. (2023) found that measures of gender inequality and gender-based violence were predictive of a country's human trafficking legal cases. Other studies have examined policies around human trafficking, finding that compliance with anti-trafficking policies is higher in countries with low corruption and greater respect around the rights of women (Cho, Dreher, and Neumayer 2014), and stronger efforts to protect victims are found in countries with a larger proportion of female parliamentarians and left-leaning parties in cabinet (Schönhöfer 2017).

Qualitative studies also reflect these issues stemming from gender inequality. Interviews with villagers in Vietnam highlight daughters' vulnerability to child labor, as parents elected to keep their sons in school while sending their daughters away for work (Nguyen and Gordon 2020). Case studies of the trafficking of women from post-Soviet countries to Israel reveal the role that poverty and family obligations play in women's decisions to make risky migration choices (Russell 2014). Such discriminatory practices in education and employment also contribute to the feminization of poverty, where women and children are disproportionately impoverished (Cameron and Newman 2008; Kligman and Limoncelli 2005).

The feminization of poverty can add to women's double burden, or their labor both inside and outside of the home, leading to migration for opportunity. Russell (2014) argues that women's migration has not drastically increased since 1960, but instead has shifted. Rather than migrating with husbands and partners, women now increasingly migrate alone in search of jobs. With this shift women have increasingly become significant remittance senders, with households and even entire communities dependent on the wages sent back from these migrants (Russell 2014). For example, research shows that women migrating from Mexico and El Salvador to the United States faced limited economic opportunities and lacked gender protections in their home countries, and there was an expectation they would send remittances once they reached their destination (Noyori-Corbett and Moxley 2016). Under such circumstances, the concept of "feminization of survival" is used to refer to family and community reliance on women to migrate for economic sustenance (Sassen 2002). Also referred to as "survival migrants," it is this combination of a need for income, demand for workers, and tightening migration restrictions in destination countries that leave these migrants at risk of trafficking victimization. For women, these circumstances are only magnified by gender-based employment discrimination that pushes them into informal economic sectors, which lack legal migration routes and leave women vulnerable to trafficking victimization (Aronowitz 2017; Chuang 2006a). In these ways, feminist theory can highlight the ways that gender creates unique vulnerabilities, though it should again be emphasized that not all human trafficking victims are women and girls.

Women as Perpetrators

In addition to understanding the ways that gender organizes social life and creates vulnerabilities tied to victimization, feminist criminology can also be used to understand gender and offending. Studies have begun to examine women's involvement in human trafficking as offenders, rather than simply victims. From the 2020 UNODC Global Report on Trafficking in Persons we know that the majority of persons investigated or arrested, prosecuted, and/or convicted of trafficking in persons are men, comprising over 60 percent of the total. However, 36 percent of those prosecuted for trafficking were women and were more likely to be involved in the recruitment phase. Data on federal human trafficking charges filed by US attorneys between 1994 and 2014 shows that of the 555 women and 4,966 men charged, the majority were charged with higher penalty sex trafficking offenses, at 67 percent and 90 percent, respectively. However, women were more likely than men to be charged with lower penalty sex trafficking offenses that did not involve minors or the use of force compared to men (Judge and Doherty 2022).

Research on women's involvement as perpetrators shows that there is no one typical profile. Instead, women's roles vary by geographic location and from case to case (McCarthy 2020). The role that women play in trafficking networks is often shaped by the cultural context and its associated race, class, and gender roles (Arsovska and Begum 2014; McCarthy 2020; Shen 2016). Women working as prostitutes may use caregiving roles to recruit other girls and women, talking with them and taking care of them, and then exerting control and manipulation over them, with or without a male companion (Kleemans, Kruisbergen, and Kouwenberg 2014). Similarly, a study of women's involvement in trafficking cases in Russia showed that women utilized their gendered roles as caregivers and nurturers working in hospitals to convince mothers to give up their newborns and then facilitate illegal adoption (McCarthy 2020). By contrast, women work more as supporters in trafficking networks in the Balkan regions, with researchers attributing this ancillary role to long-standing patriarchal beliefs about the submission of women to men (Arsovska and Begum 2014).

For many women, romantic relationships with their male co-offenders or previous involvement in sex work themselves is common (Broad 2015; Wijkman and Kleemans 2019). Pathways for women's involvement in sex trafficking involve substance use disorders, abuse, childhood exploitation, lack of education, and a lack of economic and social supports (Love et al. 2021). As discussed in chapter 3, there is overlap between trafficking victims and offenders, and being a trafficking victim can influence women's later involvement as an offender (Broad 2015). However, studies have also found that, much like men, women involved in trafficking can also simply be motivated by economic profit (Arsovska and Allum 2014; Shen 2016).

Several studies have also worked to categorize the roles of women in human trafficking into various types. In their study of eighty-nine court cases in the Netherlands, Siegel and de Blank (2010) find three categories based on women's roles and relationships with male traffickers. The majority of cases were categorized as supporters, which includes women who work in facilitating roles, such as recruitment or supervising, and participate out of loyalty or fear. For cases categorized as partners-in-crime, the women maintained a more equal relationship with the man, ranging from married couples working together to more business-like arrangements. Finally, the least common category of madams involved older women who played the primary role in coordinating all human trafficking activities.

Roe-Sepowitz et al. (2015) used forty-nine case studies of women prosecuted for sex trafficking of minors to identify five typologies unique in their use of violence, codefendants, and actions. This included 39 percent girlillas, 23 percent handlers, 18 percent bottoms, 14 percent madams/business partners, and 6 percent caretakers. Girlillas were unique in their use of violence and force against female minor victims, while handlers participated in traditional trafficking behaviors such as recruitment and transportation. The term bottom is used to refer to women who have previously been a sex worker and are trusted by the male pimp to assist in the trafficking through actions such as maintaining control, renting rooms and posting ads, or transportation. The typology of madams and business partners is reflective of Siegel and de Blank's (2010) categories of madams and partners-in-crime, while caretakers reflect those women who do not force the minors into prostitution, but generally look out for their well-being while they are involved in sex work.

Using data from forty-four prosecutions of sex trafficking involving female traffickers, Veldhuizen-Ochodničanová and Jeglic (2021) find that 48 percent of cases involved women in positions of leadership. They established four patterns of leadership, including co-leaders with a male trafficker (19%), madams running a brothel (12%), ringleaders (9%), and solo leaders (9%). The remaining women were involved in sex trafficking operations in a nonleadership position. This includes bottoms (33%), aiders and abettors (16%), and recruiters or smugglers (2%).

Queer Criminology

Queer criminology is a critical perspective that draws attention to crime and the criminal justice system as they sit in relation to members of the LGBTQ community. This includes ways that the LGBTQ community is stigmatized and criminalized, victimization experiences and encounters with the criminal justice system, and the criminal justice careers of LGBTQ individuals (Buist, Lenning, and Ball 2018). Queer criminology can be used to critically examine the way that human trafficking is studied. For example, sex trafficking is typically thought of in heteronormative ideals, with a female seller and male buyer. This influences the questions that are included in surveys and interviews, identification of victims, and policies that exclude male victims of sex trafficking (Robertson and Sgoutas 2012).

Much of the sex trafficking literature focuses on cisgender females, despite evidence of high prevalence rates among cisgender males, transgender youth, and gender nonconforming youth (Tomasiewicz 2018). As discussed in chapter 2, LGBTQ youth face harassment and bullying in schools, family rejection and abandonment leading to homelessness, and other forms of abuse that make them vulnerable to trafficking (Xian, Chock, and Dwiggins 2017). One study of 215 homeless young adults aged eighteen to twenty-five in Arizona found that LGBTQ+ young adults were twice as likely to have been sex trafficked compared to their heterosexual counterparts (Hogan and Roe-Sepowitz 2023).

Trans individuals involved in sex work have also reported experiences of violence and exploitation that meet the definition of human trafficking. Yet many report that law enforcement did not recognize them as a victim, instead frequently arresting them, and that anti-trafficking services and organizations were not welcoming to trans individuals (Fehrenbacher et al. 2020). One attorney describes the way her client was treated after being arrested, despite having the T nonimmigrant status granted to foreign victims of trafficking: "When she explained she was a victim of trafficking, the officer laughed at her, made transphobic comments, and told her she was going to be deported" (Egyes 2019, 15). With reactions such as these, many trans individuals remained engaged in survival sex work due to limited economic opportunities (Fehrenbacher et al. 2020).

Queer criminology thus highlights the need for anti-trafficking practices and policies that are affirming to the LGBTQ population, addressing that they may have different needs and require different services from their heterosexual or cisgender peers (Tomasiewicz 2018). This includes training for criminal justice officials and eliminating barriers to services for survivors (Egyes 2019). This is still an uphill battle, highlighted by recent federal legislation. In 2015, the US Senate was working on reauthorizing the Runaway and Homeless Youth Act by passing the Runaway and Homeless Youth and Trafficking Prevention Act. Included was an amendment that prohibited the denial of services to youth on the basis of race, color, religion, national origin, sex, gender identity, sexual orientation, or disability. Ultimately, the act failed to pass in the Senate due to concerns that religious service providers would face losing their funding unless they eliminated their LGBTQ discriminatory practices (Boukli and Renz 2019).

CRITICAL RACE THEORY

Feminist theory has historically struggled to incorporate the voices of the marginalized, often relegating them to the margins (Wolken 2006). In the United States, the dominant view of feminism comes from a White, middle-class, heterosexual perspective (Daly and Chesney-Lind 1988). As such, critical race theory fills an important void in the literature. Scholars such as Patricia Hill Collins, bell hooks, and Kimberlé Crenshaw have been highly influential in the development of critical race studies (Bell 2018). Critical race theory builds on legal and feminist theories to assert that racism is embedded in the social structure of American society. Further, the concept of intersectionality, coined by Kimberlé Crenshaw, is a central tenant. The concept deals with understanding how identities such as race, class, gender, and sexuality do not exist in isolation, but create overlapping systems of disadvantage and discrimination (Butler 2015a).

Intersectional Inequality

Beyond poverty and gender-based inequality, racial and ethnic discrimination also act as a link to human trafficking. Marginalization on the basis of race or ethnicity creates populations vulnerable to human trafficking as they face blocked resources, stigma, and a lack of legal protections (Bryant-Davis and Tummala-Narra 2017). But this racism also intersects with other identities, such as gender or migration status. For Indigenous women, the history of colonization and marginalization has contributed to long-term effects that influence vulnerability to victimization, including high rates of poverty, violence, and substance abuse. These issues are only further compounded by the complex state, federal, and Native jurisdictional issues of crimes committed in Indian Country (Shanley and Jordan 2017).

Racist ideologies about women can also drive demand, with Asian women stereotyped as submissive, Latinas as erotic, African women as hypersexual, and Indigenous women as uncivilized (Bryant-Davis and Tummala-Narra 2017). Interviews with Indigenous sex trafficking survivors found that 42 percent reported their pimp or buyer directing racist insults toward them while sexually aroused. This included both racist and sexist remarks, such as "savage, squaw" and "whore, slut" (Farley et al. 2011). Stereotypes about Asian women being sexually submissive drive sex tourism to countries like Thailand and the Philippines. One man blames the culture as the problem, rather than his own behavior as a sex tourist: "In the Orient, women are second class citizens, often treated in dehumanizing ways. There's nothing you can do to change it, but you can still be one of the kind and generous ones who helps [by hiring these women and girls as prostitutes]" (Todres 2009, 627). In addition to employing racialized stereotypes to justify purchasing sex, the quote from this buyer also demonstrates neutralizations discussed in chapter 5, such as denial of responsibility.

Critical race theory can also be used to explore the very real impacts that media portrayals of racial and ethnic stereotypes have, including in regard to human trafficking. Patricia Hill Collins developed the concept of controlling images to explain how raced, classed, and gendered depictions of Black women provide an ideological justification for inequality and oppression. Throughout history, these depictions have included the mammy during slavery, the Black single mother, the welfare queen, and the jezebel (Collins 2008). Many of these stereotypes can be found in media today, influencing depictions of human trafficking victims (Butler 2015b).

Initially used to justify the rape and sexual exploitation of Black women during slavery, the jezebel myth was used to portray Black women as aggressive and overly sexual (Butler 2015b). Decades later, Black women would migrate to the North in search of work, only to be pushed toward prostitution and denied the same legal protections and social services available to White women, leaving them vulnerable to sexual exploitation (Butler 2015b). In the United States today a strong association of race with crime can shape ideas about who is and is not a victim (Butler 2015a). Girls of color are stereotyped as more sexually promiscuous, even "predisposed to prostitution," and punished more harshly than White girls (Butler 2015b). Despite federal law labeling minors as victims, girls of color are often instead treated as criminals and juvenile delinquents (Phillips 2015). Black girls are more likely to be seen as willing participants in their sexual exploitation, while White girls are portrayed as innocent victims, impacting the reactions from police officers to judges (Constance-Huggins, Moore, and Slay 2022). Ultimately, these stereotypes can lead to women and girls of color facing barriers to being identified and recognized as victims of human trafficking (Butler 2015a).

Raids, Rescues, and Carceral Responses

Racial and ethnic stereotypes can also influence the response to human trafficking. Historically, the rescue narrative involved "heroic white men as protectors of vulnerable white femininity from violent men of color" (Baker 2019, 776). This is reflected in early laws around White slave panic, as discussed in chapter 1, and still contributes to ideas about the ideal victim. Throughout the 1970s, 1990s, and 2000s, concerns over juvenile prostitution centered a narrative that framed urban Black men as targeting White, middle-class girls in America's heartland (Baker 2019). More recently, attention toward human trafficking occurring outside the Western world has contributed to the stereotypical image of a woman from a "third world" country who has been coerced into working in the sex industry (Doezema 2000). The raid-and-rescue narrative that permeates many anti-trafficking organizations today leans heavily into patriarchal and racial tropes about third world victims in need of saving.

The raid-and-rescue model often stems from an anti-prostitution stance supported by evangelical Christians, law enforcement, and anti-prostitution feminists (Phillips 2015). Anti-trafficking organizations receiving funding from the United States often must accept the money with the stipulation that they cannot be seen as supporting sex workers or prostitution in any form (Ahmed and Seshu 2012). Consider the International Justice Mission, a Christian nongovernmental organization, that is heavily involved with brothel raids in India and Thailand. Sex workers are placed into homes with little regard to whether or not they are actual victims (Desyllas 2007). This heavy-handed response often undermines projects at the local level that provide services for sex workers or target the conditions that make women vulnerable. For example, HIV outreach and care for sex workers in India is severely disrupted by brothel raids that interrupt treatment and harm carefully built relationships of trust. Women are often forced into rehabilitation programs that more closely resemble jails and further expose the women to abuse (Ahmed and Seshu 2012).

Many of these homes, shelters, and rehabilitation programs are funded by NGOs rather than the government. They frequently make use of detention or do not allow the victims of trafficking to leave the shelter grounds with few exceptions, and generally only with supervision (Gallagher and Pearson 2010). The justification for the detention of these women and girls rests on the argument that they are unruly, vulnerable, and in need of reform (Lee 2014). While these shelters can provide the necessary supports and services that victims need, some are functionally more similar to jails, making no distinction between sex workers and trafficking victims.

Shelters in Cambodia and Thailand have come under criticism for being "closed" shelters that essentially detain victims under the justification that it is for their protection (Gallagher and Pearson 2010). Interviews with individuals about their experiences in these Cambodian shelters have also revealed abusive behaviors and stigmatization by staff, feelings of imprisonment, and mixed experiences with counseling (Tsai, Lim, and Nhanh 2020, 2022). In Thailand, women who were taken from raids to such shelters report intrusive and distressing conditions, including invasive medical tests and periods of detention lasting up to two years (Lee 2014). The end result of such treatment is not the protection of victims, but rather victims avoiding detection by authorities in order to evade detention and being driven back to the same conditions that led them to sex work in the first place (Gallagher and Pearson 2010; Lee 2014).

CHAPTER RESOURCES

1. Visit the National Conference of State Legislatures (NCSL) Human Trafficking Enactment Database here: https://www.ncsl.org/civil-and-criminal-justice/human-trafficking-enactment-database. Under Topics, select Prevention and Awareness. Select a particular State if desired, but be sure to set the Year to All. Read about some of the legislation passed on this topic. Considering what you have learned, do you think this legislation is tackling the root issues of human trafficking in order to have effective prevention? What do you think effective prevention would look like under law?

2. Watch a video about human trafficking in Thailand's fishing industry. For example, you can watch "Slavery at Sea: Thai Fishing Industry Turns to Trafficking" from the *Guardian* here: https://www.youtube .com/watch?v=qNwoqLB_wKs. Or you can view "Pirates and Slaves" from the Environmental Justice Foundation here: https://www .youtube.com/watch?v=SVRUXWRJLVc. How does globalization

play a role in this trafficking? What would a conflict criminologist say about this situation?

1. As a class, discuss what role media portrayals of human trafficking have played in shaping your previous knowledge of human trafficking. Contrast different forms of media, such as films, the news, and social media. Did these portrayals match the construction of the ideal victim and/or ideal offender?

2. What are some of the problems with a retributive justice approach to human trafficking? What are procedural justice, restorative justice, and transitional justice, and how can they provide an alternative approach?

3. How can critical theories be used to understand how someone's identity (e.g., gender, sexuality, race/ethnicity) shapes their vulnerability to human trafficking? How does looking at these identities from an intersectional perspective change things?

SEVEN

Integrationist Perspectives

This chapter explores the relationship that integrationist perspectives share with human trafficking. Integrated theories highlight the ways that factors from multiple theories can be combined to understand crime and victimization more holistically. The two integrationist perspectives to be discussed in this chapter include life course and developmental theories and social-ecological theory stemming from the public health model.

LIFE COURSE AND DEVELOPMENTAL THEORIES

Developmental and life course theories emphasize the ways that individual development and social structures can change over the life course, creating pathways toward or away from criminal behavior. For example, in studying the life course, developmental criminologists may be interested in onset or entrance into crime, continuity or persistence in crime, and desistance or exiting from crime (Bohm and Vogel 2015).

One such theory is Sampson and Laub's age-graded theory of informal social control, which combines the life course perspective with social control theory. Their theory argues that changes in social ties, particularly those related to work, family, and community, can be used to understand changes in the behavioral patterns of criminals (Sampson and Laub 1990). Social structural factors, such as socioeconomic disadvantage or family disruption, impact social bonds and social capital, or relationships that can provide resources to reduce the likelihood of crime (Bohm and Vogel 2015).

Under the life course perspective, these social bonds change throughout the stages of life. Focusing on the timing and duration of important life events emphasizes trajectories and transitions (Sampson and Laub 1992). Trajectories are long-term patterns of behavior, such as one's career or educational achievements. Trajectories are marked by a sequence of transitions, or specific events, such as getting a new job or getting married. Major life events may act as turning points, altering trajectories and creating new pathways.

Regarding human trafficking, this perspective is helpful in examining longitudinally how major events and risk factors across the life course can increase an individual's vulnerability to trafficking victimization. Developmental and life course theories are also useful for understanding both entry into and exiting from trafficking, as well as differences across the life course, such as juvenile risk factors versus adult risk factors.

Many studies that take a life course or developmental perspective focus on identifying risk factors for trafficking, or those things that make individuals more vulnerable to victimization. Childhood sexual abuse and running away have been identified as critical risk factors for youth who sell sex (Kaestle 2012). Negative relationships with caregivers, including experiencing abuse or neglect, have also been identified as risk factors for domestic minor sex trafficking (O'Brien 2018). Similarly, another study found that adolescent sexual victimization, younger age at first alcohol/drug use, experiencing intimate partner violence, and a stigmatization of the sexual self were all associated with adolescent commercial sexual exploitation (Reid 2014). These risk factors are hypothesized to influence an adolescent's interaction with their environment in ways that increase risks.

At the same time, studies have also identified factors that protect against victimization. For example, school connectedness, such as being happy at school and feeling a part of school, can have a protective effect on adolescents selling and buying sex (Kaestle 2012). Interpersonal relationships can often act as either risk or protective factors. Interpersonal relationships that promote self-worth and boundary setting, particularly around sex, are important factors in mitigating risks for domestic minor sex trafficking (O'Brien 2018). Such relationships can also be important in promoting resiliency and preventing returning to a trafficking situation.

Age-Graded and Gendered Pathways

Using the lens of life course theory, Reid (2012) reviewed research on sex trafficking to understand how pathways and vulnerabilities can differ by age, gender, and nationality. Victims of domestic and international sex trafficking share many common risk factors, such as poverty, inadequate education and employment opportunities, and a history of violence and abuse. For international victims, however, being undocumented and not speaking the language acted as additional risk factors that further isolated victims. There were also many similarities across gender, with both male and female victims who were homeless, in foster care, or experiencing abuse or family dysfunction and who had limited school involvement being at increased risk for sex trafficking. Two differences, however, include that boys were more likely to report involvement in more serious types of delinquency and less likely to be under the control of a trafficker or pimp. Comparisons by age also revealed differences, with exposure to and normalization of prostitution being associated with earlier age of initial involvement, along with factors such as running away and adverse home environments. A later age of onset was associated with risk factors related to resource needs, such as having children. Ultimately, this review highlights how the age-graded theory of informal social control predicts the ways structural factors related to the home and environment influence social control processes in childhood and social capital in adulthood. Without these relationships and resources, individuals face increased vulnerability to sex trafficking victimization (Reid 2012).

As with Reid's review, many studies have endeavored to compare risk factors to identify age-graded and gendered pathways for victimization. One study of youth who reported being paid for sex found that risk factors for both male and female adolescents and young adults operated similarly (Reid and Piquero 2014). Adverse relationships with caregivers, sexual assault, and younger age at first sex were associated with a younger age of entry into commercial sexual exploitation. Factors related to social capital, such as less education, criminal environments, and substance use, were associated with a later age of entry. These findings parallel another study on age-graded pathways into prostitution. Women who entered as adolescents were more likely to report childhood abuse and normalization of prostitution, while those who entered as adults were more likely to do so for addiction or survival purposes (Cobbina and Oselin 2011).

Similarly, Chohaney (2016) applied life course theory to study risk factors for domestic minor and adult sex trafficking in Ohio. Structural factors that affected social control processes were influential for adolescents, with characteristics such as difficulty in school, time spent in juvenile detention, and conflict with parents increasing the odds of being forced into sex trafficking. Among adults, factors that increased the odds of trafficking were structurally related to a lack of social capital, including homelessness, unsuccessful attempts to exit sex work, and age. Based on these findings, Chohaney suggests that education and resources that target at-risk youth and assistance that reduces barriers to exit for adults may be beneficial in reducing sex trafficking.

Entry and Exit

In addition to understanding how risks differ by factors such as age and gender, life course and developmental theories are also useful for examining the process by which individuals enter and exit trafficking. Interviews with sixty-one US teenagers who were prostituted and trafficked identified key themes of vulnerability, including being abandoned and homeless, experiencing sexual and physical violence, and negative interactions with criminal justice system actors. Entry often involved survival-focused coping, where risks had to be negotiated. For example, youth described how the streets were not safe to stay on, but neither was going home, so going with a stranger who offered shelter was the best offer they found in a bad situation (Williams 2010).

Other research has identified similar routes into the sex trade for minors, with survival needs such as food, clothing, and housing, along with the fulfillment of emotional needs or drug use, being cited as an entry pathway (Lutnick 2016). These structural and social contexts play a role in initiation, while various types of relationships shape movement in and out of the sex trade. Peers, family, intimate partners, and pimps can influence youth's exposure to violence, manipulation, and abuse (Lutnick 2016). Regarding how youth exit from trading sex, positive relationships can play a role by helping to fulfill youths' needs and allowing them to disconnect from the trade. At the same time, emotional attachments to others still involved, or if basic needs are no longer met, can lead to youth being drawn back to reengaging in sex work (Lutnick 2016).

A review of thirteen empirical studies found that exiting sex trafficking can also be broken down by various levels that can contain factors that facilitate or hinder the exit process (Ferrari 2021). At the individual level, factors such as spirituality, self-confidence and self-esteem, and a desire to take one's life back for future plans can facilitate leaving, while feelings of shame and uselessness can hinder exiting. At the relational level, the presence of mentors and being connected to both formal and informal sources of social support further enable individuals to leave sex trafficking. Feeling stigmatized, rejected, or invalidated can thwart efforts to leave. Structurally, studies show that group and individual programs from social agencies can encourage exit by promoting a sense of safety, skills, and self-efficacy, in addition to access to jobs. Such programs are important, as low socioeconomic status has been identified as a factor that can set individuals back, even leading to a relapse back into victimization.

Ultimately, much of the developmental and life course research in regard to human trafficking has focused on sex trafficking, and specifically youth involvement in the commercial sex trade. There is a lack of research on how age-graded and gendered pathways may differ for labor trafficking victims or what risk and protective factors might look like for nonsexual forms of exploitation.

SOCIAL-ECOLOGICAL THEORY

A growing approach to understanding human trafficking is the public health model. Human trafficking has been described as a growing epidemic, and the lens of public health allows examining this issue as a "disease." One paper describes the parallels:

> Trafficking physically, psychologically, and emotionally sickens those individuals and communities that are afflicted by it. . . . Frontline responders such as labor inspectors, police officers, and civil society actors "diagnose" cases through victim identification, triage these cases, and provide service referrals just as healthcare professionals do for diseases. Trafficking survivors receive various forms of treatment, including medical care, to recover from their experience. There are many risk factors associated with trafficking and being exposed to compounding vulnerabilities magnifies overall risk—similar to comorbidities in traditional health problems. Like many infectious diseases such as HIV/AIDS and tuberculosis, human trafficking disproportionately affects the most marginalized and vulnerable populations (Gallo, Konrad, and Thinyane 2022, 116).

In essence, the public health approach involves shifting away from law and punishment as the primary tools for addressing trafficking (Todres 2010). Instead, a public health approach emphasizes generating more precise prevalence estimates, identifying at-risk populations, implementing various prevention strategies, and evaluating and improving programs (Greenbaum 2017; Rothman et al. 2017; Such et al. 2020).

This perspective can be advantageous to the field of human trafficking in several ways. This includes promoting interdisciplinary and cross-agency collaboration (Rothman et al. 2017). The issue of human trafficking has been addressed by a variety of disciplines, each with their own perspective (Russell 2018). Multidisciplinary work can create a better understanding of the larger picture around the issue. Partnerships with multiple agencies beyond just law enforcement can lead to novel solutions that better serve the needs of victims. Further, public health research methods can help generate improved estimates of trafficked populations (Fedina and DeForge 2017). Community-centered and community-based participatory research methods have been used to access and identify the often hidden population of trafficking victims, with respondent-driven sampling being used to study both labor and sex trafficking (Curtis et al. 2008; Zhang 2012). Finally, the emphasis on evaluating what works and creating research-led solutions improves outcomes for policies and programs. This is particularly important given that a U.S. Government Accountability Office report found that among twenty-three international anti-trafficking projects, most failed to assess if they were actually achieving their stated goals (Todres 2010). One study of service providers in Kansas City utilized public health surveillance, which involves the ongoing collection of data to inform action, to identify what survivors needed from agencies in order to successfully exit from trafficking (Schwarz and Britton 2015).

Theoretically, however, the public health approach is often informed by social-ecological theory. The framework for this approach stems from Bronfenbrenner's (1979) original work using ecological systems theory to understand human development. The social-ecological approach describes the complex and interconnected factors that contribute to the identified public health problem by examining four main levels: the individual, the relational, the communal, and the societal (Alpert and Chin 2017). This theoretical approach again expands consideration beyond the criminal justice system, arguing that a focus only on investigations, arrests, and prosecutions is a limited measure of success (Albright and D'Adamo 2017a). Instead, efforts at intervention and prevention need to address all four levels to truly be successful at addressing the root causes of and vulnerabilities to trafficking (Greenbaum 2017).

For example, the social-ecological framework has been applied to child sex trafficking to examine how factors at each level interact and contribute to vulnerability (Finigan-Carr et al. 2019; Greenbaum 2020a). At the individual level, factors of personal history are important. This include things like a history of child abuse or neglect, homelessness or running away, substance abuse, and being LGBTQ. At the relational level, family dysfunction, trauma bonds, and deviant peer networks matter in exposing the child to relationships that leave them vulnerable to exploitation. Violence, prostitution, drugs, and sex tourism in a community are contexts that also matter. Involvement in the child welfare and juvenile justice systems are other communal factors that increase risk for child sex trafficking. Finally, at the societal level are factors related to gender- or race-based discrimination; inequalities related to health, wealth, and education; and broader beliefs, values, and policies around the issue of child sex trafficking.

Such a framework has also been used to understand how the needs of survivors vary by level of intervention. Interventions at the individual level include therapy, substance abuse treatment, and daily living skills, while the relational and communal levels include group treatment, family therapy, educational and vocational support, social supports, and community connections (Hopper 2017a). Broader societal-level supports include welcoming survivors to positions of leadership and organizational changes to emphasize trauma-informed and culturally adapted interventions (Hopper 2017a). Interviews with survivors on factors that influenced their ability to exit the sex trade and reintegrate with their communities also highlight factors working at multiple levels. At the micro-level, physical and mental health problems became motivations to leave, while at the meso-level supportive interpersonal relationships helped build secure attachments and independence. At the macro-level, establishing a life outside of the sex trade increased resiliency, positive thinking, and ongoing motivations for change (Cecchet and Thoburn 2014).

Prevention efforts can also be improved by targeting each of the four levels (Todres 2010). Prevention at the individual level might focus on providing empowerment and tools to reduce risk of exploitation, such as education programs for at-risk youth. At the relational level, mentoring programs can provide positive friendships, encourage youth to stay in school, and reduce risky behavior. Targeted awareness campaigns can work to reduce negative social norms in a community, such as the purchasing of sex. Prevention at the societal level involves programs that address the root causes of trafficking, including inequality, poverty, and discrimination. For example, school lunch programs in poor communities can reduce malnutrition, resulting in better school performance and lower truancy (Todres 2010). Additional prevention measures are discussed in this chapter's policy box.

As was discussed in chapter 1, modern legislation on human trafficking has framed the issue within the context of the three Ps: prosecution of offenders, protection of victims, and prevention of trafficking. However, as has been seen throughout this book, the predominant framing of human trafficking as a crime and justice problem has meant that there has been more attention given to prosecution, and to a lesser extent protection (Chuang 2006a). Prevention has rarely been the focus. As discussed in chapter 6, even within the major international instrument on human trafficking, the Palermo Protocol, prosecution obligations are written as mandatory, while protection and prevention are couched in terms of endeavors and considerations (Chuang 2006a; Todres 2009).

Prevention policies and programs may target supply or demand. Supply-based prevention strategies include programs that raise awareness of human trafficking, increase political interest and resources to combat trafficking, provide legal alternatives for migration, or reduce the factors thought to make individuals vulnerable to trafficking, such as poverty and discrimination (Shinkle 2007). Awareness campaigns have been among the most commonly used prevention strategy, though with mixed results. Campaigns highlighting the risks of migration may even be counterproductive, as target audiences view them as manipulation designed to keep them out of wealthier countries or become less fearful and more interested in seeking work abroad (Chuang 2006a; Shinkle 2007). These campaigns may also play into stereotypes about what ideal victims and ideal offenders look like, while obscuring the larger, structural factors at play (O'Brien 2016). In order for awareness campaigns to be more effective, studies have noted that they should be targeted and clear in their messaging, focusing on particular groups and emphasizing local contexts (Bryant and Landman 2020).

With governments framing trafficking as a problem of crime, prostitution, and border control, little attention has been given to the root factors that leave individuals vulnerable to trafficking. While demand reduction campaigns may place blame on the men who buy sex, the larger societal structures that contribute to demand for cheap goods and cheap labor frequently remain invisible (O'Brien 2016). The public health model draws attention beyond the individual to consider relational, communal, and societal levels as well. Prevention can be further refined at each of these levels with programs that reduce vulnerabilities, enhance resiliency, mitigate risks, and even provide long-term guidance to help prevent revictimization (Alpert and Chin 2017).

Further, a public health model approach highlights the importance of evaluating the effectiveness of programs and policies. Few anti-trafficking interventions have been evaluated to date. One review of ninety evaluations produced between 2000 and 2015 found that among the evaluations that do exist, the majority do not meet established standards of evaluation and lack transparency in their methodology and conclusions (Bryant and Landman 2020). Similarly, another review of forty-nine evaluations found that outcomes go unreported and the methods used lack the rigor needed to draw conclusions about program effectiveness (Davy 2016). Under the public health model, multiple stakeholders are encouraged to work together to design, implement, and evaluate anti-trafficking strategies at multiple levels. Consider the My Life My Choice program, which targets girls at risk for commercial sexual exploitation in Boston by providing group sessions led by professionals and survivors that work to shape knowledge, attitudes, and skills. One evaluation of the program found a statistically significant decrease in risky sexual behavior and positive increases in self-esteem (Greenbaum 2020b). Such programs can target not just the individual level, but include institutions such as schools, community centers, and businesses. Societal structures can also be targeted to decrease risks through programs that address education, poverty, housing, and migrant rights (Schwarz et al. 2019).

What kind of prevention program would you design and how would you evaluate it? Consider what policies should be implemented outside the sphere of the criminal justice system.

CHAPTER RESOURCES

1. Watch the story of GEMS founder Rachel Lloyd in the video "Human Trafficking Victim Rachel Lloyd Helps Other Survivors" by Real Women/Real Stories here: https://www.youtube.com/watch?v=cGJoi3h2rvs. Identify and discuss the age-graded and gendered pathway that increased Rachel's risk for exploitation.

2. The Fair Food Program aims to prevent farm labor exploitation by ensuring workers are protected regarding wages, hours, health, safety, and more. You can read about how the program works and what the

standards of the Code of Conduct are in the most recent State of the Program Report on their website: https://fairfoodprogram.org/results/. What is the program and what are some elements of the code? What are some of the mechanisms the program has in place to ensure the code is being followed? Do you think this program is a good example of preventative measures against exploitation and trafficking? Why or why not?

CHAPTER DISCUSSION QUESTIONS

1. Identify some of the entry and exit factors for sex trafficking. How might entry and exit factors look different for labor trafficking victims?

2. What are the four levels of the social-ecological model? Design a policy or program that would address human trafficking for each level of the model.

BIBLIOGRAPHY

AAI (Airline Ambassadors International). 2022. "Human Trafficking." AAI, February 6, 2022. https://airlineamb.org/human-trafficking/.

Agnew, Robert. 1992. "Foundation for a General Strain Theory of Crime and Delinquency." *Criminology* 30 (1): 47–88. https://doi.org/10.1111/j.1745-9125.1992.tb01093.x.

Ahmed, Aziza, and Meena Seshu. 2012. "'We Have the Right Not to Be "Rescued" . . .': When Anti-Trafficking Programmes Undermine the Health and Well-Being of Sex Workers." *Anti-Trafficking Review,* no. 1 (June). https://doi.org/10.14197/atr.201219.

Akee, Randall, Arnab K. Basu, Arjun Bedi, and Nancy H. Chau. 2014. "Transnational Trafficking, Law Enforcement, and Victim Protection: A Middleman Trafficker's Perspective." *Journal of Law and Economics* 57 (2): 349–86. https://doi.org/10.1086/675404.

Akee, Randall, Arnab K. Basu, Nancy H. Chau, and Melanie Khamis. 2010. "Ethnic Fragmentation, Conflict, Displaced Persons and Human Trafficking: An Empirical Analysis." In *Migration and Culture: Frontiers of Economics and Globalization,* edited by G. S. Epstein and I. N. Gang, 8:691–716. Bingley, UK: Emerald Group.

Albert, Kendra, Emily Armbruster, Elizabeth Brundige, Elizabeth Denning, Kimberly Kim, Lorelei Lee, Lindsey Ruff, Korica Simon, and Yueyu Yang. 2020. "FOSTA in Legal Context." *Columbia Human Rights Law Review* 52 (3): 1084–1158.

Albright, Erin, and Kate D'Adamo. 2017a. "Decreasing Human Trafficking through Sex Work Decriminalization." *AMA Journal of Ethics* 19 (1): 122–26. https://doi.org/10.1001/journalofethics.2017.19.1.sect2–1701.

———. 2017b. "The Media and Human Trafficking: A Discussion and Critique of the Dominant Narrative." In *Human Trafficking Is a Public Health Issue: A Paradigm Expansion in the United States,* edited by Makini Chisolm-Straker and Hanni Stoklosa, 363–78. Cham, Switzerland: Springer International. https://doi.org/10.1007/978–3–319–47824–1_21.

Allert, Jeanne L. 2022. "Justice Professionals' Lens on Familial Trafficking Cases." *Criminal Justice Review* 47 (2): 208–24. https://doi.org/10.1177/07340168211024719.

Alpert, Elaine J., and Sharon E. Chin. 2017. "Human Trafficking: Perspectives on Prevention." In *Human Trafficking Is a Public Health Issue: A Paradigm Expansion in the United States,* edited by Makini Chisolm-Straker and Hanni Stoklosa, 379–400. Cham, Switzerland: Springer International. https://doi.org/10.1007/978-3-319-47824-1_22.

Anderson, Valerie R., Kara England, and William S. Davidson. 2017. "Juvenile Court Practitioners' Construction of and Response to Sex Trafficking of Justice System Involved Girls." *Victims & Offenders* 12 (5): 663–81. https://doi.org/10.1080/15564886.2016.1185753.

Anthony, Brittany. 2018. *On-Ramps, Intersections, and Exit Routes: A Roadmap for Systems and Industries to Prevent and Disrupt Human Trafficking.* Polaris Project. https://polarisproject.org/wp-content/uploads/2018/08/A-Roadmap-for-Systems-and-Industries-to-Prevent-and-Disrupt-Human-Trafficking-Social-Media.pdf.

Antonopoulos, Georgios A., and John A. Winterdyk. 2005. "Techniques of Neutralizing the Trafficking of Women—A Case Study of an Active Trafficker in Greece." *European Journal of Crime, Criminal Law and Criminal Justice* 13 (2): 136–47.

Aransiola, Joshua Oyeniyi, and Christina Zarowsky. 2014. "Street Children, Human Trafficking and Human Security in Nigeria: Competing Discourses of Vulnerability and Danger." *African Population Studies* 27 (2): 398–410. https://doi.org/10.11564/27-2-484.

Armstrong, Stephanie, V. Jordan Greenbaum, Cristina López, and Julie Barroso. 2020. "Preparedness to Identify and Care for Trafficked Persons in South Carolina Hospitals: A State-Wide Exploration." *Journal of Human Trafficking* 6 (3): 281–308. https://doi.org/10.1080/23322705.2019.1603747.

Aronowitz, Alexis A. 2001. "Smuggling and Trafficking in Human Beings: The Phenomenon, the Markets That Drive It and the Organisations That Promote It." *European Journal on Criminal Policy and Research* 9 (2): 163–95. https://doi.org/10.1023/A:1011253129328.

———. 2009. "The Smuggling–Trafficking Nexus and the Myths Surrounding Human Trafficking." In *Sociology of Crime, Law and Deviance: Immigration, Crime and Justice,* edited by William F. Mcdonald, 13:107–28. Bingley, UK: Emerald Group. https://doi.org/10.1108/S1521-6136(2009)0000013010.

———. 2017. *Human Trafficking: A Reference Handbook.* Santa Barbara, CA: ABC-CLIO.

———. 2019. "Regulating Business Involvement in Labor Exploitation and Human Trafficking." *Journal of Labor and Society* 22 (1): 145–64. https://doi.org/10.1111/wusa.12372.

Aronowitz, Alexis A., and Mounia Chmaitilly. 2020. "Human Trafficking: Women, Children, and Victim-Offender Overlap." Oxford Research Encyclopedia of Criminology and Criminal Justice, October 27, 2020. https://doi.org/10.1093/acrefore/9780190264079.013.609.

Aronowitz, Alexis A., Gerda Theuermann, and Elena Tyurykanova. 2010. *Analysing the Business Model of Trafficking in Human Beings to Better Prevent the Crime.* Vienna, Austria: OSCE Office of the Special Representative and Co-ordinator for Combating Trafficking in Human Beings.

Aronowitz, Alexis A., and Maaike Elza Veldhuizen. 2021. "The Human Trafficking–Organized Crime Nexus." In *The Routledge Handbook of Transnational Organized Crime,* 2nd ed., edited by Felia Allum and Stan Gilmour, 232–52. New York: Routledge.

Arsovska, Jana, and Felia Allum. 2014. "Introduction: Women and Transnational Organized Crime." *Trends in Organized Crime* 17 (1): 1–15. https://doi.org /10.1007/s12117–014–9223-y.

Arsovska, Jana, and Popy Begum. 2014. "From West Africa to the Balkans: Exploring Women's Roles in Transnational Organized Crime." *Trends in Organized Crime* 17 (1): 89–109. https://doi.org/10.1007/s12117–013–9209–1.

Austin, Rachel, and Amy Farrell. 2017. "Human Trafficking and the Media in the United States." Oxford Research Encyclopedia of Criminology and Criminal Justice, April 26, 2017. https://doi.org/10.1093/acrefore/9780190264079.013.290.

Avdeyeva, Olga A. 2012. "Does Reputation Matter for States' Compliance with International Treaties? States Enforcement of Anti-Trafficking Norms." *International Journal of Human Rights* 16 (2): 298–320. https://doi.org/10.1080/1364298 7.2010.540240.

Baird, Kyla, and Jennifer Connolly. 2021. "Recruitment and Entrapment Pathways of Minors into Sex Trafficking in Canada and the United States: A Systematic Review." *Trauma, Violence, & Abuse* 24 (1): 189–202. https://doi.org/10.1177 /15248380211025241.

Baker, Aryn. 2015. "Why the Blood Diamond Trade Won't Die." *TIME.Com,* 2015. https://time.com/blood-diamonds/.

Baker, Carrie N. 2014. "An Intersectional Analysis of Sex Trafficking Films." *Meridians* 12 (1): 208–26. https://doi.org/10.2979/meridians.12.1.208.

———. 2019. "Racialized Rescue Narratives in Public Discourses on Youth Prostitution and Sex Trafficking in the United States." *Politics & Gender* 15 (4): 773–800. https://doi.org/10.1017/S1743923X18000661.

Baldwin, Susie B., Anne E. Fehrenbacher, and David P. Eisenman. 2015. "Psychological Coercion in Human Trafficking: An Application of Biderman's Framework." *Qualitative Health Research* 25 (9): 1171–81. https://doi.org/10.1177 /1049732314557087.

Bales, Kevin. 2004. *Disposable People : New Slavery in the Global Economy.* 2nd ed. Berkeley: University of California Press.

———. 2007. "What Predicts Human Trafficking?" *International Journal of Comparative and Applied Criminal Justice* 31 (2): 269–79. https://doi.org/10.1080/019 24036.2007.9678771.

Bales, Kevin, Laura T. Murphy, and Bernard W. Silverman. 2020. "How Many Trafficked People Are There in Greater New Orleans? Lessons in Measurement." *Journal of Human Trafficking* 6 (4): 375–87. https://doi.org/10.1080/23322705.2019.1634936.

Ball, Michael, Chris N. Bayer, Michael McCoy, Stefan Reed, Jasper Trautsch, and Jiahua Xu. 2015. *Corporate Compliance with the California Transparency in Supply Chains Act of 2010.* Development International. https://28696c7d-66ef-4bd0–86e3-c319e9b535e4.filesusr.com/ugd/f0f801_0276d7c94ebe453f8648b91dd3589 8ba.pdf.

Ballucci, Dale, and Felicia Stathakis. 2022. "Re-conceptualizing Success: Investigating Specialized Units Responses to the Sexual Trafficking of Female Victim-Survivors." *Feminist Criminology* 17 (5): 661–83. https://doi.org/10.1177/15570851221114396.

Bang, Naomi Jiyoung. 2013. "Unmasking the Charade of the Global Supply Contract: A Novel Theory of Corporate Liability in Human Trafficking and Forced Labor Cases." *Houston Journal of International Law* 35 (2): 255–322.

Barnhart, Melynda H. 2009. "Sex and Slavery: An Analysis of Three Models of State Human Trafficking Legislation." *William & Mary Journal of Women and the Law* 16 (1): 83–132.

Barrick, Kelle, Pamela K. Lattimore, Wayne J. Pitts, and Sheldon X. Zhang. 2013. *Indicators of Labor Trafficking among North Carolina Migrant Farmworkers.* RTI International. https://www.ojp.gov/pdffiles1/nij/grants/244204.pdf.

———. 2014. "When Farmworkers and Advocates See Trafficking But Law Enforcement Does Not: Challenges in Identifying Labor Trafficking in North Carolina." *Crime, Law and Social Change* 61 (2): 205–14. https://doi.org/10.1007/s10611-013-9509-z.

Barrick, Kelle, Meg Panichelli, Barrot Lambdin, Minh Dang, and Alexandra Lutnick. 2021. "Law Enforcement Identification of Potential Trafficking Victims." *Journal of Crime and Justice* 44 (5): 579–94. https://doi.org/10.1080/07356 48X.2020.1837204.

Baxter, Alexandra Louise Anderson. 2020. "When the Line between Victimization and Criminalization Blurs: The Victim-Offender Overlap Observed in Female Offenders in Cases of Trafficking in Persons for Sexual Exploitation in Australia." *Journal of Human Trafficking* 6 (3): 327–38. https://doi.org/10.1080/2332 2705.2019.1578579.

Beccaria, Cesare. 1963. *On Crimes and Punishments.* Translated by Henry Paolucci. Englewood Cliffs, NJ: Prentice-Hall.

Becker, Howard S. 1963. *Outsiders: Studies in the Sociology of Deviance.* New York: Free Press.

Beckman, Marlene D. 1983. "The White Slave Traffic Act: The Historical Impact of a Criminal Law Policy on Women." *Georgetown Law Journal* 72 (3): 1111–42.

Beeson, Jodie G. 2015. "Psychology of Human Trafficking." In *Combating Human Trafficking: A Multidisciplinary Approach,* edited by Michael J. Palmiotto, 47–60. Boca Raton, FL: CRC Press. https://doi.org/10.1201/b17709-5.

Bell, Katherine. 2018. "Critical Race Theory." *Feminist Media Histories* 4 (April): 57–60. https://doi.org/10.1525/fmh.2018.4.2.57.

Berger, Stephanie M. 2012. "No End in Sight: Why the 'End Demand' Movement Is the Wrong Focus for Efforts to Eliminate Human Trafficking." *Harvard Journal of Law & Gender* 35 (2): 523–70.

Bernat, Frances P., and Tatyana Zhilina. 2010. "Human Trafficking: The Local Becomes Global Human Sex Trafficking—Introduction." *Women and Criminal Justice* 20 (1/2): 2–9.

Bernstein, Elizabeth. 2010. "Militarized Humanitarianism Meets Carceral Feminism: The Politics of Sex, Rights, and Freedom in Contemporary Antitrafficking Campaigns." *Signs: Journal of Women in Culture and Society* 36 (1): 45–71. https://doi.org/10.1086/652918.

———. 2012. "Carceral Politics as Gender Justice? The 'Traffic in Women' and Neoliberal Circuits of Crime, Sex, and Rights." *Theory and Society* 41 (3): 233.

Bessell, Sarah. 2018. *Fact Sheet: Human Trafficking and Domestic Violence*. Human Trafficking Legal Center. https://www.htlegalcenter.org/wp-content/uploads /Human-Trafficking-and-Domestic-Violence-Fact-Sheet.pdf.

Boerman, Thomas, and Adam Golob. 2021. "Gangs and Modern-Day Slavery in El Salvador, Honduras and Guatemala: A Non-Traditional Model of Human Trafficking." *Journal of Human Trafficking* 7 (3): 241–57. https://doi.org/10.1080/233 22705.2020.1719343.

Boggiani, Michele. 2015. "When Is a Trafficking Victim a Trafficking Victim: Anti-Prostitution Statutes and Victim Protection." *Cleveland State Law Review* 64 (4): 915–64.

Bohm, Robert M., and Brenda L. Vogel. 2015. *A Primer on Crime and Delinquency Theory*. 4th ed. Durham, NC: Carolina Academic Press. https://cap-press.com /books/isbn/9781611636857/A-Primer-on-Crime-and-Delinquency-Theory-Fourth-Edition.

Boris, Eileen, and Heather Berg. 2014. "Protecting Virtue, Erasing Labor: Historical Responses to Trafficking." In *Human Trafficking Reconsidered: Rethinking the Problem, Envisioning New Solutions,* edited by Kimberly Kay Hoang and Rhacel Salazar Parrenas, 19–40. New York: International Debate Education Association.

Bouché, Vanessa. 2015. *A Report on the Use of Technology to Recruit, Groom and Sell Domestic Minor Sex Trafficking Victims*. Thorn. https://www.thorn.org /wp-content/uploads/2015/02/Survivor_Survey_r5.pdf.

———. 2017. *An Empirical Analysis of the Intersection of Organized Crime and Human Trafficking in the United States*. National Institute of Justice. https://nij.ojp.gov /library/publications/empirical-analysis-intersection-organized-crime-and-human-trafficking-united.

Bouché, Vanessa, and Sean M. Crotty. 2018. "Estimating Demand for Illicit Massage Businesses in Houston, Texas." *Journal of Human Trafficking* 4 (4): 279–97. https://doi.org/10.1080/23322705.2017.1374080.

Bouché, Vanessa, Amy Farrell, and Dana Wittmer. 2015. *Identifying Effective Counter-Trafficking Programs and Practices in the U.S.: Legislative, Legal, and Public Opinion Strategies That Work*. U.S. Department of Justice. https://www.ojp.gov /pdffiles1/nij/grants/249670.pdf.

Bouché, Vanessa, and Stephanie Shady. 2017. "A Pimp's Game: A Rational Choice Approach to Understanding the Decisions of Sex Traffickers." *Women & Criminal Justice* 27 (2): 91–108. https://doi.org/10.1080/08974454.2016.1250701.

Boukli, Avi, and Flora Renz. 2019. "Deconstructing the Lesbian, Gay, Bisexual, Transgender Victim of Sex Trafficking: Harm, Exceptionality and Religion–Sexuality Tensions." *International Review of Victimology* 25 (1): 71–90. https://doi.org/10.1177/0269758018772670.

Braithwaite, John. 1989. *Crime, Shame and Reintegration.* Cambridge: Cambridge University Press.

Brennan, Denise. 2008. "Competing Claims of Victimhood? Foreign and Domestic Victims of Trafficking in the United States." *Sexuality Research and Social Policy* 5 (4): 45–61. https://doi.org/10.1525/srsp.2008.5.4.45.

———. 2017. "Fighting Human Trafficking Today: Moral Panics, Zombie Data, and the Seduction of Rescue Combating Human Trafficking: Current Trends and Cutting Edge Issues—Articles & Essays." *Wake Forest Law Review* 52 (2): 477–96.

Broad, Rose. 2015. "'A Vile and Violent Thing': Female Traffickers and the Criminal Justice Response." *British Journal of Criminology* 55 (6): 1058–75. https://doi.org/10.1093/bjc/azv072.

Bronfenbrenner, Urie. 1979. *The Ecology of Human Development: Experiments by Nature and Design.* Cambridge, MA: Harvard University Press.

Bruckmüller, Karin. 2020. "Trafficking of Human Beings for Organ (Cells and Tissue) Removal." In *The Palgrave International Handbook of Human Trafficking,* edited by John Winterdyk and Jackie Jones, 319–37. Cham, Switzerland: Springer International. https://doi.org/10.1007/978-3-319-63058-8_20.

Bryant, Katharine, and Todd Landman. 2020. "Combatting Human Trafficking since Palermo: What Do We Know about What Works?" *Journal of Human Trafficking* 6 (2): 119–40. https://doi.org/10.1080/23322705.2020.1690097.

Bryant-Davis, Thema, and Pratyusha Tummala-Narra. 2017. "Cultural Oppression and Human Trafficking: Exploring the Role of Racism and Ethnic Bias." *Women & Therapy* 40 (1–2): 152–69. https://doi.org/10.1080/02703149.2016.1210964.

Budiani-Saberi, Debra A., Kallakurichi Rajendiran Raja, Katie C. Findley, Ponsian Kerketta, and Vijay Anand. 2014. "Human Trafficking for Organ Removal in India: A Victim-Centered, Evidence-Based Report." *Transplantation* 97 (4): 380–84. https://doi.org/10.1097/01.TP.0000438624.83472.55.

Buist, Carrie L., Emily Lenning, and Matthew Ball. 2018. "Queer Criminology." In *Routledge Handbook of Critical Criminology,* 2nd ed., edited by Walter S. DeKeseredy and Molly Dragiewicz, 96–106. New York: Routledge.

Bureau of International Labor Affairs. 2020. *2020 List of Goods Produced by Child Labor or Forced Labor.* Bureau of International Labor Affairs, U.S. Department of Labor. https://www.dol.gov/sites/dolgov/files/ILAB/child_labor_reports/tda2019/2020_TVPRA_List_Online_Final.pdf.

Burgess, Robert L., and Ronald L. Akers. 1966. "A Differential Association-Reinforcement Theory of Criminal Behavior." *Social Problems* 14 (2): 128–47. https://doi.org/10.2307/798612.

Burke, Mary C., Barbara Amaya, and Kelly Dillon. 2020. "Sex Trafficking as Structural Gender-Based Violence: Overview and Trauma Implications." In *The Pal-*

grave *International Handbook of Human Trafficking,* edited by John Winterdyk and Jackie Jones, 451–65. Cham, Switzerland: Springer International. https://doi .org/10.1007/978-3-319-63058-8_22.

Burnitis, Caitlyn. 2019. "Facing the Future with FOSTA: Examining the Allow States and Victims to Fight Online Sex Trafficking Act of 2017." *University of Miami Race and Social Justice Law Review* 10 (2): 139–66.

Butler, Cheryl Nelson. 2015a. "A Critical Race Feminist Perspective on Prostitution & Sex Trafficking in America." *Yale Journal of Law and Feminism* 27 (1): 95–140.

———. 2015b. "The Racial Roots of Human Trafficking." *UCLA Law Review* 62 (6): 1464–1514.

Cameron, Erinn C., Fiona J. Cunningham, Samantha L. Hemingway, Sherri L. Tschida, and Kristine M. Jacquin. 2023. "Indicators of Gender Inequality and Violence against Women Predict Number of Reported Human Trafficking Legal Cases across Countries." *Journal of Human Trafficking* 9 (1): 79–93. https://doi .org/10.1080/23322705.2020.1852000.

Cameron, Lisa, Jennifer Seager, and Manisha Shah. 2021. "Crimes against Morality: Unintended Consequences of Criminalizing Sex Work." *Quarterly Journal of Economics* 136 (1): 427–69. https://doi.org/10.1093/qje/qjaa032.

Cameron, Sally, and Edward Newman. 2008. "Introduction: Understanding Human Trafficking." In *Trafficking in Humans: Social, Cultural and Political Dimensions,* edited by Sally Cameron and Edward Newman, 1–18. Tokyo: United Nations University Press.

Carpenter, Ami, and Jamie Gates. 2016. *Nature and Extent of Gang Involvement in Sex Trafficking in San Diego County.* National Institute of Justice. https://www .ojp.gov/ncjrs/virtual-library/abstracts/nature-and-extent-gang-involvement-sex- trafficking-san-diego-county.

Casassa, Kaitlin, Logan Knight, and Cecilia Mengo. 2022. "Trauma Bonding Perspectives from Service Providers and Survivors of Sex Trafficking: A Scoping Review." *Trauma, Violence, & Abuse* 23 (3): 969–84. https://doi.org/10.1177/1524838020985542.

Cecchet, Stacy J., and John Thoburn. 2014. "The Psychological Experience of Child and Adolescent Sex Trafficking in the United States: Trauma and Resilience in Survivors." *Psychological Trauma: Theory, Research, Practice, and Policy* 6 (5): 482–93. https://doi.org/10.1037/a0035763.

Centeno, Miguel A., and Joseph N. Cohen. 2010. *Global Capitalism: A Sociological Perspective.* Cambridge: Polity Press.

Chacón, Jennifer M. 2006. "Misery and Myopia: Understanding the Failures of U.S. Efforts to Stop Human Trafficking Part IV—Asylum, Refugees, and Human Rights." *Immigration and Nationality Law Review* 27:331–96.

Chakoian, Kaitie, Resham Sethi, and Jessica Santos. 2021. *Trauma-Informed Practice in the Field: Recommendations for Human Trafficking Service Providers.* Brandeis University Institute for Economic and Racial Equity. https://heller.brandeis .edu/iere/pdfs/trauma-informed-practice-in-the-field-1.pdf.

Chambers, Ronald, Matthew Gibson, Sarah Chaffin, Timothy Takagi, Nancy Nguyen, and Toussaint Mears-Clark. 2022. "Trauma-Coerced Attachment and

Complex PTSD: Informed Care for Survivors of Human Trafficking." *Journal of Human Trafficking* (January): 1–10. https://doi.org/10.1080/23322705.2021.2012386.

Chapkis, Wendy. 2003. "Trafficking, Migration, and the Law: Protecting Innocents, Punishing Immigrants." *Gender & Society* 17 (6): 923–37. https://doi.org/10.1177/0891243203257477.

———. 2005. "Soft Glove, Punishing Fist: The Trafficking Victims Protection Act of 2000." In *Regulating Sex: The Politics of Intimacy and Identity,* edited by Elizabeth Bernstein and Laurie Schaffner, 51–66. New York: Routledge.

Chin, John J., Anna J. Kim, Lois Takahashi, and Douglas J. Wiebe. 2015. "Do Sexually Oriented Massage Parlors Cluster in Specific Neighborhoods? A Spatial Analysis of Indoor Sex Work in Los Angeles and Orange Counties, California." *Public Health Reports* 130 (5): 533–42. https://doi.org/10.1177/003335491513000516.

Cho, Seo-Young. 2015. "Modeling for Determinants of Human Trafficking: An Empirical Analysis." *Social Inclusion: Lisbon* 3 (1): 2–21.

Cho, Seo-Young, Axel Dreher, and Eric Neumayer. 2013. "Does Legalized Prostitution Increase Human Trafficking?" *World Development* 41 (January): 67–82. https://doi.org/10.1016/j.worlddev.2012.05.023.

———. 2014. "Determinants of Anti-Trafficking Policies: Evidence from a New Index." *Scandinavian Journal of Economics* 116 (2): 429–54. https://doi.org/10.1111/sjoe.12055.

Cho, Seo-Young, and Krishna Chaitanya Vadlamannati. 2012. "Compliance with the Anti-Trafficking Protocol." *European Journal of Political Economy* 28 (2): 249–65. https://doi.org/10.1016/j.ejpoleco.2011.12.003.

Chohaney, Michael L. 2016. "Minor and Adult Domestic Sex Trafficking Risk Factors in Ohio." *Journal of the Society for Social Work and Research* 7 (1): 117–41. https://doi.org/10.1086/685108.

Choi. 2010. "Human Trafficking for Sexual Exploitation in the UK: Case Study of Eastern Europe and the Baltic States' Women." *International Area Review* 13 (1): 105–26. https://doi.org/10.1177/223386591001300106.

Chong, Natividad Gutiérrez. 2014. "Human Trafficking and Sex Industry: Does Ethnicity and Race Matter?" *Journal of Intercultural Studies* 35 (2): 196–213. https://doi.org/10.1080/07256868.2014.885413.

Christie, Nils. 1986. "The Ideal Victim." In *From Crime Policy to Victim Policy: Reorienting the Justice System,* edited by Ezzat A. Fattah, 17–30. London: Palgrave Macmillan. https://doi.org/10.1007/978-1-349-08305-3_2.

Chuang, Janie. 2006a. "Beyond a Snapshot: Preventing Human Trafficking in the Global Economy." *Indiana Journal of Global Legal Studies* 13 (1): 137–63. https://doi.org/10.2979/gls.2006.13.1.137.

———. 2006b. "The United States as Global Sheriff: Using Unilateral Sanctions to Combat Human Trafficking." *Michigan Journal of International Law* 27 (2): 437–94.

———. 2010. "Rescuing Trafficking from Ideological Capture: Prostitution Reform and Anti-Trafficking Law and Policy." *University of Pennsylvania Law Review* 158 (6): 1655–1728.

———. 2014. "Exploitation Creep and the Unmaking of Human Trafficking Law." *American Journal of International Law* 108 (4): 609–49. https://doi.org/10.5305/amerjintelaw.108.4.0609.

Clarke, Ronald V. 2008. "Situational Crime Prevention." In *Environmental Criminology and Crime Analysis,* edited by Richard Wortley and Lorraine Mazerolle, 200–216. New York: Willan.

Cloward, Richard A., and L. E. Ohlin. 1960. *Delinquency and Opportunity: A Study of Delinquent Gangs.* Glencoe, IL: Free Press.

Cobbina, Jennifer E., and Sharon S. Oselin. 2011. "It's Not Only for the Money: An Analysis of Adolescent versus Adult Entry into Street Prostitution." *Sociological Inquiry* 81 (3): 310–32. https://doi.org/10.1111/j.1475-682X.2011.00375.x.

Cockbain, Ella, and Kate Bowers. 2019. "Human Trafficking for Sex, Labour and Domestic Servitude: How Do Key Trafficking Types Compare and What Are Their Predictors?" *Crime, Law and Social Change* 72 (1): 9–34. https://doi.org/10.1007/s10611-019-09836-7.

Cockbain, Ella, Kate Bowers, and Galina Dimitrova. 2018. "Human Trafficking for Labour Exploitation: The Results of a Two-Phase Systematic Review Mapping the European Evidence Base and Synthesising Key Scientific Research Evidence." *Journal of Experimental Criminology* 14 (3): 319–60. https://doi.org/10.1007/s11292-017-9321-3.

Cockbain, Ella, and Richard Wortley. 2015. "Everyday Atrocities: Does Internal (Domestic) Sex Trafficking of British Children Satisfy the Expectations of Opportunity Theories of Crime?" *Crime Science* 4 (1): 35. https://doi.org/10.1186/s40163-015-0047-0.

Cohen, Lawrence E., and Marcus Felson. 1979. "Social Change and Crime Rate Trends: A Routine Activity Approach." *American Sociological Review* 44 (4): 588–608. https://doi.org/10.2307/2094589.

Cole, Jennifer. 2018. "Service Providers' Perspectives on Sex Trafficking of Male Minors: Comparing Background and Trafficking Situations of Male and Female Victims." *Child and Adolescent Social Work Journal* 35 (4): 423–33. https://doi.org/10.1007/s10560-018-0530-z.

Cole, Jennifer, and Ginny Sprang. 2015. "Sex Trafficking of Minors in Metropolitan, Micropolitan, and Rural Communities." *Child Abuse & Neglect* 40 (February): 113–23. https://doi.org/10.1016/j.chiabu.2014.07.015.

Collins, Patricia Hill. 2008. *Black Feminist Thought: Knowledge, Consciousness, and the Politics of Empowerment.* 1st ed. New York: Routledge.

Constance-Huggins, Monique, Shaneé Moore, and ZaDonna M. Slay. 2022. "Sex Trafficking of Black Girls: A Critical Race Theory Approach to Practice." *Journal of Progressive Human Services* 33 (1): 62–74. https://doi.org/10.1080/10428232.2021.1987755.

Constantinou, Angelo. 2016. "Is Crime Displacement Inevitable? Lessons from the Enforcement of Laws against Prostitution-Related Human Trafficking in Cyprus." *European Journal of Criminology* 13 (2): 214–30. https://doi.org/10.1177/1477370815617190.

Contreras, Paola Michelle, Diya Kallivayalil, and Judith Lewis Herman. 2017. "Psychotherapy in the Aftermath of Human Trafficking: Working Through the Consequences of Psychological Coercion." *Women & Therapy* 40 (1–2): 31–54. http://dx.doi.org/10.1080/02703149.2016.1205908.

Conway, Kyle. 2020. *Sixty Years of Boom and Bust: The Impact of Oil in North Dakota, 1958–2018.* Grand Forks: Digital Press at the University of North Dakota.

Copley, Lauren. 2014. "Neutralizing Their Involvement: Sex Traffickers' Discourse Techniques." *Feminist Criminology* 9 (1): 45–58. http://dx.doi.org/10.1177/1557085113501849.

Cornish, Derek Blaikie, and R. V. G. Clarke. 1986. *The Reasoning Criminal: Rational Choice Perspectives on Offending.* New York: Springer-Verlag.

Corrin, Chris. 2005. "Transitional Road for Traffic: Analysing Trafficking in Women from and through Central and Eastern Europe." *Europe-Asia Studies* 57 (4): 543–60.

Crotty, Sean M., and Vanessa Bouché. 2018. "The Red-Light Network: Exploring the Locational Strategies of Illicit Massage Businesses in Houston, Texas." *Papers in Applied Geography* 4 (2): 205–27. https://doi.org/10.1080/23754931.2018.1425633.

CTDC (Counter Trafficking Data Collaborative). 2021. "26 Visualisations." https://www.ctdatacollaborative.org/visualisations.

Culkin, Laurie. 2015. "Exchanging Cooperation for Visas: Flaws in U.S. Immigration System Criminalizes Trafficking Victims." *University of Baltimore Journal of International Law* 3 (2): 115–36.

Curtis, Ric, Karen Terry, Meredith Dank, Kirk Dombrowski, and Bilal Khan. 2008. *Commercial Sexual Exploitation of Children in New York City, Volume One: The CSEC Population in New York City: Size, Characteristics, and Needs.* Center for Court Innovation, John Jay College of Criminal Justice. https://www.ojp.gov/pdffiles1/nij/grants/225083.pdf.

D'Adamo, Kate. 2016. "Prioritising Prosecutions Is the Wrong Approach." *Anti-Trafficking Review,* no. 6 (May): 111–13. https://doi.org/10.14197/atr.20121668.

Dagistanli, Selda, and Sanja Milivojevic. 2013. "Appropriating the Rights of Women: Moral Panics, Victims and Exclusionary Agendas in Domestic and Cross-Borders Sex Crimes." *Women's Studies International Forum* 40 (September): 230–42. https://doi.org/10.1016/j.wsif.2013.09.001.

Daly, Kathleen, and Meda Chesney-Lind. 1988. "Feminism and Criminology." *Justice Quarterly* 5 (4): 497–538. https://doi.org/10.1080/07418828800089871.

Dank, Meredith, P. Mitchell Downey, Cybele Kotonias, Debbie Mayer, Colleen Owens, Laura Pacifici, and Lilly Yu. 2016. *Estimating the Size and Structure of the Underground Commercial Sex Economy in Eight Major US Cities.* Urban Institute. https://www.urban.org/research/publication/estimating-size-and-structure-underground-commercial-sex-economy-eight-major-us-cities.

Dank, Meredith, Jennifer Yahner, Kuniko Madden, Banuelos Isela, Lilly Yu, Andrea Ritchie, Michyll Mora, and Brendan Conner. 2015. *Surviving the Streets of New York: Experiences of LGBTQ Youth, YMSM, and YWSW Engaged in Survival Sex*. Urban Institute. https://www.urban.org/research/publication/surviving-streets-new-york-experiences-lgbtq-youth-ymsm-and-ywsw-engaged-survival-sex/view/full_report.

Davis, Kathleen YS. 2006. *Human Trafficking and Modern Day Slavery in Ohio*. Polaris Project. https://d1wqtxts1xzle7.cloudfront.net/3458835/Ohio-Report-on-Trafficking-with-cover-page-v2.pdf?Expires=1647283397&Signature=GJOeD-NMcGOifAbEfPDx3xlf5arDlGEnVLrpxaoVrBCPtir5KnCy7J249JoaymTNJR QyhsmICMTwjqnHb1ozA6l4D1Qn2i~MHrp4zeQp5ejXCThrON8cTFecMv A1ILvaoqz9MioZ-rU-Z6mwMRwol78cMRL5RySKkQkf6MavFUoD2iFRrW ~FUq15TN~tRreu1X8emSvoaHOpCmFVit-zcpA38DdzXdxVHi67zyf9lv6x-SQx7pffVrd6wIXY1mfzju7fpsXTuJhAf-ROLYtKaqqpHbh4ppOPJrMsIL87B 3iKraDMBVNvts~JVr69P8wrVgQ1rWiO46hdISvPhj7nSV5A__& Key-Pair-Id=APKAJLOHF5GGSLRBV4ZA.

Davy, Deanna. 2016. "Anti–Human Trafficking Interventions: How Do We Know If They Are Working?" *American Journal of Evaluation* 37 (4): 486–504. https://doi.org/10.1177/1098214016630615.

Derks, Annuska, Roger Henke, and Ly Vanna. 2006. *Review of a Decade of Research on Trafficking in Persons, Cambodia*. Asia Foundation. https://asiafoundation.org/resources/pdfs/CBTIPreview.pdf.

Desyllas, Moshoula Capous. 2007. "A Critique of the Global Trafficking Discourse and U.S. Policy." *Journal of Sociology and Social Welfare* 34 (4): 57–80.

de Vries, Ieke, and Amy Farrell. 2018. "Labor Trafficking Victimizations: Repeat Victimization and Polyvictimization." *Psychology of Violence* 8 (5): 630–38. https://doi.org/10.1037/vio0000149.

de Vries, Ieke, Megan Amy Jose, and Amy Farrell. 2020. "It's Your Business: The Role of the Private Sector in Human Trafficking." In *The Palgrave International Handbook of Human Trafficking*, edited by John Winterdyk and Jackie Jones, 745–62. Cham, Switzerland: Springer International. https://doi.org/10.1007/978-3-319-63058-8_45.

Diaz, Madelyn, Lin Huff-Corzine, and Jay Corzine. 2022. "Demanding Reduction: A County-Level Analysis Examining Structural Determinants of Human Trafficking Arrests in Florida." *Crime & Delinquency* 68 (1): 28–51. https://doi.org/10.1177/0011128720962710.

DoCarmo, Tania E. 2020. "Ethical Considerations for Studying Human Trafficking." In *The Palgrave International Handbook of Human Trafficking*, edited by John Winterdyk and Jackie Jones, 177–94. Cham, Switzerland: Springer International. https://doi.org/10.1007/978-3-319-63058-8_8.

Doezema, Jo. 2000. "Loose Women or Lost Women? The Re-emergence of the Myth of White Slavery in Contemporary Discourses of Trafficking in Women." *Gender Issues* 18 (1): 23–50. https://doi.org/10.1007/s12147-999-0021-9.

————. 2002. "Who Gets to Choose? Coercion, Consent, and the UN Trafficking Protocol." *Gender and Development* 10 (1): 20–27.

————. 2010. *Sex Slaves and Discourse Masters: The Construction of Trafficking.* New York: Zed Books. https://www.bloomsbury.com/us/sex-slaves-and-discourse-masters-9781848134133/.

Doychak, Kendra, and Chitra Raghavan. 2020. "'No Voice or Vote:' Trauma-Coerced Attachment in Victims of Sex Trafficking." *Journal of Human Trafficking* 6 (3): 339–57. https://doi.org/10.1080/23322705.2018.1518625.

Dryhurst, Karin. 2012. "Liability up the Supply Chain: Corporate Accountability for Labor Trafficking." *New York University Journal of International Law and Politics* 45 (2): 641–76.

Dubrawski, Artur, Kyle Miller, Matthew Barnes, Benedikt Boecking, and Emily Kennedy. 2015. "Leveraging Publicly Available Data to Discern Patterns of Human-Trafficking Activity." *Journal of Human Trafficking* 1 (1): 65–85. https://doi.org/10.1080/23322705.2015.1015342.

Duncan, Alexandra C., and Dana DeHart. 2019. "Provider Perspectives on Sex Trafficking: Victim Pathways, Service Needs, & Blurred Boundaries." *Victims & Offenders* 14 (4): 510–31. https://doi.org/10.1080/15564886.2019.1595241.

Durkheim, Émile. 1951. *Suicide: A Study in Sociology.* Edited by George Simpson. Translated by John A. Spaulding and George Simpson. New York: Free Press.

Eargle, Lisa A., and Jessica M. Doucet. 2021. "Investigating Human Trafficking within the United States: A State-Level Analysis of Prevalence and Correlates." *Sociation* 20 (1): 13–26.

Edwards, Emily E., Jennifer S. Middleton, and Jennifer Cole. 2022. "Family-Controlled Trafficking in the United States: Victim Characteristics, System Response, and Case Outcomes." *Journal of Human Trafficking,* 1–19. https://doi.org/10.1080/23322705.2022.2039866.

Egyes, Lynly S. 2019. "Borders and Intersections: The Unique Vulnerabilities of LGBTQ Immigrants to Trafficking." In *Broadening the Scope of Human Trafficking Research: A Reader,* 2nd ed., edited by Erin C. Heil and Andrea J. Nichols, 1–18. Durham, NC: Carolina Academic Press.

End Slavery Now. 2015. "Shamere McKenzie." End Slavery Now, January 3, 2015. http://endslaverynow.org/blog/articles/shamere-mckenzie/.

Ezell, Laura. 2016. "Human Trafficking in Multinational Supply Chains: A Corporate Director's Fiduciary Duty to Monitor and Eliminate Human Trafficking Violations Notes." *Vanderbilt Law Review* 69 (2): 499–544.

Farley, Melissa, Nicole Matthews, Sarah Deer, Guadalupe Lopez, Christine Stark, and Eileen Hudon. 2011. *Garden of Truth: The Prostitution and Trafficking of Native Women in Minnesota.* St. Paul: Minnesota Indian Women's Sexual Assault Coalition and Prostitution Research & Education. https://www.niwrc.org/sites/default/files/images/resource/Garden-of-Truth.pdf.

Farr, Kathryn. 2004. *Sex Trafficking: The Global Market in Women and Children.* New York: Worth.

Farrell, Amy, Vanessa Bouché, and Dana Wolfe. 2019. "Assessing the Impact of State Human Trafficking Legislation on Criminal Justice System Outcomes." *Law & Policy* 41 (2): 174–97. http://dx.doi.org/10.1111/lapo.12124.

Farrell, Amy, Katherine Bright, Ieke de Vries, Rebecca Pfeffer, and Meredith Dank. 2020. "Policing Labor Trafficking in the United States." *Trends in Organized Crime* 23 (1): 36–56. https://doi.org/10.1007/s12117-019-09367-6.

Farrell, Amy, Monica J. DeLateur, Colleen Owens, and Stephanie Fahy. 2016. "The Prosecution of State-Level Human Trafficking Cases in the United States." *Anti-Trafficking Review,* no. 6 (May): 48–70. https://doi.org/10.14197/atr.20121664.

Farrell, Amy, and Stephanie Fahy. 2009. "The Problem of Human Trafficking in the U.S.: Public Frames and Policy Responses." *Journal of Criminal Justice* 37 (6): 617–26. https://doi.org/10.1016/j.jcrimjus.2009.09.010.

Farrell, Amy, and Brianne Kane. 2020. "Criminal Justice System Responses to Human Trafficking." In *The Palgrave International Handbook of Human Trafficking,* edited by John Winterdyk and Jackie Jones, 641–57. Cham, Switzerland: Springer International. https://doi.org/10.1007/978-3-319-63058-8_40.

Farrell, Amy, Jack McDevitt, and Stephanie Fahy. 2010. "Where Are All the Victims? Understanding the Determinants of Official Identification of Human Trafficking Incidents." *Criminology & Public Policy* 9 (2): 201–33. https://doi.org/10.1111/j.1745-9133.2010.00621.x.

Farrell, Amy, Colleen Owens, and Jack McDevitt. 2014. "New Laws but Few Cases: Understanding the Challenges to the Investigation and Prosecution of Human Trafficking Cases." *Crime, Law and Social Change* 61 (2): 139–68. https://doi.org/10.1007/s10611-013-9442-1.

Farrell, Amy, and Rebecca Pfeffer. 2014. "Policing Human Trafficking: Cultural Blinders and Organizational Barriers." *Annals of the American Academy of Political and Social Science* 653 (1): 46–64. https://doi.org/10.1177/0002716213515835.

Farrell, Amy, Rebecca Pfeffer, and Katherine Bright. 2015. "Police Perceptions of Human Trafficking." *Journal of Crime and Justice* 38 (3): 315–33. https://doi.org/10.1080/0735648X.2014.995412.

Farrell, Amy, and Jessica Reichert. 2017. "Using U.S. Law-Enforcement Data: Promise and Limits in Measuring Human Trafficking." *Journal of Human Trafficking* 3 (1): 39–60. https://doi.org/10.1080/23322705.2017.1280324.

Fedina, Lisa. 2015. "Use and Misuse of Research in Books on Sex Trafficking: Implications for Interdisciplinary Researchers, Practitioners, and Advocates." *Trauma, Violence, & Abuse* 16 (2): 188–98. https://doi.org/10.1177/1524838014523337.

Fedina, Lisa, and Bruce R. DeForge. 2017. "Estimating the Trafficked Population: Public-Health Research Methodologies May Be the Answer." *Journal of Human Trafficking* 3 (1): 21–38. https://doi.org/10.1080/23322705.2017.1280316.

Feehs, Kyleigh, and Alyssa Currier Wheeler. 2021. *2020 Federal Human Trafficking Report.* Human Trafficking Institute. https://www.traffickinginstitute.org/wp-content/uploads/2021/06/2020-Federal-Human-Trafficking-Report-Low-Res.pdf.

Fehrenbacher, Anne E., Jennifer Musto, Heidi Hoefinger, Nicola Mai, P. G. Macioti, Calogero Giametta, and Calum Bennachie. 2020. "Transgender People and

Human Trafficking: Intersectional Exclusion of Transgender Migrants and People of Color from Anti-trafficking Protection in the United States." *Journal of Human Trafficking* 6 (2): 182–94. https://doi.org/10.1080/23322705.2020.1690116.

Feingold, David A. 2011. "Trafficking in Numbers: The Social Construction of Human Trafficking Data." In *Sex, Drugs, and Body Counts: The Politics of Numbers in Global Crime and Conflict,* edited by Peter Andreas and Kelly M. Greenhill, 46–74. Ithaca, NY: Cornell University Press. https://doi.org/10.7591/9780801458309–005.

Ferrari, Chiara. 2021. "The Factors Involved in the Exit from Sex Trafficking: A Review." *Journal of International Women's Studies* 22 (5): 195–209.

Finigan-Carr, Nadine, Melissa Johnson, Michael Pullmann, C. Stewart, and Anne Fromknecht. 2019. "A Traumagenic Social Ecological Framework for Understanding and Intervening with Sex Trafficked Children and Youth." *Child and Adolescent Social Work Journal* 36 (February). https://doi.org/10.1007/s10560–018–0588–7.

Finklea, Kristin, Adrienne L. Fernandes-Alcantara, and Alison Siskin. 2015. *Sex Trafficking of Children in the United States: Overview and Issues for Congress.* Congressional Research Service, January 28, 2015. https://sgp.fas.org/crs/misc/R41878.pdf.

Finn, Kathleen, Erica Gajda, Thomas Perin, and Carla Fredericks. 2017. "Responsible Resource Development and Prevention of Sex Trafficking: Safeguarding Native Women and Children on the Fort Berthold Reservation." *Harvard Journal of Law & Gender* 40 (1): 1–51.

FitzGerald, Sharron A. 2016. "Vulnerable Geographies: Human Trafficking, Immigration and Border Control in the UK and Beyond." *Gender, Place and Culture* 23 (2): 181–97.

Franchino-Olsen, Hannabeth. 2021a. "Frameworks and Theories Relevant for Organizing Commercial Sexual Exploitation of Children/Domestic Minor Sex Trafficking Risk Factors: A Systematic Review of Proposed Frameworks to Conceptualize Vulnerabilities." *Trauma, Violence, & Abuse* 22 (2): 306–17. https://doi.org/10.1177/1524838019849575.

———. 2021b. "Vulnerabilities Relevant for Commercial Sexual Exploitation of Children/Domestic Minor Sex Trafficking: A Systematic Review of Risk Factors." *Trauma, Violence, & Abuse* 22 (1): 99–111. https://doi.org/10.1177/1524838018821956.

Franchino-Olsen, Hannabeth, Hannah A. Silverstein, Nicole F. Kahn, and Sandra L. Martin. 2020. "Minor Sex Trafficking of Girls with Disabilities." *International Journal of Human Rights in Healthcare* 13 (2): 97–108. https://doi.org/10.1108/IJHRH-07–2019–0055.

Frank, Michael J., and G. Zachary Terwilliger. 2015. "Gang-Controlled Sex Trafficking." *Virginia Journal of Criminal Law* 3 (2): 342–434.

Fraser, Campbell. 2016. "An Analysis of the Emerging Role of Social Media in Human Trafficking: Examples from Labour and Human Organ Trading." *International Journal of Development Issues* 15 (2): 98–112. https://doi.org/10.1108/IJDI-12–2015–0076.

Gallagher, Anne T. 2010. *The International Law of Human Trafficking*. New York: Cambridge University Press.

———. 2011. "Improving the Effectiveness of the International Law of Human Trafficking: A Vision for the Future of the US Trafficking in Persons Reports." *Human Rights Review* 12 (3): 381–400. https://doi.org/10.1007/s12142-010-0183-6.

———. 2016. "Editorial: The Problems and Prospects of Trafficking Prosecutions: Ending Impunity and Securing Justice." *Anti-Trafficking Review*, no. 6 (May): 1–11. https://doi.org/10.14197/atr.20121661.

———. 2017. "What's Wrong with the Global Slavery Index?" *Anti-Trafficking Review*, no. 8 (April). https://doi.org/10.14197/atr.20121786.

Gallagher, Anne, and Elaine Pearson. 2010. "The High Cost of Freedom: A Legal and Policy Analysis of Shelter Detention for Victims of Trafficking." *Human Rights Quarterly* 32 (1): 73–114.

Gallo, Michael, Renata A. Konrad, and Hannah Thinyane. 2022. "An Epidemiological Perspective on Labor Trafficking." *Journal of Human Trafficking* 8 (2): 113–34. https://doi.org/10.1080/23322705.2020.1815474.

Gerassi, Lara B., and Andrea Nichols. 2018. *Sex Trafficking and Commercial Sexual Exploitation: Prevention, Advocacy, and Trauma-Informed Practice*. New York: Springer.

Gibbons, Judith L. 2017. "Human Trafficking and Intercountry Adoption." *Women & Therapy* 40 (1–2): 170–89. https://doi.org/10.1080/02703149.2016.1210965.

Global Witness. 2007. *Loopholes in the Kimberley Process*. Global Witness, October 2007. https://cdn.globalwitness.org/archive/files/import/loopholes_in_the_kimberley_process.pdf.

———. 2013. "The Kimberley Process." Global Witness, April 1, 2013. https:///en/campaigns/conflict-diamonds/kimberley-process/.

Goode, Erich, and Nachman Ben-Yehuda. 1994. "Moral Panics: Culture, Politics, and Social Construction." *Annual Review of Sociology* 20:149–71.

Goodey, Jo. 2008. "Human Trafficking: Sketchy Data and Policy Responses." *Criminology & Criminal Justice* 8 (4): 421–42. https://doi.org/10.1177/1748895808096471.

Gotch, Katherine. 2016. "Preliminary Data on a Sample of Perpetrators of Domestic Trafficking for Sexual Exploitation: Suggestions for Research and Practice." *Journal of Human Trafficking* 2 (1): 99–109. https://doi.org/10.1080/23322705.2016.1136539.

Goździak, Elżbieta M. 2015. "Data Matters: Issues and Challenges for Research on Trafficking." In *Global Human Trafficking: Critical Issues and Contexts,* edited by Molly Dragiewicz, 23–37. New York: Routledge.

Goździak, Elżbieta, and Micah N. Bump. 2008. *Data and Research on Human Trafficking: Bibliography of Research-Based Literature*. National Institute of Justice. https://www.ncjrs.gov/pdffiles1/nij/grants/224392.pdf.

Goździak, Elżbieta, and Sarah Graveline. 2015. *In Search of Data and Research on Human Trafficking: Analysis of Research-Based Literature (2008–2014)*. Washington, DC: Institute for the Study of International Migration. https://doi.org/10.13140/RG.2.1.1861.8724.

Greenbaum, Jordan. 2017. "Introduction to Human Trafficking: Who Is Affected?" In *Human Trafficking Is a Public Health Issue: A Paradigm Expansion in the United States,* edited by Makini Chisolm-Straker and Hanni Stoklosa, 1–14. Cham, Switzerland: Springer International. https://doi.org/10.1007/978–3–319–47824–1_1.

———. 2020a. "A Public Health Approach to Global Child Sex Trafficking." *Annual Review of Public Health* 41 (1): 481–97. https://doi.org/10.1146/annurev-publhealth-040119–094335.

———. 2020b. "The Public Health Approach to Human Trafficking Prevention." *Georgia State University Law Review* 36 (4): 1059–74.

Gregoriou, Christiana, and Ilse A. Ras. 2018. "Representations of Transnational Human Trafficking: A Critical Review." In *Representations of Transnational Human Trafficking: Present-Day News Media, True Crime, and Fiction,* edited by Christiana Gregoriou, 1–24. Cham, Switzerland: Springer International. https://doi.org/10.1007/978–3–319–78214–0_1.

Gruber, Aya, Amy J. Cohen, and Kate Mogulescu. 2016. "Penal Welfare and the New Human Trafficking Intervention Courts." *Florida Law Review* 68 (5): 1333–1402.

Guerette, Rob T., and Kate J. Bowers. 2009. "Assessing the Extent of Crime Displacement and Diffusion of Benefits: A Review of Situational Crime Prevention Evaluations." *Criminology* 47 (4): 1331–68. https://doi.org/10.1111/j.1745–9125.2009.00177.x.

Gulati, Girish J. 2011. "News Frames and Story Triggers in the Media's Coverage of Human Trafficking." *Human Rights Review* 12 (3): 363–79. https://doi.org/10.1007/s12142–010–0184–5.

Hacker, Daphna. 2015. "Strategic Compliance in the Shadow of Transnational Anti-Trafficking Law." *Harvard Human Rights Journal* 28 (1): 11–64.

Hadjiyanni, Tasoulla, Melanie Povlitzki, and Hannah Preble. 2014. "The Placeness of Sex Trafficking: Instilling Consciousness through Minnesota's Experience." *Journal of Interior Design* 39 (1): 1–16. https://doi.org/10.1111/joid.12019.

Hagan, Frank E., and Leah E. Daigle. 2020. *Introduction to Criminology: Theories, Methods, and Criminal Behavior.* 10th ed. Thousand Oaks, CA: Sage. https://us.sagepub.com/en-us/nam/introduction-to-criminology/book259210.

Hagen, Leslie A., and Benjamin L. Whittemore. 2017. "Combatting Trafficking of Native Americans and Alaska Natives Human Trafficking." *United States Attorneys' Bulletin* 65 (6): 149–68.

Hamilton, Carl. 2019. "Human Trafficking Survivor Tells Her Story in Elkton." *Cecil Daily,* April 19, 2019. https://www.cecildaily.com/news/local_news/human-trafficking-survivor-tells-her-story-in-elkton/article_dce1795d-4a48–598f-b1db-4fa58480824b.html.

Hannan, Madeline, Kathryn Martin, Kimberly Caceres, and Nina Aledort. 2017. "Children at Risk: Foster Care and Human Trafficking." In *Human Trafficking Is a Public Health Issue: A Paradigm Expansion in the United States,* edited by Makini Chisolm-Straker and Hanni Stoklosa, 105–21. Cham, Switzerland: Springer International. https://doi.org/10.1007/978–3–319–47824–1_7.

Harcourt, Christine, Jody O'Conner, Sandra Egger, Christopher K. Fairley, Handan Wand, Marcus Y. Chen, Lewis Marshall, John H. Kaldor, and Basil Donovan. 2010. "The Decriminalisation of Prostitution Is Associated with Better Coverage of Health Promotion Programs for Sex Workers." *Australian and New Zealand Journal of Public Health* 34 (5): 382–86.

Hargreaves-Cormany, Holly, James Beasley, Terri Patterson, Kara Meadows, Princess-Kasharáe Middleton, Ellen Wood, Jonathan Alicchio, and Nathanael Gaspar. 2022. "Psychopathy in Human Trafficking Offenders: Current Trends and Challenges." In *Psychopathy and Criminal Behavior,* edited by Paulo Barbosa Marques, Mauro Paulino, and Laura Alho, 369–87. Cambridge, MA: Academic Press. https://doi.org/10.1016/B978-0-12-811419-3.00021-2.

Hargreaves-Cormany, Holly A., and Terri D. Patterson. 2016. "Characteristics of Survivors of Juvenile Sex Trafficking: Implications for Treatment and Intervention Initiatives." *Aggression and Violent Behavior* 30 (September–October): 32–39. https://doi.org/10.1016/j.avb.2016.06.012.

Hargreaves-Cormany, Holly A., Terri D. Patterson, and Yvonne E. Muirhead. 2016. "A Typology of Offenders Engaging in the Sex Trafficking of Juveniles (STJ): Implications for Risk Assessment." *Aggression and Violent Behavior* 30 (September–October): 40–47. https://doi.org/10.1016/j.avb.2016.06.011.

Heil, Erin C. 2017. "Intercountry Adoption and Child Trafficking." In *Broadening the Scope of Human Trafficking,* edited by Erin C. Heil and Andrea J. Nichols, 75–89. Durham, NC: Carolina Academic Press.

Heil, Erin, and Andrea Nichols. 2014. "Hot Spot Trafficking: A Theoretical Discussion of the Potential Problems Associated with Targeted Policing and the Eradication of Sex Trafficking in the United States." *Contemporary Justice Review* 17 (4): 421–33. https://doi.org/10.1080/10282580.2014.980966.

Heil, Erin C., and Andrea J. Nichols. 2015. *Human Trafficking in the Midwest: A Case Study of St. Louis and the Bi-State Area.* Durham, NC: Carolina Academic Press. http://www.cap-press.com/books/isbn/9781611636383/Human-Trafficking-in-the-Midwest.

Heinrich, Kelly Hyland. 2010. "Ten Years after the Palermo Protocol: Where Are Protections for Human Trafficking?" *Human Rights Brief* 18 (1): 1–5.

Hennig, Jana, Sarah Craggs, Frank Laczko, and Fred Larsson. 2007. *Trafficking in Human Beings and the 2006 World Cup in Germany.* International Organization for Migration. https://www.iom.int/sites/g/files/tmzbdl486/files/2018-07/mrs29THBWCG.pdf.

Hindelang, Michael J., Michael R. Gottfredson, and James Garofalo. 1978. *Victims of Personal Crime—An Empirical Foundation for a Theory of Personal Victimization.* Cambridge, MA: Ballinger. https://www.ojp.gov/ncjrs/virtual-library/abstracts/victims-personal-crime-empirical-foundation-theory-personal.

Hirschi, Travis. 2009. *Causes of Delinquency.* New Brunswick, NJ: Transaction.

Hogan, Kimberly A., and Dominique Roe-Sepowitz. 2023. "LGBTQ+ Homeless Young Adults and Sex Trafficking Vulnerability." *Journal of Human Trafficking* 9 (1): 63–78. https://doi.org/10.1080/23322705.2020.1841985.

Hollis, Meghan E., Marcus Felson, and Brandon C. Welsh. 2013. "The Capable Guardian in Routine Activities Theory: A Theoretical and Conceptual Reappraisal." *Crime Prevention and Community Safety* 15 (1): 65–79. https://doi.org/10.1057/cpcs.2012.14.

Hopper, E. K., and L. D. Gonzalez. 2018. "A Comparison of Psychological Symptoms in Survivors of Sex and Labor Trafficking." *Behavioral Medicine* 44 (3): 177–88. https://doi.org/10.1080/08964289.2018.1432551.

Hopper, Elizabeth K. 2017a. "The Multimodal Social Ecological (MSE) Approach: A Trauma-Informed Framework for Supporting Trafficking Survivors' Psychosocial Health." In *Human Trafficking Is a Public Health Issue: A Paradigm Expansion in the United States,* edited by Makini Chisolm-Straker and Hanni Stoklosa, 153–83. Cham, Switzerland: Springer International. https://doi.org/10.1007/978-3-319-47824-1_10.

———. 2017b. "Trauma-Informed Psychological Assessment of Human Trafficking Survivors." *Women & Therapy* 40 (1–2): 12–30. https://doi.org/10.1080/02703149.2016.1205905.

Hoyle, Carolyn, Mary Bosworth, and Michelle Dempsey. 2011. "Labelling the Victims of Sex Trafficking: Exploring the Borderland between Rhetoric and Reality." *Social & Legal Studies* 20 (3): 313–29. https://doi.org/10.1177/0964663911405394.

Hua, Julietta. 2011. *Trafficking Women's Human Rights.* Minneapolis: University of Minnesota Press.

Huff-Corzine, Lin, Sarah Ann Sacra, Jay Corzine, and Rachel Rados. 2017. "Florida's Task Force Approach to Combat Human Trafficking: An Analysis of County-Level Data." *Police Practice & Research* 18 (3): 245–58. https://doi.org/10.1080/15614263.2017.1291567.

Hughes, Donna M. 2000. "The 'Natasha' Trade: The Transnational Shadow Market of Trafficking in Women." *Journal of International Affairs; New York* 53 (2): 625–51.

Human Rights Watch. 2018. "Hidden Chains: Rights Abuses and Forced Labor in Thailand's Fishing Industry." Human Rights Watch, January 23, 2018. https://www.hrw.org/report/2018/01/23/hidden-chains/rights-abuses-and-forced-labor-thailands-fishing-industry.

Hupp Williamson, Sarah. 2017. "Institutional Anomie and Socialist Feminist Theory: A Process Analysis of Trafficking in Post-socialist Countries." In *Broadening the Scope of Human Trafficking,* edited by Erin C. Heil and Andrea J. Nichols, 231–57. Durham, NC: Carolina Academic Press.

———. 2022. *Human Trafficking in the Era of Global Migration: Unravelling the Impact of Neoliberal Economic Policy.* Bristol, UK: Bristol University Press.

Husseman, Jeannette, Colleen Owens, Hanna Love, Lilly Yu, Evelyn McCoy, Abbey Flynn, and Kyla Woods. 2018. *Bending Towards Justice: Perceptions of Justice among Human Trafficking Survivors.* Washington, DC: Urban Institute. https://www.ojp.gov/pdffiles1/nij/grants/251631.pdf.

ILO (International Labour Office). 2013. *Caught at Sea: Forced Labour and Trafficking in Fisheries.* Geneva: ILO. http://site.ebrary.com/id/10795029.

———. 2014. *Profits and Poverty: The Economics of Forced Labour.* Geneva: International Labour Organization.

Jac-Kucharski, Alicja. 2012. "The Determinants of Human Trafficking: A US Case Study." *International Migration* 50 (6): 150–65. https://doi.org/10.1111/j.1468-2435.2012.00777.x.

Jacobs, Beth, and Stephanie Richard. 2016. *National Survivor Network Members Survey: Impact of Criminal Arrest and Detention on Survivors of Human Trafficking.* National Survivor Network. https://nationalsurvivornetwork.org/wp-content/uploads/2017/12/VacateSurveyFinal.pdf.

Jagoe, Caroline, Pei Ying Natalie Toh, and Gillian Wylie. 2022. "Disability and the Risk of Vulnerability to Human Trafficking: An Analysis of Case Law." *Journal of Human Trafficking,* 1–15. https://doi.org/10.1080/23322705.2022.2111507.

Jakobsson, Niklas, and Andreas Kotsadam. 2013. "The Law and Economics of International Sex Slavery: Prostitution Laws and Trafficking for Sexual Exploitation." Working Papers in Economics, no. 458. University of Gothenburg, Department of Economics. https://econpapers.repec.org/paper/hhsgunwpe/0458.htm.

Jampawan, Wicha. 2018. "Prevention of Trafficking in Persons for Forced Sea Fishery Work in Thailand." *Asian Review* 31 (1): 66–81.

Jiang, Bo, and Gary LaFree. 2017. "Social Control, Trade Openness and Human Trafficking." *Journal of Quantitative Criminology* 33 (4): 887–913. https://doi.org/10.1007/s10940-016-9316-7.

Joarder, Mohammad Abdul Munim, and Paul W. Miller. 2014. "The Experiences of Migrants Trafficked from Bangladesh." *Annals of the American Academy of Political and Social Science* 653 (1): 141–61. https://doi.org/10.1177/0002716213518722.

Johnston, Anne, Barbara Friedman, and Meghan Sobel. 2015. "Framing an Emerging Issue: How U.S. Print and Broadcast News Media Covered Sex Trafficking, 2008–2012." *Journal of Human Trafficking* 1 (3): 235–54.

Jones, Tonisha, and Brian Kingshott. 2016. "A Feminist Analysis of the American Criminal Justice System's Response to Human Trafficking." *Criminal Justice Studies* 29 (3): 272–87. https://doi.org/10.1080/1478601X.2016.1178642.

Judge, Shana M., and Yuka Kawahito Doherty. 2022. "The Demographic Characteristics of Federal Trafficking Defendants: Who Are the Offenders?" *Journal of Human Trafficking,* 1–24. https://doi.org/10.1080/23322705.2022.2104572.

Junod, Anne, Jeffrey Jacquet, Felix Fernando, and Lynette Flage. 2017. "Life in the Goldilocks Zone: Perceptions of Place Disruption on the Periphery of the Bakken Shale." *Society & Natural Resources* 31 (November): 1–18. https://doi.org/10.1080/08941920.2017.1376138.

Jurek, Alicia L., and William R. King. 2020. "Structural Responses to Gendered Social Problems: Police Agency Adaptations to Human Trafficking." *Police Quarterly* 23 (1): 25–54. https://doi.org/10.1177/1098611119873093.

Kaestle, Christine E. 2012. "Selling and Buying Sex: A Longitudinal Study of Risk and Protective Factors in Adolescence." *Prevention Science* 13 (3): 314–22. https://doi.org/10.1007/s11121-011-0268-8.

Kakar, Suman. 2017. *Human Trafficking*. Durham, NC: Carolina Academic Press.

Kakar, Suman, Wendy Dressler, and Brent Blakeman. 2019. "The Hospitality Indus-try and Sex Trafficking: The Mutual Relationship between Hotels and Motels and Sex Trafficking." In *Broadening the Scope of Human Trafficking Research: A Reader,* 2nd ed., edited by Erin C. Heil and Andrea J. Nichols, 111–32. Durham, NC: Carolina Academic Press.

Kangaspunta, Kristiina, Fabrizio Sarrica, Raggie Johansen, Jesper Samson, Agata Rybarska, and Kelly Whelan. 2018. *Global Report on Trafficking in Persons 2018, Booklet 2: Trafficking in Persons in the Context of Armed Conflict*. Global Report on Trafficking in Persons, UNODC. https://www.unodc.org/unodc/en/data-and-analysis/glotip-2018.html.

Kara, Siddharth. 2010a. "Designing More Effective Laws against Human Trafficking." *Northwestern University Journal of International Human Rights* 9 (2): 123–48.

———. 2010b. *Sex Trafficking: Inside the Business of Modern Slavery*. New York: Columbia University Press.

———. 2017. *Modern Slavery: A Global Perspective*. New York: Columbia Univer-sity Press. https://doi.org/10.7312/kara15846.

Karakuş, Önder, and Oğuzhan Başıbüyük. 2010. "Social Disorganization Theory and Human Trafficking: A Systemic Control Approach to the Phenomenon." *Turkish Journal of Police Studies* 12 (2): 23–41.

Karakuş, Önder, and Edmund F. McGarrell. 2011. "A Quantitative Analysis of the Cross-National Distribution of Human Trafficking." *Turkish Journal of Police Studies* 13 (2): 97–122.

Kempadoo, Kamala. 2001. "Women of Color and the Global Sex Trade: Transna-tional Feminist Perspectives." *Meridians* 1 (2): 28–51.

———. 2007. "The War on Human Trafficking in the Caribbean." *Race & Class* 49 (2): 79.

Kendis, Becca. 2019. "Human Trafficking and Prostitution Courts: Problem Solv-ing or Problematic Comment." *Case Western Reserve Law Review* 69 (3): 805–41.

Kennedy, M. Alexis, Carolin Klein, Jessica T. K. Bristowe, Barry S. Cooper, and John C. Yuille. 2007. "Routes of Recruitment." *Journal of Aggression, Maltreat-ment & Trauma* 15 (2): 1–19. https://doi.org/10.1300/J146v15n02_01.

Kenyon, Samuel D., and Youngyol Yim Schanz. 2014. "Sex Trafficking: Examining Links to Prostitution and the Routine Activity Theory." *International Journal of Criminology and Sociology* 3: 61–76. https://doi.org/10.6000/1929-4409.2014 .03.05.

Kleemans, Edward R., Edwin W. Kruisbergen, and Ruud F. Kouwenberg. 2014. "Women, Brokerage and Transnational Organized Crime: Empirical Results from the Dutch Organized Crime Monitor." *Trends in Organized Crime* 17 (1): 16–30. https://doi.org/10.1007/s12117-013-9203-7.

Kligman, Gail, and Stephanie Limoncelli. 2005. "Trafficking Women after Social-ism: From, to, and through Eastern Europe." *Social Politics: International Studies in Gender, State and Society* 12 (1): 118–40.

Koegler, Erica, Whitney Howland, Patric Gibbons, Michelle Teti, and Hanni Stoklosa. 2020. "'When Her Visa Expired, the Family Refused to Renew It,' Intersections of Human Trafficking and Domestic Violence: Qualitative Document Analysis of Case Examples from a Major Midwest City." *Journal of Interpersonal Violence,* September, 0886260520957978. https://doi.org/10.1177/0886260520957978.

KTRK. 2018. "American Airlines Agent Saves 2 Girls from Alleged Human Trafficking Suspect." ABC13 Houston, February 18, 2018. https://abc13.com/american-airlines-ticketing-agent-saves-two-girls-from-human-trafficking-denice-miracle/3086779/.

Kulig, Teresa C., and Leah C. Butler. 2019. "From 'Whores' to 'Victims': The Rise and Status of Sex Trafficking Courts." *Victims & Offenders* 14 (3): 299–321. https://doi.org/10.1080/15564886.2019.1595242.

Laczko, Frank, and Marco A. Gramegna. 2003. "Developing Better Indicators of Human Trafficking." *Brown Journal of World Affairs* 10 (1): 179–94.

Lammasniemi, Laura. 2020. "International Legislation on White Slavery and Anti-Trafficking in the Early Twentieth Century." In *The Palgrave International Handbook of Human Trafficking,* edited by John Winterdyk and Jackie Jones, 67–78. Cham, Switzerland: Springer International. https://doi.org/10.1007/978-3-319-63058-8_112.

Langhorn, Mark. 2018. "Human Trafficking and Sexual Servitude: Organised Crime's Involvement in Australia." *Salus Journal* 6 (1): 25.

Le, Luong, and Caitlin Wyndham. 2022. "What We Know about Human Traffickers in Vietnam." *Anti-Trafficking Review,* no. 18 (April): 33–48. https://doi.org/10.14197/atr.201222183.

Lederer, Laura J. 2011. "Sold for Sex: The Link between Street Gangs and Trafficking in Persons." *Protection Project Journal of Human Rights and Civil Society,* 1–20. https://www.nawj.org/uploads/pdf/conferences/2015-Midyear/CLE/link_between_street_gangs_and_trafficking.pdf.

Lee, Maggy. 2011. *Trafficking and Global Crime Control.* London: SAGE.

———. 2014. "Gendered Discipline and Protective Custody of Trafficking Victims in Asia." *Punishment & Society* 16 (2): 206–22. https://doi.org/10.1177/1462474513517019.

Lewis-O'Connor, Annie, and Elaine J. Alpert. 2017. "Caring for Survivors Using a Trauma-Informed Care Framework." In *Human Trafficking Is a Public Health Issue: A Paradigm Expansion in the United States,* edited by Makini Chisolm-Straker and Hanni Stoklosa, 309–23. Cham, Switzerland: Springer International. https://doi.org/10.1007/978-3-319-47824-1_18.

Limoncelli, Stephanie A. 2009a. "Human Trafficking: Globalization, Exploitation, and Transnational Sociology." *Sociology Compass* 3 (1): 72–91. https://doi.org/10.1111/j.1751-9020.2008.00178.x.

———. 2009b. "The Trouble with Trafficking: Conceptualizing Women's Sexual Labor and Economic Human Rights." *Women's Studies International Forum* 32 (4): 261–69. https://doi.org/10.1016/j.wsif.2009.05.002.

Loibl, Elvira. 2020. "Child Trafficking for Adoption Purposes: A Criminological Analysis of the Illegal Adoption Market." In *The Palgrave International Handbook of Human Trafficking,* edited by John Winterdyk and Jackie Jones, 401–17. Cham, Switzerland: Springer International. https://doi.org/10.1007/978–3–319–63058–8_97.

Love, Debra A., Annie I. Fukushima, Tiana N. Rogers, Ethan Petersen, Ellen Brooks, and Charles R. Rogers. 2021. "Challenges to Reintegration: A Qualitative Intrinsic Case Study of Convicted Female Sex Traffickers." *Feminist Criminology,* October. https://doi.org/10.1177/15570851211045042.

Lugo, Kristina. 2020. "Gang Sex Trafficking in the United States." In *The Palgrave International Handbook of Human Trafficking,* edited by John Winterdyk and Jackie Jones, 521–40. Cham, Switzerland: Springer International. https://doi.org/10.1007/978–3–319–63058–8_31.

Lung, For-Wey, Tsung-Jen Lin, Yi-Ching Lu, and Bih-Ching Shu. 2004. "Personal Characteristics of Adolescent Prostitutes and Rearing Attitudes of Their Parents: A Structural Equation Model." *Psychiatry Research* 125 (3): 285–91. https://doi.org/10.1016/j.psychres.2003.12.019.

Lutnick, Alexandra. 2016. *Domestic Minor Sex Trafficking: Beyond Victims and Villains.* New York: Columbia University Press. https://doi.org/10.7312/lutn16920.

Lutnick, Alexandra, and Deborah Cohan. 2009. "Criminalization, Legalization or Decriminalization of Sex Work: What Female Sex Workers Say in San Francisco, USA." *Reproductive Health Matters* 17 (34): 38–46. https://doi.org/10.1016/S0968-8080(09)34469-9.

Lutya, Thozama Mandisa. 2010. "Lifestyles and Routine Activities of South African Teenagers at Risk of Being Trafficked for Involuntary Prostitution." *Journal of Child & Adolescent Mental Health* 22 (2): 91–110. https://doi.org/10.2989/17280583.2010.528578.

Macias-Konstantopoulos, Wendy, and Zheng B. Ma. 2017. "Physical Health of Human Trafficking Survivors: Unmet Essentials." In *Human Trafficking Is a Public Health Issue: A Paradigm Expansion in the United States,* edited by Makini Chisolm-Straker and Hanni Stoklosa, 185–210. Cham, Switzerland: Springer International. https://doi.org/10.1007/978-3-319-47824-1_11.

Mahalingam, Ravi, and Jatswan S. Sidhu. 2021. "Inside the Crime of Sex Trafficking in Sabah, Malaysia." *Journal of Human Trafficking* 7 (3): 308–24. https://doi.org/10.1080/23322705.2019.1710069.

Mahmoud, Toman Omar, and Christoph Trebesch. 2010. "The Economics of Human Trafficking and Labour Migration: Micro-Evidence from Eastern Europe." *Journal of Comparative Economics* 38 (2): 173–88. https://doi.org/10.1016/j.jce.2010.02.001.

Makin, David A., and Caroline Bye. 2018. "Commodification of Flesh: Data Visualization Techniques and Interest in the Licit Sex Industry." *Deviant Behavior* 39 (1): 46–63. https://doi.org/10.1080/01639625.2016.1260383.

Malarek, Victor. 2011. *The Natashas: The New Global Sex Trade.* Toronto: Penguin Canada.

Marchionni, Doreen Marie. 2012. "International Human Trafficking: An Agenda-Building Analysis of the US and British Press." *International Communication Gazette* 74 (2): 145–58. https://doi.org/10.1177/1748048511432600.

Marinova, Nadejda K., and Patrick James. 2012. "The Tragedy of Human Trafficking: Competing Theories and European Evidence." *Foreign Policy Analysis* 8 (3): 231–53. https://doi.org/10.1111/j.1743-8594.2011.00162.x.

Martin, Kimberly, Kelle Barrick, Nicholas J. Richardson, Dan Liao, and David Heller. 2019. "Violent Victimization Known to Law Enforcement in the Bakken Oil-Producing Region of Montana and North Dakota, 2006–2012." RTI International, February 2019. https://www.ojp.gov/ncjrs/virtual-library/abstracts/violent-victimization-known-law-enforcement-bakken-oil-producing.

Martin, Lauren, and Annie Hill. 2019. "Debunking the Myth of 'Super Bowl Sex Trafficking': Media Hype or Evidenced-Based Coverage." *Anti-Trafficking Review,* no. 13, 13–29.

Maskew, Trish. 2005. "Child Trafficking and Intercountry Adoption: The Cambodian Experience." *Cumberland Law Review* 35 (3): 619–38.

Matthews, Rick. 2011. "Marxist Criminology." In *Routledge Handbook of Critical Criminology,* edited by Walter S. DeKeseredy and Molly Dragiewicz, 110–21. New York: Routledge. https://doi.org/10.4324/9780203864326-15.

McCarthy, Lauren A. 2020. "A Gendered Perspective on Human Trafficking Perpetrators: Evidence from Russia." *Journal of Human Trafficking* 6 (1): 79–94. https://doi.org/10.1080/23322705.2019.1571302.

McDonald, Gavin G., Christopher Costello, Jennifer Bone, Reniel B. Cabral, Valerie Farabee, Timothy Hochberg, David Kroodsma, Tracey Mangin, Kyle C. Meng, and Oliver Zahn. 2021. "Satellites Can Reveal Global Extent of Forced Labor in the World's Fishing Fleet." *Proceedings of the National Academy of Sciences* 118 (3): 1–9. https://doi.org/10.1073/pnas.2016238117.

McNeal, Brittani A., and Jeffery T. Walker. 2016. "Parental Effects on the Exchange of Sex for Drugs or Money in Adolescents." *American Journal of Criminal Justice* 41 (4): 710–31. http://dx.doi.org/10.1007/s12103-015-9313-7.

Mehlman-Orozco, Kimberly. 2015. "Safe Harbor Legislation for Juvenile Victims of Sex Trafficking: A Myopic View of Improvements in Practice." *Social Inclusion* 3 (1): 52–62. https://doi.org/10.17645/si.v3i1.56.

Meier, Patricia J. 2008. "Small Commodities: How Child Traffickers Exploit Children and Families in Intercountry Adoption and What the United States Must Do to Stop Them." *Journal of Gender, Race & Justice* 12 (1): 185–224.

Merry, Sally Engle. 2016. *The Seductions of Quantification: Measuring Human Rights, Gender Violence, and Sex Trafficking.* Chicago: University of Chicago Press, 2016.

Merton, Robert K. 1938. "Social Structure and Anomie." *American Sociological Review* 3 (5): 672–82. https://doi.org/10.2307/2084686.

Messner, Steven F., and Richard Rosenfeld. 2013. *Crime and the American Dream.* 5th ed. Belmont, CA: Wadsworth Cengage Learning.

Miller, Kyle, Emily Kennedy, and Artur Dubrawski. 2016. "Do Public Events Affect Sex Trafficking Activity?" *arXiv:1602.05048 [stat.AP]*, February. http://arxiv.org/abs/1602.05048.

Mishra, Veerendra. 2015. *Combating Human Trafficking: Gaps in Policy and Law.* New Delhi, India: SAGE.

Mitchell, Kimberly J., David Finkelhor, and Janis Wolak. 2010. "Conceptualizing Juvenile Prostitution as Child Maltreatment: Findings from the National Juvenile Prostitution Study." *Child Maltreatment* 15 (1): 18–36. https://doi.org/10.1177/1077559509349443.

Mletzko, Deborah, Lucia Summers, and Ashley N. Arnio. 2018. "Spatial Patterns of Urban Sex Trafficking." *Journal of Criminal Justice* 58 (September): 87–96. https://doi.org/10.1016/j.jcrimjus.2018.07.008.

Mo, Cecilia Hyunjung. 2018. "Perceived Relative Deprivation and Risk: An Aspiration-Based Model of Human Trafficking Vulnerability." *Political Behavior* 40 (1): 247–77. https://doi.org/10.1007/s11109-017-9401-0.

Mollema, N., and S. S. Terblanche. 2017. "The Effectiveness of Sentencing as a Measure to Combat Human Trafficking." *South African Journal of Criminal Justice* 30 (2): 198–223. https://doi.org/10.10520/EJC-a96e28dea.

Motivans, Mark, and Howard N. Snyder. 2018. *Federal Prosecution of Human-Trafficking Cases, 2015.* U.S. Department of Justice, Bureau of Justice Statistics, June 2018. https://bjs.ojp.gov/content/pub/pdf/fphtc15.pdf.

Musto, Jennifer. 2016. *Control and Protect: Collaboration, Carceral Protection, and Domestic Sex Trafficking in the United States.* Oakland: University of California Press. https://search.ebscohost.com/login.aspx?direct=true&AuthType=ip,shib&db=e000xna&AN=1132446&site=ehost-live&scope=site&custid=wgc1.

Muzzatti, Stephen L., and Emma M. Smith. 2018. "Cultural Criminology." In *Routledge Handbook of Critical Criminology,* 2nd ed., edited by Walter S. DeKeseredy and Molly Dragiewicz, 107–19. New York: Routledge. https://doi.org/10.4324/9781315622040-10.

National Gang Intelligence Center. 2015. *National Gang Report 2015.* Department of Justice. https://www.fbi.gov/file-repository/stats-services-publications-national-gang-report-2015.pdf/view.

New, Stephen John. 2015. "Modern Slavery and the Supply Chain: The Limits of Corporate Social Responsibility?" *Supply Chain Management: An International Journal* 20 (6): 697–707. https://doi.org/10.1108/SCM-06-2015-0201.

Nguyen, Bich Ngoc, and Mark Gordon. 2020. "Human Trafficking and Gender Inequality in Remote Communities of Central Vietnam." *Journal of Social Change* 12 (1). https://doi.org/10.5590/JOSC.2020.12.1.11.

Nhan, Johnny, and Kendra N. Bowen. 2020. "Policing Internet Sex Trafficking." *Journal of Qualitative Criminal Justice & Criminology* 9 (1): 1–25. https://doi.org/10.21428/88de04a1.2d5eb46e.

Nichols, Andrea J. 2016. *Sex Trafficking in the United States: Theory, Research, Policy, and Practice.* New York: Columbia University Press.

———. 2017. "Global Inequality and Human Trafficking: The Organ and Tissue Trade." In *Broadening the Scope of Human Trafficking,* edited by Erin C. Heil and Andrea J. Nichols, 25–41. Durham, NC: Carolina Academic Press.

Nichols, Andrea J., and Erin C. Heil. 2015. "Challenges to Identifying and Prosecuting Sex Trafficking Cases in the Midwest United States." *Feminist Criminology* 10 (1): 7–35. https://doi.org/10.1177/1557085113519490.

———. 2022. "Human Trafficking of People with a Disability: An Analysis of State and Federal Cases." *Dignity: A Journal of Analysis of Exploitation and Violence* 7 (1). https://doi.org/10.23860/dignity.2022.07.01.01.

Norwood, Jeremy S. 2020. "Labor Exploitation of Migrant Farmworkers: Risks for Human Trafficking." *Journal of Human Trafficking* 6 (2): 209–20. https://doi.org/10.1080/23322705.2020.1690111.

Noyori-Corbett, Chie, and David P. Moxley. 2016. "Inequality of Women as a Factor Influencing Migration from Countries of Origin to the United States and Its Implications for Understanding Human Trafficking." *International Social Work* 59 (6): 890–903. https://doi.org/10.1177/0020872815580047.

O'Brien, Erin. 2016. "Human Trafficking Heroes and Villains: Representing the Problem in Anti-Trafficking Awareness Campaigns." *Social & Legal Studies* 25 (2): 205. http://dx.doi.org/10.1177/0964663915593410.

O'Brien, Jennifer E. 2018. "'Sometimes, Somebody Just Needs Somebody—Anybody—to Care:' The Power of Interpersonal Relationships in the Lives of Domestic Minor Sex Trafficking Survivors." *Child Abuse & Neglect* 81: 1–11.

O'Brien, Jennifer E., and Wen Li. 2020. "The Role of the Internet in the Grooming, Exploitation, and Exit of United States Domestic Minor Sex Trafficking Victims." *Journal of Children and Media* 14 (2): 187–203. https://doi.org/10.1080/17482798.2019.1688668.

Office to Monitor and Combat Trafficking in Persons. 2022. "3Ps: Prosecution, Protection, and Prevention." U.S. Department of State. https://www.state.gov/3ps-prosecution-protection-and-prevention/.

Oselin, Sharon S. 2014. *Leaving Prostitution: Getting Out and Staying Out of Sex Work.* New York: NYU Press.

Outshoorn, Joyce. 2005. "The Political Debates on Prostitution and Trafficking of Women." *Social Politics: International Studies in Gender, State and Society* 12 (1): 141–55.

———. 2015. "The Trafficking Policy Debates." In *Global Human Trafficking: Critical Issues and Contexts,* edited by Molly Dragiewicz, 7–22. New York: Routledge.

Owens, Colleen, Meredith Dank, Amy Farrell, Justin Breaux, Isela Banuelos, Rebecca Pfeffer, Ryan Heitsmith, Katie Bright, and Jack McDevitt. 2014. *Understanding the Organization, Operation, and Victimization Process of Labor Trafficking in the United States.* Urban Institute. https://www.urban.org/research/publication/understanding-organization-operation-and-victimization-process-labor-trafficking-united-states/view/full_report.

Pajnik, Mojca. 2010. "Media Framing of Trafficking." *International Feminist Journal of Politics* 12 (1): 45–64. https://doi.org/10.1080/14616740903429114.

Paraskevas, Alexandros, and Maureen Brookes. 2018. "Nodes, Guardians and Signs: Raising Barriers to Human Trafficking in the Tourism Industry." *Tourism Management* 67 (August): 147–56. https://doi.org/10.1016/j.tourman.2018.01.017.

Park, Robert Ezra, and Ernest Watson Burgess. 1925. *The City.* Chicago: University of Chicago Press.

Passas, Nikos, and Robert Agnew. 1997. *The Future of Anomie Theory.* Boston: Northeastern University Press.

Patritti, Carina. 2010. "Restoring Human Trafficking Victims through Victim-Offender Dialogue." *Cardozo Journal of Conflict Resolution* 12 (1): 217–44.

Peters, Alicia W. 2013. "'Things That Involve Sex Are Just Different': US Anti-Trafficking Law and Policy on the Books, in Their Minds, and in Action." *Anthropological Quarterly* 86 (1): 221–55.

Petrunov, Georgi. 2014. "Human Trafficking in Eastern Europe: The Case of Bulgaria." *Annals of the American Academy of Political and Social Science* 653 (1): 162–82.

Phillips, Jasmine. 2015. "Black Girls and the (Im)Possibilities of a Victim Trope: The Intersectional Failures of Legal and Advocacy Interventions in the Commercial Sexual Exploitation of Minors in the United States." *UCLA Law Review* 62 (6): 1642–75.

Pickles, John, and Shengjun Zhu. 2013. "The California Transparency in Supply Chains Act." SSRN Scholarly Paper. Capturing the Gains Working Paper 15. https://doi.org/10.2139/ssrn.2237437.

Pierce, Sarah C. 2010. "Turning a Blind Eye: U.S. Corporate Involvement in Modern Day Slavery." *Journal of Gender, Race & Justice* 14 (2): 577–600.

Planitzer, Julia, and Nora Katona. 2017. "Criminal Liability of Corporations for Trafficking in Human Beings for Labour Exploitation." *Global Policy* 8 (4): 505–11. https://doi.org/10.1111/1758-5899.12510.

Planitzer, Julia, Nora Katona, Barbara Linder, and Karin Lukas. 2018. "Corporate Liability for Trafficking in Human Beings: Gaps in Application and Ways Forward." *Journal of Trafficking and Human Exploitation* 2 (1): 19–41. https://doi.org/10.7590/245227718X15260460483724.

Polaris Project. 2016. *Sex Trafficking and LGBTQ+ Youth.* Polaris Project, May 1, 2016. https://polarisproject.org/resources/sex-trafficking-and-lgbtq-youth/.

———. 2019. *Human Trafficking at Home: Labor Trafficking of Domestic Workers.* Polaris Project, July 1, 2019. https://polarisproject.org/resources/human-trafficking-at-home-labor-trafficking-of-domestic-workers/.

Pollock, Joycelyn M., and Valerie Hollier. 2010. "T Visas: Prosecution Tool or Humanitarian Response?" *Women & Criminal Justice* 20 (1–2): 127–46. https://doi.org/10.1080/08974451003641172.

Potter, Kathleen, Judy Martin, and Sarah Romans. 1999. "Early Developmental Experiences of Female Sex Workers: A Comparative Study." *Australian and New Zealand Journal of Psychiatry* 33 (6): 935–40. https://doi.org/10.1046/j.1440-1614.1999.00655.x.

Raby, Kyla, and Nerida Chazal. 2022. "The Myth of the 'Ideal Offender': Challenging Persistent Human Trafficking Stereotypes through Emerging Australian Cases." *Anti-Trafficking Review,* no. 18 (April): 13–32. https://doi.org/10.14197/atr.201222182.

Rajaram, Shireen S., and Sriyani Tidball. 2018. "Survivors' Voices—Complex Needs of Sex Trafficking Survivors in the Midwest." *Behavioral Medicine* 44 (3): 189–98. https://doi.org/10.1080/08964289.2017.1399101.

Rao, Smriti, and Christina Presenti. 2012. "Understanding Human Trafficking Origin: A Cross-Country Empirical Analysis." *Feminist Economics* 18 (2): 231–63. https://doi.org/10.1080/13545701.2012.680978.

Raphael, Jody. 2020. "Parents as Pimps: Survivor Accounts of Trafficking of Children in the United States." *Dignity: A Journal of Analysis of Exploitation and Violence* 4 (4). https://doi.org/10.23860/dignity.2019.04.04.07.

Raphael, Jody, and Brenda Myers-Powell. 2010. *From Victims to Victimizers: Interviews with 25 Ex-pimps in Chicago.* Schiller DuCanto & Fleck Family Law Center of DePaul University College of Law. https://law.depaul.edu/academics/centers-institutes-initiatives/schiller-ducanto-fleck-family-law-center/Documents/interview_ex_pimps.pdf.

Reed, Shon M., M. Alexis Kennedy, Michele R. Decker, and Andrea N. Cimino. 2019. "Friends, Family, and Boyfriends: An Analysis of Relationship Pathways into Commercial Sexual Exploitation." *Child Abuse & Neglect* 90 (April): 1–12. https://doi.org/10.1016/j.chiabu.2019.01.016.

Reid, Joan A. 2011. "An Exploratory Model of Girl's Vulnerability to Commercial Sexual Exploitation in Prostitution." *Child Maltreatment* 16 (2): 146–57. https://doi.org/10.1177/1077559511404700.

———. 2012. "Exploratory Review of Route-Specific, Gendered, and Age-Graded Dynamics of Exploitation: Applying Life Course Theory to Victimization in Sex Trafficking in North America." *Aggression and Violent Behavior* 17 (3): 257–71. https://doi.org/10.1016/j.avb.2012.02.005.

———. 2014. "Risk and Resiliency Factors Influencing Onset and Adolescence-Limited Commercial Sexual Exploitation of Disadvantaged Girls: Risks Influencing Commercial Sexual Exploitation." *Criminal Behaviour and Mental Health* 24 (5): 332–44. https://doi.org/10.1002/cbm.1903.

———. 2016. "Entrapment and Enmeshment Schemes Used by Sex Traffickers." *Sexual Abuse* 28 (6): 491–511. https://doi.org/10.1177/1079063214544334.

———. 2018. "Sex Trafficking of Girls with Intellectual Disabilities: An Exploratory Mixed Methods Study." *Sexual Abuse* 30 (2): 107–31.

Reid, Joan A., Michael T. Baglivio, Alex R. Piquero, Mark A. Greenwald, and Nathan Epps. 2017. "Human Trafficking of Minors and Childhood Adversity in Florida." *American Journal of Public Health* 107 (2): 306–11. https://doi.org/10.2105/AJPH.2016.303564.

Reid, Joan A., Juliana Huard, and Rachael A. Haskell. 2015. "Family-Facilitated Juvenile Sex Trafficking." *Journal of Crime and Justice* 38 (3): 361–76. https://doi.org/10.1080/0735648X.2014.967965.

Reid, Joan A., and Shayne Jones. 2011. "Exploited Vulnerability: Legal and Psychological Perspectives on Child Sex Trafficking Victims." *Victims & Offenders* 6 (2): 207–31. https://doi.org/10.1080/15564886.2011.557327.

Reid, Joan A., and Alex R. Piquero. 2014. "Age-Graded Risks for Commercial Sexual Exploitation of Male and Female Youth." *Journal of Interpersonal Violence* 29 (9): 1747–77. https://doi.org/10.1177/0886260513511535.

———. 2016. "Applying General Strain Theory to Youth Commercial Sexual Exploitation." *Crime & Delinquency* 62 (3): 341–67. https://doi.org/10.1177/0011128713498213.

Renzetti, Claire M. 2011. "Feminist Perspectives in Criminology." In *Routledge Handbook of Critical Criminology,* edited by Walter S. DeKeseredy and Molly Dragiewicz, 110–21. New York: Routledge. https://doi.org/10.4324/9780203864326–15.

Richter, Marlise, and Wim Delva. 2011. *"Maybe It Will Be Better Once This World Cup Has Passed."* United Nations Population Fund. http://www.migration.org.za/wp-content/uploads/2017/08/%E2%80%9CMaybe-it-will-be-better-once-this-World-Cup-has-passed%E2%80%9D.pdf.

Ritzer, George. 2010. *Globalization: A Basic Text.* Malden, MA: Wiley-Blackwell.

Robertson, Mary A., and Arlene Sgoutas. 2012. "Thinking beyond the Category of Sexual Identity: At the Intersection of Sexuality and Human-Trafficking Policy." *Politics & Gender* 8 (3): 421–29. https://doi.org/10.1017/S1743923X12000414.

Roby, Jini L., and Stephanie Matsumura. 2002. "If I Give You My Child, Aren't We Family?" *Adoption Quarterly* 5 (4): 7–31. https://doi.org/10.1300/J145v05n04_02.

Rodriguez, Nickera. 2021. "The Plight of Cyntoia Brown: Can Safe Harbor Laws Prevent the Prosecution of Child Sex Trafficking Victims?" *University of Florida Journal of Law & Public Policy* 31 (3): 459–80.

Rodríguez-López, Silvia. 2018. "(De)Constructing Stereotypes: Media Representations, Social Perceptions, and Legal Responses to Human Trafficking." *Journal of Human Trafficking* 4 (1): 61–72. https://doi.org/10.1080/23322705.2018.1423447.

———. 2020. "Telling Victims from Criminals: Human Trafficking for the Purposes of Criminal Exploitation." In *The Palgrave International Handbook of Human Trafficking,* edited by John Winterdyk and Jackie Jones, 303–18. Cham, Switzerland: Springer International. https://doi.org/10.1007/978–3–319–63058–8_17.

Roe-Sepowitz, Dominique Eve, James Gallagher, Markus Risinger, and Kristine Hickle. 2015. "The Sexual Exploitation of Girls in the United States: The Role of Female Pimps." *Journal of Interpersonal Violence* 30 (16): 2814–30. https://doi.org/10.1177/0886260514554292.

Roe-Sepowitz, Dominique E., Kristine E. Hickle, Jaime Dahlstedt, and James Gallagher. 2014. "Victim or Whore: The Similarities and Differences between Victim's Experiences of Domestic Violence and Sex Trafficking." *Journal of Human Behavior in the Social Environment* 24 (8): 883–98. https://doi.org/10.1080/10911359.2013.840552.

Roetzel, Lara, Tifanie Petro, and Erica Ramstad. 2019. "Beyond the Cages: Sex Trafficking in South Dakota." *South Dakota Law Review* 64 (3): 346–66.

Rosenblatt, Katariina. 2014. "Determining the Vulnerability Factors, Lures and Recruitment Methods Used to Entrap American Children into Sex Trafficking." *Sociology and Criminology-Open Access* 02 (01). https://doi.org/10.4172/2375-4435.1000108.

Rothe, Dawn L., and David O. Friedrichs. 2015. *Crimes of Globalization: New Directions in Critical Criminology.* New York: Routledge.

Rothman, Emily F., Amy Farrell, Katherine Bright, and Jennifer Paruk. 2018. "Ethical and Practical Considerations for Collecting Research-Related Data from Commercially Sexually Exploited Children." *Behavioral Medicine* 44 (3): 250–58. http://dx.doi.org/10.1080/08964289.2018.1432550.

Rothman, Emily F., Hanni Stoklosa, Susie B. Baldwin, Makini Chisolm-Straker, Rumi Kato Price, and Holly G. Atkinson. 2017. "Public Health Research Priorities to Address US Human Trafficking." *American Journal of Public Health* 107 (7): 1045–47. https://doi.org/10.2105/AJPH.2017.303858.

Ruddell, Rick, and Sarah Britto. 2020. "A Perfect Storm: Violence toward Women in the Bakken Oil Patch." *International Journal of Rural Criminology* 5 (2): 204–27. https://doi.org/10.18061/1811/92030.

Russell, Amy M. 2014. "'Victims of Trafficking': The Feminisation of Poverty and Migration in the Gendered Narratives of Human Trafficking." *Societies* 4 (4): 532–48. https://doi.org/10.3390/soc4040532.

Russell, Ashley. 2018. "Human Trafficking: A Research Synthesis on Human-Trafficking Literature in Academic Journals from 2000–2014." *Journal of Human Trafficking* 4 (2): 114–36. https://doi.org/10.1080/23322705.2017.1292377.

Sampson, Robert J., and W. Byron Groves. 1989. "Community Structure and Crime: Testing Social-Disorganization Theory." *American Journal of Sociology* 94 (4): 774–802. https://doi.org/10.1086/229068.

Sampson, Robert J., and John H. Laub. 1990. "Crime and Deviance over the Life Course: The Salience of Adult Social Bonds." *American Sociological Review* 55 (5): 609–27. https://doi.org/10.2307/2095859.

———. 1992. "Crime and Deviance in the Life Course." *Annual Review of Sociology* 18:63–84.

Sanchez, Rosario V., Patricia M. Speck, and Patricia A. Patrician. 2019. "A Concept Analysis of Trauma Coercive Bonding in the Commercial Sexual Exploitation of Children." *Journal of Pediatric Nursing* 46 (May): 48–54. https://doi.org/10.1016/j.pedn.2019.02.030.

Sanford, Rachealle, Daniel E. Martínez, and Ronald Weitzer. 2016. "Framing Human Trafficking: A Content Analysis of Recent U.S. Newspaper Articles." *Journal of Human Trafficking* 2 (2): 139–55. https://doi.org/10.1080/23322705.2015.1107341.

Santamaria, Kelsey Y. 2021. *Human Trafficking: Key Federal Criminal Statutes.* Congressional Research Service, October 7, 2021. https://crsreports.congress.gov/product/pdf/IF/IF11942.

Sassen, Saskia. 2002. "Women's Burden: Counter-Geographies of Globalization and the Feminization of Survival." *Nordic Journal of International Law* 71 (2): 255–74. https://doi.org/10.1163/157181002761931378.

Saunders, Penelope, and Gretchen Soderlund. 2003. "Threat or Opportunity? Sexuality, Gender and the Ebb and Flow of Trafficking as Discourse." *Canadian Woman Studies/Les cahiers de la femme* 22 (3–4). https://cws.journals.yorku.ca/index.php/cws/article/view/6409.

Savona, Ernesto U., and Sonia Stefanizzi. 2007. *Measuring Human Trafficking: Complexities and Pitfalls.* New York: Springer Science & Business Media.

Sawadogo, Wilfried Relwende. 2012. "The Challenges of Transnational Human Trafficking in West Africa." *African Studies Quarterly; Gainesville* 13 (1/2): 95–115.

Scarpa, Silvia. 2020. "UN Palermo Trafficking Protocol Eighteen Years On: A Critique." In *The Palgrave International Handbook of Human Trafficking,* edited by John Winterdyk and Jackie Jones, 623–40. Cham, Switzerland: Springer International. https://doi.org/10.1007/978-3-319-63058-8_38.

Schaffner, Jessica E. 2014. "Optimal Deterrence: A Law and Economics Assessment of Sex and Labor Trafficking Law in the United States Federal Sentencing Challenges Post-Booker: Criminal Justice Institute Symposium—Comment." *Houston Law Review* 51 (5): 1519–54.

Schloenhardt, Andreas, and Rebekkah Markey-Towler. 2016. "Non-criminalisation of Victims of Trafficking in Persons—Principles, Promises, and Perspectives." *Groningen Journal of International Law* 4 (1): 10. https://doi.org/10.21827/59db68fc35c13.

Schmalleger, Frank. 2020. *Criminology (Justice Series).* 5th ed. Indianapolis, IN: Pearson. https://www.pearson.com/content/one-dot-com/one-dot-com/us/en/higher-education/program.html.

Schönhöfer, Johanna. 2017. "Political Determinants of Efforts to Protect Victims of Human Trafficking." *Crime, Law and Social Change* 67 (2): 153–85.

Schwarz, Corinne, Daniel Alvord, Dorothy Daley, Megha Ramaswamy, Emily Rauscher, and Hannah Britton. 2019. "The Trafficking Continuum: Service Providers' Perspectives on Vulnerability, Exploitation, and Trafficking." *Affilia* 34 (1): 116–32. https://doi.org/10.1177/0886109918803648.

Schwarz, Corinne, and Hannah E. Britton. 2015. "Queering the Support for Trafficked Persons: LGBTQ Communities and Human Trafficking in the Heartland." *Perspectives on Human Trafficking and Modern Forms of Slavery* 3 (1). https://doi.org/10.17645/si.v3i1.172.

Shanley, Erin, and Robyn Jordan. 2017. "Sex Trafficking in Indian Country." In *Human Trafficking Is a Public Health Issue: A Paradigm Expansion in the United States,* edited by Makini Chisolm-Straker and Hanni Stoklosa, 123–40. Cham, Switzerland: Springer International. https://doi.org/10.1007/978-3-319-47824-1_8.

Shavers, Anna Williams. 2012. "Human Trafficking, the Rule of Law, and Corporate Social Responsibility." *South Carolina Journal of International Law and Business* 9 (1): 39–88.

Shaw, C. R., and H. D. McKay. 1942. *Juvenile Delinquency and Urban Areas.* Chicago: University of Chicago Press.

Shelley, Louise I. 2010. *Human Trafficking: A Global Perspective.* New York: Cambridge University Press.

Shen, Anqi. 2016. "Female Perpetrators in Internal Child Trafficking in China: An Empirical Study." *Journal of Human Trafficking* 2 (1): 63–77. https://doi.org/10.1080/23322705.2016.1136537.

Shinkle, Whitney. 2007. *Preventing Human Trafficking: An Evaluation of Current Efforts.* Transatlantic Perspectives on Migration, Policy Brief #3, August 2007. Institute for the Study of International Migration.

Shively, Michael, Sarah Kuck Jalbert, Ryan Kling, William Rhodes, Peter Finn, Chris Flygare, Laura Tierney, et al. 2008. *Final Report on the Evaluation of the First Offender Prostitution Program.* National Institute of Justice, March 7, 2008. https://www.ojp.gov/pdffiles1/nij/grants/221894.pdf.

Shively, Michael, Kristina Kliorys, Kristin Wheeler, and Dana Hunt. 2012. *A National Overview of Prostitution and Sex Trafficking Demand Reduction Efforts, Final Report.* National Institute of Justice, April 30, 2012. https://www.ojp.gov/pdffiles1/nij/grants/238796.pdf.

Shively, Michael, Kamala Smith, Sarah Jalbert, and Omri Drucker. 2016. *Human Trafficking Organizations and Facilitators: A Detailed Profile and Interviews with Convicted Traffickers in the United States.*" National Institute of Justice, March 2016. https://www.ojp.gov/ncjrs/virtual-library/abstracts/human-trafficking-organizations-and-facilitators-detailed-profile.

Siegel, Dina, and Sylvia de Blank. 2010. "Women Who Traffic Women: The Role of Women in Human Trafficking Networks—Dutch Cases." *Global Crime* 11 (4): 436–47. https://doi.org/10.1080/17440572.2010.519528.

Skeldon, R. 2002. "Trafficking: A Perspective from Asia." *International Migration* 38 (3): 7–30. https://doi.org/10.1111/1468–2435.00113.

Skilbrei, May-Len, and Marianne Tveit. 2008. "Defining Trafficking through Empirical Work: Blurred Boundaries and Their Consequences." *Gender, Technology and Development* 12 (1): 9–30. http://dx.doi.org/10.1177/097185240701200103.

Smith, Stacie Reimer. 2013. "Underutilization of the T-Visa: Comparing the T-Visa to Similar Temporary Residence Programs around the World." *Georgetown Journal of Gender and the Law* 14 (3): 719–48.

Smolenski, Carol, and Sarah Ingerman. 2017. "Trafficking of Children within the United States." In *Human Trafficking Is a Public Health Issue: A Paradigm Expansion in the United States,* edited by Makini Chisolm-Straker and Hanni Stoklosa, 93–104. Cham, Switzerland: Springer International. https://doi.org/10.1007/978–3–319–47824–1_6.

Smolin, David M. 2006. "Child Laundering: How the Intercountry Adoption System Legitimizes and Incentivizes the Practices of Buying, Trafficking, Kidnapping, and Stealing Children." *Wayne Law Review* 52 (1): 113–200.

Spidel, A., C. Greaves, B. S. Cooper, H. Hervé, R. D. Hare, and J. C. Yuille. 2006. "The Psychopath as Pimp." *Canadian Journal of Police and Security Services* 4 (4): 193–99.

Sprang, Ginny, and Jennifer Cole. 2018. "Familial Sex Trafficking of Minors: Trafficking Conditions, Clinical Presentation, and System Involvement." *Journal of Family Violence* 33 (3): 185–95. https://doi.org/10.1007/s10896–018–9950-y.

Stark, Rodney. 1987. "Deviant Places: A Theory of the Ecology of Crime." *Criminology* 25 (4): 893–910.

Stickle, Wendy, Shelby Hickman, and Christine White. 2020. *Human Trafficking: A Comprehensive Exploration of Modern Day Slavery*. Thousand Oaks, CA: SAGE.

Stoklosa, Hanni, Elizabeth Showalter, Anna Melnick, and Emily F. Rothman. 2017. "Health Care Providers' Experience with a Protocol for the Identification, Treatment, and Referral of Human-Trafficking Victims." *Journal of Human Trafficking* 3 (3): 182–92. https://doi.org/10.1080/23322705.2016.1194668.

Stone, Marjorie. 2005. "Twenty-First Century Global Sex Trafficking: Migration, Capitalism, Class, and Challenges for Feminism Now." *English Studies in Canada; Edmonton* 31 (2/3): 31–38.

Such, E., C. Laurent, R. Jaipaul, and S. Salway. 2020. "Modern Slavery and Public Health: A Rapid Evidence Assessment and an Emergent Public Health Approach." *Public Health* 180 (March): 168–79. https://doi.org/10.1016/j.puhe.2019.10.018.

Surtees, Rebecca. 2008. "Traffickers and Trafficking in Southern and Eastern Europe: Considering the Other Side of Human Trafficking." *European Journal of Criminology* 5 (1): 39–68. https://doi.org/10.1177/1477370807084224.

Sutherland, Edwin H. 1947. "Differential Association." In *Classics of Criminology*, 4th ed., edited by Joseph H. Jacoby, Theresa A. Severance, and Alan S. Bruce, 299–301. Long Grove, IL: Waveland Press.

SWAN (Sex Workers Alliance Network) and GHJP (Global Health Justice Partnership). 2020. *Sex Work vs Trafficking: How They Are Different and Why It Matters*. SWAN and Yale GHJP. https://law.yale.edu/sites/default/files/area/center/ghjp/documents/issue_brief_sex_work_vs_trafficking_v2.pdf.

Swenstein, Abigail, and Kate Mogulescu. 2016. "Resisting the Carceral: The Need to Align Anti-trafficking Efforts with Movements for Criminal Justice Reform." *Anti-Trafficking Review*, no. 6 (May): 118–22. https://doi.org/10.14197/atr.201216610.

Sykes, Gresham M., and David Matza. 1957. "Techniques of Neutralization: A Theory of Delinquency." *American Sociological Review* 22 (6): 664–70. https://doi.org/10.2307/2089195.

Szablewska, Natalia, and Krzysztof Kubacki. 2018. "Anti-human Trafficking Campaigns: A Systematic Literature Review." *Social Marketing Quarterly* 24 (2): 104–22. https://doi.org/10.1177/1524500418771611.

TAT (Truckers Against Trafficking). 2020. *2020 TAT Annual Report*. TAT. https://truckersagainsttrafficking.org/wp-content/uploads/2021/01/2020-TAT-Annual-Report.pdf.

Teigen, Anne. 2018. *Prosecuting Human Traffickers: Recent Legislative Enactments*. National Conference of State Legislature. https://www.ncsl.org/Portals/1/HTML_LargeReports/Prosecuting_Traffickers_091818_32767.pdf.

Thiemann, Inga. 2016. "Villains and Victims, but No Workers: Why a Prosecution-Focussed Approach to Human Trafficking Fails Trafficked Persons." *Anti-Trafficking Review*, no. 6 (May): 126–29. https://doi.org/10.14197/atr.201216612.

Tiefenbrun, Susan W. 2006. "Updating the Domestic and International Impact of the U.S. Victims of Trafficking Protection Act of 2000: Does Law Deter Crime

International Justice and Shifting Paradigms." *Case Western Reserve Journal of International Law* 38 (2): 249–80.

Tilley, Nick. 2014. *Crime Prevention*. New York: Routledge.

Tillyer, Marie Skubak, Michael R. Smith, and Rob Tillyer. 2023. "Findings from the U.S. National Human Trafficking Hotline." *Journal of Human Trafficking* 9 (3): 398–407. https://doi.org/10.1080/23322705.2021.1925493.

Todres, Jonathan. 2009. "Law, Otherness, and Human Trafficking." *Santa Clara Law Review* 49 (3): 605–72.

———. 2010. "Moving Upstream: The Merits of a Public Health Law Approach to Human Trafficking." *North Carolina Law Review* 89 (2): 447–506.

Tomasiewicz, Meaghan. 2018. *Sex Trafficking of Transgender and Gender Nonconforming Youth in the United States*. Center for the Human Rights of Children. https://ecommons.luc.edu/chrc/16.

Tribal Insights Brief. 2016. *Human and Sex Trafficking: Trends and Responses across Indian Country*. National Congress of American Indians Policy Research Center. https://www.ncai.org/policy-research-center/research-data/prc-publications/TraffickingBrief.pdf.

Tripp, Tara M., and Jennifer McMahon-Howard. 2016. "Perception vs. Reality: The Relationship between Organized Crime and Human Trafficking in Metropolitan Atlanta." *American Journal of Criminal Justice* 41 (4): 732–64. https://doi.org/10.1007/s12103-015-9315-5.

Troshynski, Emily, and Jennifer Blank. 2019. "Interviews with Human Traffickers: Perceptions of Sex and Violence." In *Broadening the Scope of Human Trafficking Research: A Reader,* 2nd ed., edited by Erin C. Heil and Andrea J. Nichols, 1–27. Durham, NC: Carolina Academic Press. https://cap-press.com/pdf/HeilNichols2eOnlineOnlyChapters/heil%20nichols%20online%20chapter%2001%20Troshynski.pdf.

Truong, Thanh-Dam. 2003. "Gender, Exploitative Migration, and the Sex Industry: A European Perspective." *Gender, Technology and Development* 7 (1): 31–52. https://doi.org/10.1177/097185240300700102.

———. 2006. "Poverty, Gender and Human Trafficking in Sub-Saharan Africa: Rethinking Best Practices in Migration Management." UNESCO. https://unesdoc.unesco.org/ark:/48223/pf0000143227.

Tsai, Laura Cordisco, Vanntheary Lim, and Channtha Nhanh. 2020. "Perspectives of Survivors of Human Trafficking and Sexual Exploitation on Their Relationships with Shelter Staff: Findings from a Longitudinal Study in Cambodia." *British Journal of Social Work* 50 (1): 176–94. https://doi.org/10.1093/bjsw/bcz128.

———. 2022. "Perspectives of Boys on Their Experiences in Human Trafficking Shelter Programming in Cambodia." *Journal of Human Behavior in the Social Environment* 32 (1): 17–32. https://doi.org/10.1080/10911359.2020.1845902.

Tseloni, Andromachi, and Ken Pease. 2003. "Repeat Personal Victimization: Boosts or Flags." *British Journal of Criminology* 43 (1): 196–212.

Turner, Chad. 2014. "Sometimes It Is Better Not to Be Unique: The U.S. Department of State View on Intercountry Adoption and Child Trafficking and Why It Should Change." *Duke Forum for Law & Social Change (DFLSC)* 6 (1): 91–112.

Turner, Jackie, and Liz Kelly. 2009. "Trade Secrets: Intersections between Diasporas and Crime Groups in the Constitution of the Human Trafficking Chain." *British Journal of Criminology* 49 (2): 184–201.

Twis, Mary K. 2019. "Predicting Different Types of Victim-Trafficker Relationships: A Multinomial Logistic Regression Analysis." *Journal of Human Trafficking* 6 (4): 450–66. https://doi.org/10.1080/23322705.2019.1634963.

Twis, Mary K., Lynzee Kirschner, and Don Greenwood. 2021. "Trafficked by a Friend: A Qualitative Analysis of Adolescent Trafficking Victims' Archival Case Files." *Child & Adolescent Social Work Journal* 38 (6): 611–20. https://doi.org/10.1007/s10560-020-00662-8.

Tyldum, Guri. 2010. "Limitations in Research on Human Trafficking." *International Migration* 48 (5): 1–13. https://doi.org/10.1111/j.1468-2435.2009.00597.x.

Tyldum, Guri, and Anette Brunovskis. 2005. "Describing the Unobserved: Methodological Challenges in Empirical Studies on Human Trafficking." *International Migration* 43 (1/2): 17–34.

UN (United Nations). 2000a. *A Protocol to Prevent, Suppress and Punish Trafficking in Persons, Especially Women and Children, Supplementing the United Nations Convention against Transnational Organized Crime.* United Nations, Treaty Series, vol. 2237, 319, November 15, 2000. https://treaties.un.org/Pages/ViewDetails.aspx?src=TREATY&mtdsg_no=XVIII-12-a&chapter=18.

UN (United Nations). 2000b. *United Nations Convention against Transnational Organized Crime.* United Nations, Treaty Series, vol. 2225, 209, November 15, 2000. https://treaties.un.org/Pages/ViewDetails.aspx?src=TREATY&mtdsg_no=XVIII-12&chapter=18&clang=_en.

UNODC (United Nations Office of Drugs and Crime). 2009. *International Framework for Action: To Implement the Trafficking in Persons Protocol.* New York: UNODC. https://www.unodc.org/documents/human-trafficking/Framework_for_Action_TIP.pdf.

———. 2011. *The Role of Corruption in Trafficking in Persons.* Issue Paper. UNODC. https://www.unodc.org/documents/human-trafficking/2011/Issue_Paper_-_The_Role_of_Corruption_in_Trafficking_in_Persons.pdf.

———. 2020. *Global Report on Trafficking in Persons.* UNODC. https://www.unodc.org/unodc/data-and-analysis/glotip.html.

Urban, Lynn S., and Victoria Arends. 2018. "The (In)Frequency of Organized Crime Involvement: Human Trafficking in Missouri." *Journal of Gang Research* 25 (4): 23–43.

U.S. Department of State. 2015. *Trafficking in Persons Report.* U.S. Department of State, July 2015. https://2009-2017.state.gov/j/tip/rls/tiprpt/2015/index.htm.

U.S. GAO (Government Accountability Office). 2006. *Human Trafficking: Better Data, Strategy, and Reporting Needed to Enhance U.S. Antitrafficking Efforts Abroad.* U.S. GAO, July 18, 2006. https://www.gao.gov/products/gao-06-825.

Valenzuela, Robin. 2016. "The Nashville John School: Affective Governance and the Reintegrative Shaming Approach." *Human Organization* 75 (3): 249–57. https://doi.org/10.17730/1938–3525–75.3.249.

Veldhuizen-Ochodničanová, Eva, and Elizabeth L. Jeglic. 2021. "Of Madams, Mentors and Mistresses: Conceptualising the Female Sex Trafficker in the United States." *International Journal of Law, Crime and Justice* 64 (March): 100455. https://doi.org/10.1016/j.ijlcj.2020.100455.

Vermeulen, G., Y. Van Damme, and Wendy De Bondt. 2010. "Perceived Involvement of 'Organised Crime' in Human Trafficking and Smuggling." *Revue internationale de droit penal* 81 (1): 247–73.

Viuhko, Minna. 2018. "Hardened Professional Criminals, or Just Friends and Relatives? The Diversity of Offenders in Human Trafficking." *International Journal of Comparative and Applied Criminal Justice* 42 (2–3): 177–93. https://doi.org/10.1080/01924036.2017.1391106.

Vocks, Judith, and Jan Nijboer. 2000. "The Promised Land: A Study of Trafficking in Women from Central and Eastern Europe to the Netherlands." *European Journal on Criminal Policy and Research* 8 (3): 379–88. https://doi.org/10.1023/A:1008785214932.

von Hentig, Hans. 1941. *The Criminal & His Victim: Studies in the Sociobiology of Crime.* New York: Schocken Books.

Weber, Michael A., Katarina C. O'Regan, and Liana W. Rosen. 2019. *The State Department's "Trafficking in Persons" Report: Scope, Aid Restrictions, and Methodology.* Congressional Research Service, October 30, 2019. https://sgp.fas.org/crs/row/R44953.pdf.

Weiss, Ayla. 2012. "Ten Years of Fighting Trafficking: Critiquing the Trafficking in Persons Report through the Case of South Korea." *Asian-Pacific Law and Policy Journal* 13 (2): 304–39.

Weitzer, Ronald. 2007. "The Social Construction of Sex Trafficking: Ideology and Institutionalization of a Moral Crusade." *Politics & Society* 35 (3): 447–75. https://doi.org/10.1177/0032329207304319.

———. 2010. "The Movement to Criminalize Sex Work in the United States." *Journal of Law and Society* 37 (1): 61–84. https://doi.org/10.1111/j.1467–6478.2010.00495.x.

———. 2011. "Sex Trafficking and the Sex Industry: The Need for Evidence-Based Theory and Legislation Criminology." *Journal of Criminal Law and Criminology* 101 (4): 1337–70.

———. 2014. "New Directions in Research on Human Trafficking." *Annals of the American Academy of Political and Social Science* 653 (1): 6–24. https://doi.org/10.1177/0002716214521562.

———. 2015a. "Human Trafficking and Contemporary Slavery." *Annual Review of Sociology* 41 (1): 223–42. https://doi.org/10.1146/annurev-soc-073014–112506.

———. 2015b. "Researching Prostitution and Sex Trafficking Comparatively." *Sexuality Research and Social Policy* 12 (2): 81–91. https://doi.org/10.1007/s13178–014–0168–3.

————. 2020. "The Campaign against Sex Work in the United States: A Successful Moral Crusade." *Sexuality Research and Social Policy* 17 (3): 399–414. https://doi.org/10.1007/s13178-019-00404-1.

Wells, Melissa, Kimberly J. Mitchell, and Kai Ji. 2012. "Exploring the Role of the Internet in Juvenile Prostitution Cases Coming to the Attention of Law Enforcement." *Journal of Child Sexual Abuse* 21 (3): 327–42. https://doi.org/10.1080/10538712.2012.669823.

Wheaton, Elizabeth M., Edward J. Schauer, and Thomas V. Galli. 2010. "Economics of Human Trafficking." *International Migration* 48 (4): 114–41. https://doi.org/10.1111/j.1468-2435.2009.00592.x.

Whoriskey, Peter, and Rachel Siegel. 2019. "Hershey, Nestle and Mars Won't Promise Their Chocolate Is Free of Child Labor." *Washington Post,* June 5, 2019. https://www.washingtonpost.com/graphics/2019/business/hershey-nestle-mars-chocolate-child-labor-west-africa/.

Wijkman, Miriam, and Edward Kleemans. 2019. "Female Offenders of Human Trafficking and Sexual Exploitation." *Crime, Law and Social Change* 72 (1): 53–72. https://doi.org/10.1007/s10611-019-09840-x.

Williams, Linda M. 2010. "Harm and Resilience among Prostituted Teens: Broadening Our Understanding of Victimisation and Survival." *Social Policy and Society* 9 (2): 243–54. https://doi.org/10.1017/S1474746409990376.

Wilson, Michael, and Erin O'Brien. 2016. "Constructing the Ideal Victim in the United States of America's Annual Trafficking in Persons Reports." *Crime, Law and Social Change* 65 (1–2): 29–45.

Winterdyk, John. 2020. "Explaining Human Trafficking: Modern Day-Slavery." In *The Palgrave International Handbook of Human Trafficking,* edited by John Winterdyk and Jackie Jones, 1257–74. Cham, Switzerland: Springer International. https://doi.org/10.1007/978-3-319-63058-8_68.

Winters, Georgia M., Sarah Schaaf, Rasmus F. Grydehøj, Cecilia Allan, Amber Lin, and Elizabeth L. Jeglic. 2022. "The Sexual Grooming Model of Child Sex Trafficking." *Victims & Offenders* 17 (1): 60–77. https://doi.org/10.1080/15564886.2021.1926031.

Wolken, Cynthia L. 2006. "Feminist Legal Theory and Human Trafficking in the United States: Towards a New Framework." *University of Maryland Law Journal of Race, Religion, Gender & Class* 6 (2): 407–38.

Wooditch, Alese. 2011. "The Efficacy of the Trafficking in Persons Report: A Review of the Evidence." *Criminal Justice Policy Review* 22 (4): 471–93. https://doi.org/10.1177/0887403410386217.

Wright, Eric R., Ana LaBoy, Kara Tsukerman, Nicholas Forge, Erin Ruel, Renee Shelby, Madison Higbee, et al. 2021. "The Prevalence and Correlates of Labor and Sex Trafficking in a Community Sample of Youth Experiencing Homelessness in Metro-Atlanta." *Social Sciences* 10 (2): 32. https://doi.org/10.3390/socsci10020032.

Xian, Kathryn, Shaylin Chock, and Dustin Dwiggins. 2017. "LGBTQ Youth and Vulnerability to Sex Trafficking." In *Human Trafficking Is a Public Health Issue: A Paradigm Expansion in the United States,* edited by Makini Chisolm-Straker and Hanni Stoklosa, 141–52. Cham, Switzerland: Springer International. https://doi.org/10.1007/978-3-319-47824-1_9.

Yousaf, Farhan Navid, and Bandana Purkayastha. 2015. "'I Am Only Half Alive': Organ Trafficking in Pakistan amid Interlocking Oppressions." *International Sociology* 30 (6): 637–53. https://doi.org/10.1177/0268580915605648.

Zeegers, Nicolle, and Martina Althoff. 2015. "Regulating Human Trafficking by Prostitution Policy—An Assessment of the Dutch and Swedish Prostitution Legislation and Its Effects on Women's Self-Determination." *European Journal of Comparative Law and Governance* 2 (4): 351–78.

Zhang, Sheldon. 2007. *Smuggling and Trafficking in Human Beings: All Roads Lead to America.* Westport, CT: Praeger.

———. 2009. "Beyond the 'Natasha' Story—A Review and Critique of Current Research on Sex Trafficking." *Global Crime* 10 (3): 178–95.

———. 2010. *Sex Trafficking in a Border Community: A Field Study of Sex Trafficking in Tijuana, Mexico.* San Diego: San Diego State University. https://doi.org/10.1037/e725612011-001.

———. 2012. "Measuring Labor Trafficking: A Research Note." *Crime, Law and Social Change* 85 (4): 469–82.

Zhang, Sheldon, Michael W. Spiller, Brian Karl Finch, and Qin Yang. 2014. "Estimating Labor Trafficking among Unauthorized Migrant Workers in San Diego." *Annals of the American Academy of Political and Social Science* 653 (1): 65–86.

Zhang, Weiwu. 2000. "An Interdisciplinary Synthesis of Framing." Paper presented at the Annual Conference of the Association for Education in Journalism and Mass Communication, Phoenix, AZ, August 2000.

INDEX

abduction or kidnapping, 10, 85
abolitionism. *See* sex work; abolition of
Afghanistan, 16
Africa, 55, 73, 89, 91, 118, 131
age-graded theory, 135–138
Agnew, Robert, 81–82, 86
Akers, Ronald, 101
anomie theory: Émile Durkheim and, 81–82; institutional anomie theory, 88–89
anti-trafficking: efforts, 6, 12, 26, 28–31, 68, 78, 123, 129; organizations and programs, 31, 68, 111, 129, 132, 140, 143; policies and laws, 7–10, 12, 17–18, 119, 121, 125
Argentina, 118
Arizona, 129
Asia, 55, 131
Atlanta, 53, 77, 92
attachment: parental attachment, 99–101; school attachment, 99–101; social control theory and, 98–99
Australia, 43, 67, 92
awareness, 3, 9, 22, 25–27, 35, 38, 43, 48–49, 51, 68, 109, 111, 114, 116, 124; campaigns and, 26, 31, 46, 109, 113, 141–143

Backpage, 77–79
Bakken oil region, 79–80
Balkan region, 17, 91, 127
Bangladesh, 52

barriers: to exiting, 65, 102, 138; to help, 30, 53–54, 69, 129; to investigation, 27, 37, 132
Beccaria, Cesare, 33–34
Becker, Howard, 107
Bentham, Jeremy, 34
Ben-Yehuda, Nachman, 107
Bolivia, 88–89, 118
border controls, 18, 26, 31, 51, 110, 119, 142. *See also* migration
Boston, 143
Braithwaite, John, 108–109
Bronfenbrenner, Urie, 140
brothels, 6–7, 18, 25, 43, 76, 110–111, 128, 132
Brown, Cyntoia, 65–66
Bulgaria, 93
Burgess, Ernest, 71–72
Burgess, Robert L., 101
buyers, 41–42, 50, 86, 107–109, 121, 129, 131. *See also* johns

California, 39, 79, 94–96
Cambodia, 84, 86, 88–89, 118, 133
campaigns, 26, 31, 46, 109, 113, 141–143. *See also* awareness
Canada, 60, 76, 123
causes of trafficking, 13–18, 26, 84, 114–115, 140–141; corruption, 17–18, 29, 34, 45, 47, 55, 75, 89, 106, 114, 125; conflict, 16–17, 26, 38–39, 47, 75, 100, 114, 137; economic and income inequality,

Nevada, 40, 102
New York, 77
Nigeria, 73, 118
North Carolina, 75
North Dakota, 79–80

Ohio, 76, 137
Ohlin, Lloyd E., 89–90
offenders. *See* traffickers
organ trafficking, 3, 6, 9–10, 22, 62, 83–84, 86
organized crime, 17, 26, 31, 44, 90–95, 103, 110, 116, 119

Palermo Protocol (2000), 9–10, 25–27, 31, 90, 119, 142
parents. *See* family
Park, Robert, 71–72
peacemaking criminology. *See* restorative justice
peers, 53, 68–69, 86, 98, 101, 103–104, 138, 141
Philippines, 16, 47, 131
police, 18, 24, 27–28, 34, 36, 41–43, 47–78, 55–56, 74–77, 79, 93, 95–96, 106, 109, 111, 119, 131, 139; raids by, 111, 132–133. *See also* law enforcement
poverty, 11, 15–16, 47, 52, 55, 72–75, 80, 83–85, 88, 96, 114, 116–118, 122, 125–126, 130, 137, 141–143. *See also* inequality: economic and income inequality
prevention of human trafficking, 26, 31, 40, 47, 50, 87, 119–120, 122–124, 139–143; criminal justice approach, 3, 26, 111, 114, 119, 121, 123–124, 140; demand reduction, 31, 46, 107–109, 142; human rights approach, 3, 18, 25–26, 30, 119–120; root causes and, 13, 26, 31, 84, 114, 116, 121–123, 140–143. *See also* legislation
procedural justice, 123–124
prosecution, 7, 18, 22, 26–30, 34–37, 39–40, 44, 65, 67, 78, 80, 92, 116, 119–123, 125, 127–128, 140, 142
prosecutors, 35–37, 78, 116
prostitution. *See* sex work
protection, 7, 10, 16, 17–18, 26, 28–30, 41–42, 54, 64, 67, 72, 79, 88, 95,

99–101, 118–122, 125–126, 130–133, 136, 139, 142
psychological theories, 59–63
psychopathy, 60–61
public health model, 135, 139–143

qualitative methods, 23, 43, 95, 125, 140
quantitative methods, 21, 23
queer criminology, 113, 124, 128–130

race: discrimination and, 16, 80, 130, 141; stereotypes and, 115, 131–132; victims and, 7–9, 94, 109, 130–132. *See also* Indigenous
raids, 111, 132–133
rational choice theory, 43–46
rationalizations. *See* techniques of neutralization
recruitment, 7–10, 12, 19, 22–23, 26, 45–47, 52–56, 62, 64–65, 77–78, 83–86, 94, 96, 99–101, 103–105, 127–128
reintegrative shaming theory, 108–109
restorative justice, 123–124
retributive justice, 123
Rosenfeld, Richard, 82
runaways, 52–53, 80, 88, 96, 106, 129–130
Russia, 115, 118, 127

Sampson, Robert J., 72, 135–136
San Diego, 24, 95
San Francisco, 28, 108
Saudi Arabia, 120
school, 53, 71, 74, 82, 86, 88, 95–96, 100–101, 126, 129, 136–137, 141, 143. *See also* education
sentencing, 27, 56, 66, 122; deterrent effects of, 34–36. *See also* prosecution
SESTA-FOSTA (2018), 78–79
sex trafficking, 8–10, 16, 22–23, 25, 50, 56–57, 60–64, 66, 68, 73, 75–77, 80, 86, 88, 91–96; buyers and, 41, 50, 80, 86, 107–109, 121, 129, 131; commercial sexual exploitation, 10, 21, 25, 40–44, 50, 53, 56, 62, 64, 67, 74–75, 86–87, 94–95, 102–104, 108, 115, 122, 136–137, 139, 143; conflation with sex work, 11, 20, 42–43, 78, 110–111, 114; domestic minors and, 53, 62, 66, 100, 102,

victims: arrest and criminalization of, 28, 30, 45, 64–67, 116, 119, 121–123, 129; control of, 7, 23, 29, 44–45, 56–57, 59–64, 76, 91, 94–95, 102–103, 116, 127; detention of, 28, 64, 121–122, 132–133; disabilities and, 37, 50–51, 130; needs of, 23–25, 50, 54, 61, 67–69, 86, 100, 104, 114, 124, 126, 129, 133, 137–138, 140–141; as offenders, 22, 64–67, 96, 122; recruitment of, 9, 12, 23, 26, 45–47, 52–56, 62, 64–65, 78, 83–86, 94, 96, 99–101, 103–105, 127–128; repeat victimization, 54; services for, 23–24, 28, 30–31, 53, 60, 63–64, 67–69, 123–124, 129–130, 132–133, 139–140; stereotypes of, 9, 11, 25, 31, 91, 110–111, 114–116, 121, 131–132, 142

victimization theories, 50–51; deviant place theory, 55; lifestyle theory, 52–55; routine activities theory, 46–48, 52; victim precipitation theory, 51–52

Vietnam, 116, 125

Virginia, 93

visas: A-3 visas, 55; G-5 visas, 55; T visas, 29–30, 129

vulnerability, 10, 13–16, 41, 50, 53–55, 61, 64, 80, 83–84, 86–89, 100, 108, 117, 121, 123, 125–126, 130, 136–140

White Slave Traffic Act (1910). See Mann Act (1910)

White slavery, 7–8, 109, 132

women of color, 16. 121

Founded in 1893,
UNIVERSITY OF CALIFORNIA PRESS
publishes bold, progressive books and journals
on topics in the arts, humanities, social sciences,
and natural sciences—with a focus on social
justice issues—that inspire thought and action
among readers worldwide.

The UC PRESS FOUNDATION
raises funds to uphold the press's vital role
as an independent, nonprofit publisher, and
receives philanthropic support from a wide
range of individuals and institutions—and from
committed readers like you. To learn more, visit
ucpress.edu/supportus.

www.ingramcontent.com/pod-product-compliance
Lightning Source LLC
Chambersburg PA
CBHW030839270326
41928CB00007B/1124